# The ZX81™/
# TS1000™
# Home Computer Book

# The ZX81™/ TS1000™ Home Computer Book

David C. Foyt

Osborne/McGraw-Hill
Berkeley, California

Published by
Osborne/McGraw-Hill
2600 Tenth Street
Berkeley, California 94710
U.S.A.

For information on translations and book distributors outside of the U.S.A.,
please write to Osborne/McGraw-Hill at the above address.

### The ZX81™/TS1000™ Home Computer Book

1234567890  DODO  89876543

ISBN 0-88134-106-1

Judy Ziajka, Acquisitions Editor
John Heilborn, Technical Editor
Susan Schwartz, Copy Editor
KLT van Genderen, Text Design
Yashi Okita, Cover Design
Rick van Genderen, Illustrator
Richard Cash, Photographer

# Acknowledgments

The author thanks Lee Tharrett, who read first drafts of several chapters and made a number of helpful suggestions; Ruth Abrass, who provided a ZX81 on short notice for the photographs and illustrations; and Communication Intelligence Corporation for the use of their text processing equipment.

D.C.F.

# Contents

# Preface

This book is your introduction to the Timex Sinclair 1000 and Sinclair ZX81 personal computers. It describes the computers themselves and covers the common external devices and accessories, including the television display, cassette program storage, memory expansion, and printers.

The book has three main parts. Each part focuses on one kind of Timex Sinclair computer user. The first part addresses the person who plans to use commercially prepared programs but has little or no desire to program the computer. The second part teaches the programmer or prospective programmer how to use BASIC on these computers. The third part presents more advanced information about Sinclair BASIC and the Z80 microprocessor and explains how to take advantage of some of their special characteristics. These three parts are not mutually exclusive. Users of the first part may venture into the second part just to see what BASIC programming is all about. Users of the second and third parts are likely to find themselves referring to the first part from time to time.

The first two chapters answer two questions: "What is the TS1000 (or ZX81) computer?" and "How do you make it work?" The first chapter tells you what all the pieces of the computer system are and what they do. The second chapter describes the system in greater detail and tells you how to operate each component part. With this knowledge you are ready to use any of the ready-to-run programs that are available for text processing, financial analysis, bookkeeping, computer-aided instruction, and entertainment.

Chapters 3 through 6 teach you how to write your own BASIC programs. Chapter 3 begins with the fundamentals of Sinclair BASIC. Chapters 4, 5, and 6 describe the features of BASIC in greater detail, explaining what computer programming is all about and describing some of the things you can do with this knowledge.

Chapters 7 and 8 present more advanced aspects of the Timex Sinclair computers that will interest more experienced programmers and new users who have mastered the fundamentals.

The appendixes provides valuable reference information for each kind of user. Appendix A is a summary of Sinclair BASIC for readers who already understand BASIC and want to look up the details of particular commands or functions. Appendixes B through D contain general reference material for programmers, and Appendixes E through M describe more advanced aspects of these computers. Appendix N is a bibliography of other related books and magazines.

D.C.F.

Presenting the TS1000 and ZX81

# Chapter One

**T**his chapter introduces you to the TS1000 and ZX81 computers. In it you will learn about the basic functions of these computers' parts, from the microprocessor (the "brain" of the system) to the keyboard. The chapter also introduces you to the basic equipment that can be attached to your computer to make it more useful, for example, a cassette recorder (to save your programs) or more memory (to enable you to run longer and more complex programs).

## THE COMPUTER

Figure 1-1 is a picture of the Timex-Sinclair 1000 computer (hereafter called the TS1000). Figure 1-2 shows the Sinclair ZX81. These two computers are essentially identical, except that the TS1000 has more memory. This book applies equally to both computers. Where it describes one, you can assume the other works exactly the same way.

The computer contains a Z80 microprocessor chip, two kinds of memory, a built-in keyboard, and circuitry that can control a television, cassette recorder, printer, and memory expansion pack. Figure 1-3 shows the inside of the computer. You don't have to understand how the electronic components work in order to be able to use the computer, but the sections that follow discuss each of the major components briefly so that you will know their names and functions.

You may be surprised to learn that your computer has so few internal components. As you can see from Figure 1-3, the computer's circuitry consists of only four integrated circuits: the microprocessor; a custom logic circuit (called a ULA); two memory chips; and a few small components. Each chip contains a large amount of internal circuitry, most of it so small that you could not see it without the aid of a microscope.

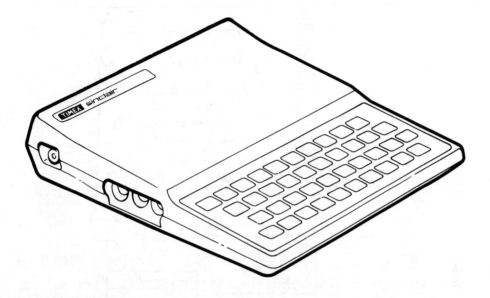

**Figure 1-1. TS1000**

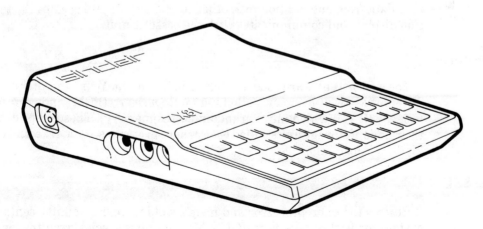

**Figure 1-2. ZX81**

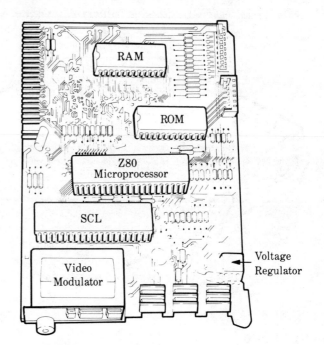

**Figure 1-3. Inside the computer**

## The Microprocessor

The *microprocessor* or CPU (Figure 1-3) is the "brain" of the computer. It executes the instructions of your program one at a time by performing arithmetic functions, comparing and manipulating numbers, and transferring data from one location to another in memory. It also creates the television display and communicates with the cassette unit.

## Memory

The *memory* chips are used for storing information. Your computer has two different kinds of memory, called *read-only memory* (ROM) and *read/write memory* (RAM, which means random-access memory). These chips contain thousands of storage units called *bytes* where programs, data, text, and other kinds of information are stored.

## The SCL

Besides the microprocessor and memory chips, your computer contains a custom-made chip called the SCL, which provides special circuitry for connecting other chips and generating the cassette, video, and keyboard signals.

The letters SCL stand for "Sinclair Computer Logic." The chip used is called a ULA (Universal Logic Array). It is programmed at the factory to perform the SCL functions.

The computer also contains a voltage regulator and a video modulator. The voltage regulator controls the power to the computer and the video modulator converts the computer display data into a standard broadcast signal so you can use your television set for the video display.

## PUTTING THE SYSTEM TOGETHER

Figure 1-4 is a picture of a typical TS1000 computer system. The system configuration of a ZX81 is identical. Your system may differ from the one pictured because some of the components shown are optional. Your television set and cassette recorder/player may also be different from the ones shown since neither Sinclair nor Timex markets their own televisions or recorders.

Only two of the components shown in Figure 1-4 are necessary for a

Figure 1-4. The TS1000 computer, memory expansion pack, cassette
    recorder/player, printer, and television screen

working computer system: the computer itself (including the built-in keyboard) and the television set. The cassette unit is used to save programs and load them into the computer from tape. The Timex 2040 printer shown prints both programs and the results of calculations onto paper.

The memory expansion pack increases the memory to 16,384 bytes (called 16K bytes in the number system used in computers). With this added memory, the computer can handle longer programs and more data.

## The Keyboard

The built-in keyboard is your main way of giving instructions to the computer. The TS1000 and ZX81 accept commands in a language called BASIC, which uses a small number of English words, along with numbers and a few other symbols, in a fairly simple and systematic way. Much of this book will explain how to use the language BASIC. For now, notice that the keyboard has all of the special words and other symbols of BASIC printed on the keys. This can make the TS1000 and ZX81 much easier to use than many other personal computers that require you to remember all the special words and type them in yourself, letter by letter.

## The Video Display

The television screen displays the interaction between you and the computer. It displays each command or keyboard character as you type it in. It also displays a special symbol called a *cursor*, which tells you what kind of information the computer expects you to enter next and where it will appear.

The screen is divided into 24 lines of 32 characters each. Although you can use just about any kind of television, a small black and white set will probably give the best picture.

## Expansion Interface

At the rear of the computer is a long, flat connector. This connector is the *expansion interface*. It is used to connect various devices to the TS1000 and ZX81 computers.

Two of the devices that connect to this interface are the 16K memory pack and the Timex 2040 or Sinclair ZX printer.

## Memory and Memory Expansion

In any computer system, the microprocessor (also called the *Central Processing Unit*, or CPU) performs all of the logical functions of the computer.

But in order for it to perform these functions, it is necessary to have a controlling program. This program can be stored in memory as either a permanent (or *nonvolatile*) program, such as the BASIC programming language, or in temporary memory, such as programs you enter.

## THE MASTER PROGRAM

The TS1000 and ZX81 computers have two different kinds of memory. *Read-only memory* (ROM) contains the master program that controls every aspect of the computer's operation. When you plug in the computer, this master program automatically takes over. When you enter commands or programs for the computer to execute (in BASIC), it is this master program in ROM that instructs the microprocessor to interpret your commands and carry them out. The ROM contains permanently stored information that was placed there at the factory, and you cannot change it.

## DATA AND PROGRAM STORAGE

The other kind of memory in your computer is called *read/write memory* (RAM), because you can change (write) its contents as well as read what was previously written into it. The letters R.A.M. are an acronym for *random-access memory*. Although both ROM and RAM can be accessed randomly, only read/write memory is called RAM. When you enter and run a program of your own, the microprocessor stores your program and the data it needs in RAM. It also keeps track of where these things are stored, so that you can find them easily when you need them.

When you turn off the power, everything stored in RAM disappears. If you saved the program on cassette before turning off the power, you can recall it by loading it into RAM; otherwise you will have to retype it.

Both ROM and RAM are made up of individual storage units called *bytes*. Each byte can contain one character, such as a letter, a punctuation mark, or a graphic symbol. The more bytes you have, the more information (programs, numbers, or text) you can store in your computer.

Memory capacity is usually described in units of Kbytes (sometimes simply called K). One Kbyte means 1024 bytes. The TS1000 and ZX81 have 8K bytes (that's 8192 bytes) of ROM. Additionally, the TS1000 has 2K bytes (2048 bytes) of RAM, while the ZX81 has 1K byte (1024 bytes) of RAM. With the optional memory expansion pack, each computer has a total of 16K, or 16,384 bytes of RAM.

T his chapter begins by telling you how to hook up your computer and make sure it is working correctly. It also describes different parts of the computer system and how to use them. These are the television display, the keyboard, the cassette recorder, the printer, and the 16K memory pack.

## SETTING UP THE SYSTEM

Find the video cable that came with the computer and plug it into the socket marked "TV" on the left side of the computer (Figure 2-1). Make sure the plug goes all the way in, so that the metal flange on the outside of the plug makes good contact with the outer surface of the socket.

Connect the television switch box terminals (marked "TV") to the VHF antenna terminals on the back of your television set (Figure 2-2). Connect the switch terminals marked "ANTENNA" to the antenna, and plug the free end of the video cable into the connector marked "COMPUTER." Set the switch to the "COMPUTER" position.

**Caution:** Always make sure the computer is disconnected from power before plugging in the memory expansion pack, the printer, or any other device that plugs into the edge connector at the back of the computer. You can do serious damage to the computer and device if you forget this.

How To Operate the TS1000 or ZX81

# Chapter Two

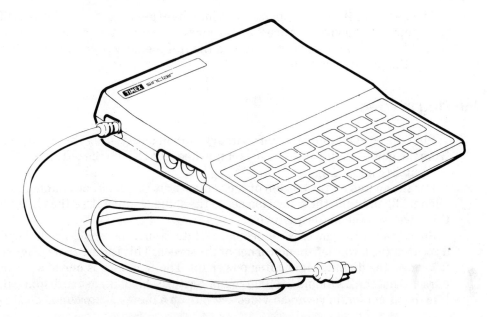

**Figure 2-1. The video cable plugs into the left side of the TS1000**

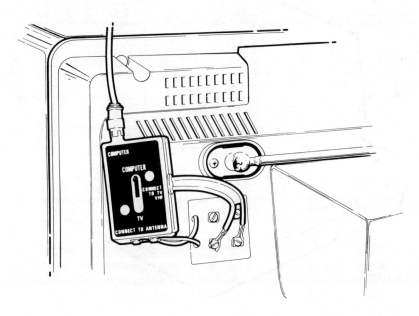

**Figure 2-2. The television switch box connects to VHF antenna terminals**

The optional 16K memory pack plugs into the edge connector on the back of the computer (shown in Figure 2-3). If your system has a Timex 2040 printer, plug it into the connector first and plug the 16K memory pack into the other side of the printer connector.

## When You Plug In Power

Plug the power supply into an ordinary 110 volt outlet. Plug the small jack from the power supply into the socket marked "9V DC" on the left side of the computer (Figure 2-4).

Use the switch on the bottom of the computer to select either channel 2 or channel 3, and tune the television set to the same channel. Use the channel that gives you the better picture.

Shortly after the power is connected, a white ▒ on a black background will appear at the lower left-hand corner of the screen. This is the *cursor*. Figure 2-5 shows the display right after power-up. The ▒ cursor is one of several cursors that the ZX81 and TS1000 computers use. All of them are displayed, like the ▒ cursor, in reversed video—white on a dark background.

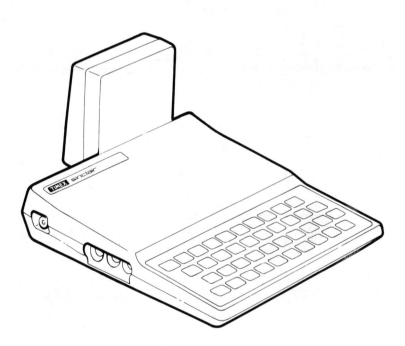

Adapted from *Timex User Manual* by Steven Vickers, © 1982 Timex Corporation

**Figure 2-3. The 16K memory pack plugs into the edge connector**

**Figure 2-4. The power supply's jack plugs into the socket 9V DC**

**Figure 2-5. Television display when computer is turned on**

Table 2-1 describes all of the possible cursor characters that you will encounter with the TS1000 or ZX81 computers.

Adjust the fine-tuning, horizontal, and vertical controls on the television set until you get a display similar to the one in Figure 2-5. Adjust the brightness and contrast for the clearest, most comfortable view.

If you run into any problems getting this display, refer to the troubleshooting guide at the back of the book.

## THE KEYBOARD

The keyboards of the TS1000 and ZX81 (Figure 2-6) have all the letters and numbers of an ordinary typewriter keyboard. Most of them are arranged in the same pattern as on a typewriter. The comma and SPACE keys, however, are at unfamiliar locations, and there is only one SHIFT key. Also, there is a key marked ENTER, which you must press at the end of each line to tell the computer that the line is complete and ready to be processed.

**Table 2-1. Cursors**

| | |
|---|---|
| | Keyword |
| | Letter or Number |
| | Function |
| | Graphics Symbols or Reversed Video |
| | Syntax Error |

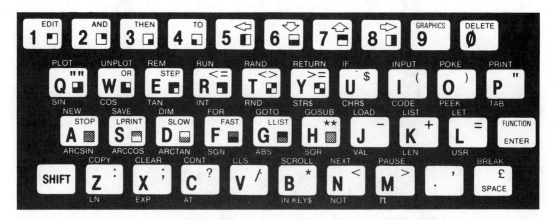

**Figure 2-6. TS1000 or ZX81 keyboard**

Many of the keys contain three or four other symbols or functions in addition to the standard letter or number. Some of these are mathematical symbols like +, –, and =, or punctuation marks such as " or ;. Other keys have special graphics symbols for drawing pictures or graphs on the screen. Other keys contain words, such as INPUT, STOP, and PEEK, which are keywords, or commands, in the BASIC programming language.

In this chapter you will learn how to select any one of the symbols on the keys, and you will see some examples of how to use them to give commands to the computer. Don't worry if you don't understand these commands. They will become clear as you follow the examples in this book.

## Letters and Keywords

BASIC
Keyword

Look at the key marked with a large capital E. It is located on the second row of keys from the top, three keys in from the left end of the row.

The word REM is a BASIC *keyword*. Keywords on the TS1000 and ZX81 are BASIC commands. The keywords, letters, and numbers are the symbols that you will use most often. The ▨ cursor that you see on the screen (Figure 2-5) indicates that the computer expects a keyword at this point. If you press the REM key now, the word REM will appear on the screen. Do it and observe the display. The ▨ cursor has disappeared, and in its place is the line:

REM ▮

The ▨ cursor means that the computer is now expecting a letter or a number instead of a keyword. If you press the E key again, it will produce the letter E instead of REM.

All of the words written above the white letter keys are BASIC keywords. If you press any letter key while the ▨ cursor is visible, the screen will display the word that is written above the letter. When the ▨ cursor is visible, the screen will display the letters themselves. The letters are printed in solid black on the white keys. All of the numbers, together with the period, ENTER, and SPACE symbols, are also printed in black. However, they do not have keywords above them, and they give the same result on the screen regardless of whether the ▨ or ▨ cursor is showing. (The BREAK written above the SPACE key is not a keyword, although it looks like one. It doesn't get printed.)

## The SHIFT Key

The SHIFT key, like the shift key of an ordinary typewriter, does not do anything by itself; it only changes the effect of pressing the other keys. Since the only letters on the TS1000 keyboard are capital letters, the SHIFT key does

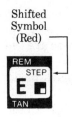

Shifted
Symbol
(Red)

not distinguish capital letters from lowercase ones. Instead, it selects the symbol that is printed in red on any other key that you press while SHIFT is held down. This book uses SHIFT- to denote a shifted key. For example, SHIFT-E will display the word **STEP** that is printed in red on the E key.

Each of the shifted keys does exactly the same thing regardless of whether the ▓ or the ▤ cursor is showing.

Some keys on the top row do not print anything on the screen when you SHIFT them. Instead, they perform special editing operations for entering and correcting programs. For example, the DELETE key (SHIFT-0) erases the last symbol you typed. Type a few symbols and then type DELETE several times. The cursor will back up and erase the symbols from the display. If you have typed more than enough symbols to fill one line, the display continues on the next line. DELETE will erase the symbols on both lines, one at a time, in the reverse of the order they were entered. DELETE will not, however, move the cursor back past the spot where it originally appeared when you connected the power.

The CURSOR-LEFT key (shown as a horizontal left arrow, ←) is similar to DELETE, but it moves the cursor backward without deleting the symbols it passes over. The CURSOR-LEFT key is obtained by pressing SHIFT-5. Type some more symbols, and then use CURSOR-LEFT to move the cursor back. SHIFT-8 (the CURSOR-RIGHT key, →) moves the cursor to the right, again leaving intact any symbols that it passes over.

The computer has an automatic insert function. When the cursor is between two symbols, any new symbol that you type will appear just to the left of the cursor, and the rest of the line will move to the right to make room for it.

The CURSOR UP and DOWN keys (SHIFT-7, ↑, and SHIFT-6, ↓) are for moving the cursor from one line to the next when you have several program lines on the screen. Chapter 3 will cover these in more detail.

## The FUNCTION Key

Function

The symbols below the white key squares are called *functions*, although some of them, such as TAB and AT, are not functions in the mathematical sense. To use the function symbols, first press the FUNCTION key (SHIFT-ENTER). Notice that a new cursor, with the symbol ▤ for FUNCTION, has appeared. Now press the TAN key. It is the same one that has REM, the letter E, and STEP on it.

You can produce any of the symbols that are written below the key squares by using the FUNCTION key, and it doesn't matter whether the ▓ or ▤ cursor was showing at the time. Remember that the FUNCTION key is a prefix key; you use it *before* pressing the key that has the symbol you want to display. This is different from the SHIFT key, which you hold down *while* you press the other key.

# The GRAPHICS Key

There is one more set of symbols on the computer keyboard. These are the special graphics symbols that are used to draw pictures and graphs. This set also includes the reverse-video versions (white characters on a black background) of the other characters.

To produce these symbols, first press the GRAPHICS key (SHIFT-9). The cursor will change to the ▣ symbol. Press the E key and the ▤ prints in reverse video. The ▣ cursor will not be reset to the ▤ cursor automatically after another key is pressed, the way the ▤ cursor was. To get the ▣ or ▤ cursor back, press GRAPHICS again.

With the ▣ cursor showing, press SHIFT-E. The character that appears on the screen is a dark square with its lower right quarter missing. It looks just like the symbol that is printed on the same keyboard key with the E. This symbol, and the others like it, are used for drawing pictures or graphs on the screen.

Graphics
Symbol —┐

```
REM
   STEP
 E ◪
TAN
```

Some of the keys on the keyboard do not have a graphics symbol on them, and they behave differently from the others when you shift them in graphics mode. The U key is an example.

Put the computer into graphics mode. Then enter SHIFT-U. You will see that the dollar sign ▤ appears in reverse video. The keys with no graphics symbols will all produce red characters in reverse video when you shift them while in graphics mode.

You have now tried all the different kinds of symbols that a key on your ZX81 or TS1000 can produce. For practice, you may want to choose a key that has all of them, such as W, and try to display each symbol that it contains.

# The ENTER Key

While you were trying out the different key combinations described above, the computer did not interpret any of your entries as commands. This is because it was waiting for you to press ENTER before executing any command.

To see how ENTER works, press the PRINT key, followed by the number 8. The screen now reads

```
PRINT 8▤
```

Now press ENTER. The computer does exactly what the command said to do: it prints the number 8 at the top of the screen.

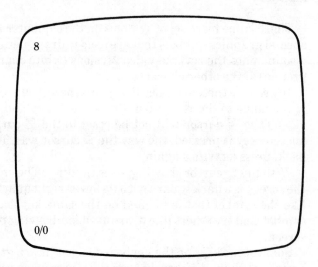

8

0/0

The numbers 0/0 at the bottom of the screen are a code to tell you whether any errors occurred while the command was being executed. You will learn more about them later.

There is no longer a cursor on the screen, but the computer will behave exactly as if it had the ▨ cursor. As soon as you type something else, the correct cursor will appear.

## ERRORS AND THE ▨ CURSOR

The computer can display one more cursor, and it is probably the most useful one of all. It tells you when you have made a mistake in typing a line. Most computers will let you type almost anything you want into a program, even if it violates the rules of the BASIC programming language and will cause an error later when you try to run the program. The TS1000 or ZX81, however, finds as many errors for you as it can and marks them with the ▨ cursor.

To demonstrate how this works, first DELETE anything you may have typed in on the bottom line. Make sure the ▨ cursor is showing, and then type

```
PRINT 4"
```

Remember to use the key with the PRINT symbol on it instead of trying to type the individual letters of the word. SHIFT the same key to produce the quotation symbol after the 4.

Now press ENTER. The computer refuses to accept the line—the line does not appear at the top of the screen. The ⊟ cursor appears to the left of the quotation symbol because the symbol is not "legal" in this context:

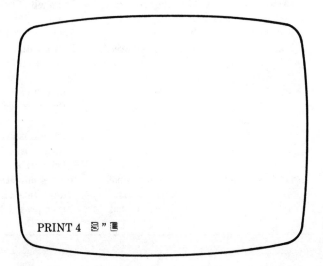

The computer will put the ⊟ cursor to the left of the first item that it detects is in error. Since it can't know exactly what you meant to enter, however, the ⊟ may appear farther to the left or right than the actual beginning of your error.

Delete the quotation symbol and watch the ⊟ cursor disappear. Now type a comma and a 5. The line should look like this:

```
PRINT 4,5▊
```

Press ENTER and the computer will print the numbers 4 and 5 at the top of the screen.

Remember, though, that no computer can catch every programming mistake that anyone could possibly make. The computer will mark with the ⊟ cursor any *syntax* errors—things that violate the rules of BASIC—that it detects *within a single line*. It will make sure that you do not enter numbers or single letters where a keyword is expected (remember the ⊟ and ▊ cursors). But the computer cannot find errors that involve the relationships between different lines of your program until the program actually runs. In addition, since the computer has no way of knowing what you intended, it may occasionally execute valid programs that do something you didn't want.

Table 2-2 summarizes the functions of the various symbols on the keyboard. Use this table as a guide to the multiple functions on the keys.

## Table 2-2. Keyboard Symbols

| Symbol | Keyboard Location | How to Display It | Example |
|--------|-------------------|-------------------|---------|
| Keyword | Above key square | Press with ▨ showing | REM |
| Letter or number | On key square | Press with ▥ showing | E |
| Red symbol | On key square | Press with SHIFT | STEP |
| Function | Below key square | Prefix with FUNCTION key | TAN |
| Reversed video | For letter or number | Turn ▤ on with GRAPHICS key, then press selected key | ▤ ▉ |
| Graphics symbol | On some key squares | Turn ▤ on with GRAPHICS key, then press selected key with SHIFT | |
| Reversed video | For shifted symbol on keys without graphics symbol | Turn ▤ on with GRAPHICS key, then press selected key with SHIFT | ▤ |

# YOUR FIRST PROGRAM

Now that you know how to use all the features of the keyboard, you are ready to write your first program. First delete any symbols left on the screen. Then type NEW (on the A key) and press the ENTER key to make sure the computer is clear and ready for a program. To enter the program, type in the lines at the end of the next paragraph, exactly as they appear on the page. Type only the words between quotation marks. All of the others are on the keyboard as keywords, like NEW, or as functions, like AT. Don't type any spaces between words or symbols (except between quotation marks). The computer will provide all the spaces that you need automatically.

Some of the program lines are too long to fit on a single line of the screen. Don't worry about that; the computer will automatically go to the next line when you get to the end of a line. Just remember to press ENTER whenever you get to the end of one of the lines as they are shown. If you make a mistake, simply re-enter the line correctly and it will replace the incorrect one.[1]

```
  5 SLOW
 10 PRINT "I NEVER MAKE MASTAKE
S"
 20 PAUSE 200
 30 PRINT AT 2,7;"WHOOPS"
 40 PAUSE 100
```

[1] Adapted from a program by A. Kohlenberg, *Syntax ZX80* (The Harvard Group, Bolton Road, Harvard, Mass., 01451, May 1982), p. 17.

```
 50 FOR Y=25 TO 14 STEP -1
 60 PRINT AT 2,Y;"█"
 70 PRINT AT 2,Y;" "
 80 NEXT Y
 90 PRINT AT 0,14;"█"
100 FOR A=18 TO 0 STEP -1
110 PRINT AT A,14;"I"
120 PRINT AT A,14;" "
130 NEXT A
140 PRINT AT 0,14;"I"
150 PRINT AT 10,8;"WELL, HARDLY
EVER"
```

Now press RUN, then press ENTER, and watch the program run.


## USING A CASSETTE PLAYER

Your TS1000 or ZX81 comes equipped with jacks for connecting a cassette
recorder/player. These jacks are on the left side of the computer and are
clearly marked MIC and EAR (Figure 2-7). You can save and load programs
that you write with the ZX81 or the TS1000, or you can buy and load
prerecorded tapes with many kinds of programs on them.

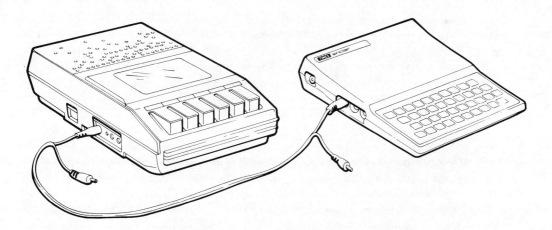

Figure 2-7. A cassette recorder plugged into the TS1000

## Choosing a Recorder and Tapes

Almost any cassette unit that is used for recording and playing music and speech will work just fine with the ZX81 or TS1000, as long as it has microphone and earphone jacks that match the cables supplied with the computer. It's convenient if your player has a tape counter that keeps track of where you are on the tape. This makes it easier to go directly to the program you want.

Be sure to use short (30 minutes or less), high-quality audio cassettes. In fact, cassettes with only five or ten minutes of playing time are actually better than longer ones, since you can rewind them quickly. They make it easier to go from one taped program to another and to use both sides without having to wait for the computer to read through many programs to get to the right one.

## Using Prerecorded Programs

If you have program tapes for your TS1000, you can begin using the programs on the tapes now, even before you read about how to program the computer.

Before attempting to load a program from tape, try listening to one of the tapes to see what it sounds like. You will not be able to recognize the individual commands of the program by the way they sound, but what you hear will help you to find the best adjustment of the cassette player's tone and volume controls.

Begin with the tone control set all the way toward treble and the volume control fairly low. Place the cassette in the cassette player and rewind the cassette to the beginning. Depress the PLAY button on the cassette player and listen. There may be a brief period of silence at the beginning while the tape leader passes through. Then you should hear a low-pitched humming sound. This sound was made by the computer that recorded the tape while it was waiting for the command to record.

Before long the hum will stop and there will be a 5-second period of silence, followed by an unpleasant screeching noise. The silent period marks the beginning of the program. If the player is not completely silent during this period, there is either a bad connection between the player and the computer or you have a source of interference, such as electrical machinery, nearby. In some cases you can read tapes successfully despite interference by adjusting the tone control to make this silent period as quiet as possible. The best thing to do, though, is to eliminate the source of the interference.

The screeching noise after the silent period is the recorded program itself. Adjust the volume so that the noise is unpleasantly loud, but not quite deafening, and stop the cassette player. Now you are ready to load a taped program into the computer. Rewind the cassette and connect one of the cables supplied with the computer to the jack on the computer marked "EAR" (Figure 2-7). Connect the other end of the cable to the EAR or EARPHONE jack of your cassette player. It's best not to connect a cable to the MIC jacks while you are loading a tape, since some cassette players will not work properly with both cables connected.

If the television screen has anything but the ▦ cursor on it, use DELETE to erase the symbols on the screen, type NEW (using the NEW key), and press ENTER. Now press the LOAD key (the same key as the letter J), followed twice by SHIFT-P. The screen should look like this:

```
LOAD ""▦
```

The two quote symbols tell the computer to load the first program that it finds on the tape. If you know the name that was given to the program when it was recorded, you can type that name between the quotes. The computer then will search through the tape until it finds a program by that name, even if it is not the first one. Now press ENTER and you will see a pattern of lines on the screen, like the one in Figure 2-8. This video pattern occurs because the computer uses some of the same circuits for the cassette signals that it uses for the video. You can use this pattern to monitor the computer's progress in loading the tape.

**Figure 2-8. Screen pattern before a taped program is located**

Next, depress the PLAY button on the cassette player and watch the television screen. When you get to the place where you heard the hum on the tape, the pattern will change slightly. It will change again when you reach the 5-second silent period. Then, when you reach the beginning of the previous screeching noise, the screen will begin to show a pattern of much more distinctive dark and light bands. Figure 2-9 is an example of the screen during this program-loading operation. The exact appearance of the screen will depend on the television settings and the program that is being read.

If you don't see these changes in the pattern, turn up the volume on the cassette recorder until you do. If you still don't see them, check to make sure that the cable is connected to the EAR jack at both ends, that it is making good contact, and that there is nothing plugged into the MIC jacks. Some cassette players make a better connection if you first push the plug in all the way, then pull it back out very slightly.

Once you have the cassette player controls adjusted, you can go back and load the tape correctly, without interruptions. Rewind the cassette, press the BREAK key to get back to the ▦ cursor, enter the LOAD " " command again, and start the tape. This time let the player run until the video pattern stops. The display should return to normal, with the program ready for use. If the program was purchased, follow the instructions that came with it. If there are no instructions, simply press the RUN key (the same as the R key), followed by ENTER.

Figure 2-9. Screen pattern while a taped program is being loaded

## Labeling Your Programs

After using your computer for a few days or weeks, you will probably have many different program tapes. If you don't make labels for the cassettes, you can quickly lose track of what you have and which tape a particular program is on. To avoid this, each time you save a program on a cassette, label the cassette with the name of the program. It's also a good idea to include the tape counter reading and a short description of what the program does.

## Caring for Cassettes

If a music cassette gets a little bit of dust on it, or if you accidentally touch the recording surface of the tape, you won't notice the small change in the way the music sounds. But cassettes are really very delicate, and even this small amount of damage can completely ruin a computer program stored on a tape. So be careful to rewind the cassette and put it back into its protective case when you are through with it. Don't touch the tape surface itself, and keep the cassette away from motors, kitchen appliances, and any other source of magnetic fields.

Because tapes can be damaged despite your precautions, record your programs twice, using different tapes. That way you will have a backup copy if one of them gets damaged.

## Write-Protecting Cassettes

You will probably use several different cassettes with your TS1000 or ZX81. Some cassettes will be "scratch" cassettes, used to make temporary copies of new programs while you are first writing or testing them. Others will have finished programs that you want to keep indefinitely. To prevent anyone (including yourself) from accidentally destroying one of the programs, you can write-protect them.

Figure 2-10 shows the write-protect notches on a cassette. New cassettes have plugs in the notches so that you can record on the tape. There is one notch for each side of the tape. To determine which tab is the correct one for the side that you want to protect, hold the cassette so that the exposed tape is away from you and the desired side of the cassette is facing up. The tab on the right side corresponds to the side that is facing up (Figure 2-10). After you have recorded the permanent version of a program you want to keep, simply punch out the tab for that side of the cassette.

Most recorders are able to detect a missing tab and will not record on a cassette that is protected in this way. It would be a good idea, though, to

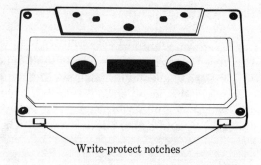

Write-protect notches

**Figure 2-10. Write-protect notches on cassette tape**

write-protect a scratch tape and try writing onto it, just to make sure that your recorder has this feature.

If you change your mind and decide to record onto a cassette that you previously protected, you can always unprotect it by covering the notch with adhesive tape.[2]


## USING A PRINTER

The printer is an optional accessory for the TS1000 or ZX81. It is not required for the computer to work properly, but it does provide a convenient way of making listings of programs, printing out the results of calculations, or making permanent graphs or pictures. Although several different printers are available, this book will describe only two: the Timex 2040 (available in the USA) and the Sinclair ZX (available in Canada and Europe). If you choose a different printer, make sure it is advertised specifically for use with the TS1000 or ZX81, and follow the manufacturer's instructions to use it. There are hundreds of printers on the market. Don't assume that one of them will work with the TS1000 or ZX81 unless the manufacturer says it will.

If your system includes a Timex 2040 or Sinclair ZX printer, plug it into the expansion interface at the back of the computer. Remember to disconnect the power first to avoid damaging the computer or the printer.

The ZX printer uses rolls of a special metallized paper. The 2040 printer uses a special thermal paper. Neither printer will work with ordinary paper.

[2] Lon Poole, Martin McNiff, and Steven Cook, *Apple II User's Guide* (Berkeley: Osborne/McGraw-Hill, 1981), p. 20.

You can use the program you entered earlier in this chapter to try out the printer. Once the program is in the computer, just press LLIST (SHIFT-G), followed by ENTER, and watch the printer print a copy of the program. With the ZX printer, don't worry if the printer is fairly noisy and the screen flickers while printing is in progress. Both of these are perfectly normal. When the printer stops, use the button to advance the paper until the entire listing is out. Then tear the paper free against the notched plastic strip. You can also use the COPY command (on the z key) to print a copy of whatever is on the screen at any time.

## USING THE 16K MEMORY PACK

Figure 2-3 shows how to connect the 16K memory pack to the computer. If you have both the memory pack and the printer, use the edge connector to connect the printer to the computer instead. Then plug the memory pack into the printer's connector.

The memory pack simply provides more read/write memory (RAM) for storing programs and data. You don't need any special instructions for using it, since the computer automatically determines how much memory it has. If you enter a program so long that it begins to fill up all the available memory, you will notice that the television display gets shorter and shorter, until only one line (or just part of one line) is visible at the top of the screen. With the memory pack, you can enter many more program lines before this begins to happen.

With the memory pack attached, you may also notice a longer pause between the time when you plug in the power and the time when the ▤ cursor first appears on the screen. The computer tests its memory during this pause, and with more memory, the testing takes a little longer.

To verify that the memory pack is working correctly, enter the following line:

```
PRINT PEEK 16388+256*PEEK 16389
```

This command prints out a number called RAMTOP, which tells how much memory the computer found when it did its memory test. With the memory pack attached, the number 32768 should appear. Without the memory pack, you should see either 18432 (for the TS1000, which has 2K of RAM) or 17408 (for the ZX81, which has 1K of RAM).

Getting Started with BASIC

# Chapter
# Three

In this chapter you will begin to learn how to give commands and write programs for your TS1000 or ZX81 computer. Like most personal computers today, your computer is designed to understand the programming language called BASIC.

A programming language is a way of giving instructions to the computer. Each of these instructions (also called commands or statements) usually tells the computer to do one fairly simple operation, like adding numbers together or printing something on the screen. You can combine these simple instructions in different ways to do many different kinds of things.

Some books on programming begin by telling you everything about each of the different statements in the language first, and then giving you all the rules for combining the statements into programs. But the best way to learn about computer programming is not to memorize lists of statements and rules. It's much easier and more fun to start by trying out a few of the most useful commands and learning how to use them to make short programs. That's what this chapter is about. Later chapters will build your knowledge by adding more commands and combining them in different ways, and explaining particular topics, such as graphics and animation. Appendix A is a complete summary of Sinclair BASIC. After you have learned about BASIC by running programs and writing some programs of your own, the summary will make it easy to look up particular commands when you need them.

## ENTERING COMMANDS

First, be sure you have set up your computer correctly. Chapter 2 tells you how to do this. It also tells you how to use the computer's keyboard to produce the different kinds of symbols that you see on the keys. All of the special words that Sinclair BASIC uses appear on the keyboard. Don't try to type out the individual words for the commands; if you do, the display probably will not show the same thing that you typed, and the computer will not do what you meant it to do. If you're not sure how to enter all the different kinds of keyboard symbols, have another look at Chapter 2.

Now make sure that the display screen looks like the picture in Figure 2-7. If it doesn't, unplug the power, wait a few seconds, and plug it back in. The ▦ cursor tells you that the computer is ready for a BASIC command.

## Displaying Numbers and Text

One of the necessary operations of a computer is to display numbers or words on the screen. Otherwise, there would be no way to tell whether the program did what it was supposed to do, or what answer it came up with when it was finished.

To print a number on the screen, simply press the key with the word PRINT on it, then press a number key (such as 7), and finally press ENTER. The command says "PRINT 7," and the computer does exactly that: it prints the number 7 on the screen. Here's how the screen should look before and after you press ENTER:

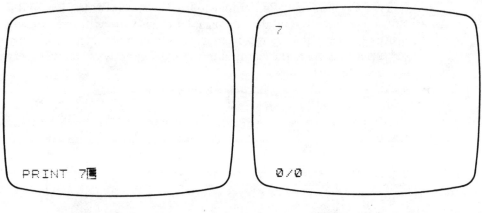

Before pressing ENTER                    After pressing ENTER

Every line of BASIC must end with the ENTER key; the computer waits for the ENTER before it tries to obey the command. This book doesn't use any special symbol for ENTER. Most of the time it will not even remind you to use it. So remember that the ENTER is necessary at the end of every line.

Fortunately, the PRINT command can do more than just print a single digit on the screen. Try each of the following commands, one at a time. Remember to end each line with ENTER.

```
PRINT 1492


PRINT -3.14


PRINT 2+3
```

As you can see, the computer knows all about positive and negative numbers and decimal fractions, and it can do arithmetic. (There's a limit to how big the numbers can be, but the limit is so large that you usually don't have to worry about it.) You can also instruct the computer to print at a particular place on the screen, or to print numbers in neat columns on successive lines. Chapter 5 will tell you how.

Numbers are not the only things that you can ask the computer to display on the television screen. In fact, it will display any line of text that you want it to display. All you have to do is to put quotation marks around the text and use a PRINT command, like this:

```
PRINT "I CAN DISPLAY ANYTHING YO
U WANT ME TO"
```

Type this line now. Remember to use the special PRINT key and to use the SHIFT key for the quotation marks. Of course you will have to type out the words between the quotation marks, one letter at a time. When you press ENTER at the end, the computer displays exactly what was between the quotes, like this:

```
PRINT "I CAN DISPLAY ANYTHING YO
U WANT ME TO"




















0/0
```

You will find many uses for PRINT statements like the one just given. If you write a program that balances your checkbook, computes compound interest, or calculates numbers for any other reason, you will probably want the computer to print some text along with the numbers that it calculates, in order to show clearly what each number is. If you write a program to display a chess board or to play an animated game, you will use PRINT statements with graphics characters between the quotation marks to draw the chess pieces or animated objects on the screen.

You might like to experiment a bit with the PRINT statement. Make sure you remember how to produce the graphics characters on the screen (see Chapter 2). Then try putting some of them into a PRINT statement.

If your system includes the Timex 2040 or Sinclair ZX printer, you can also experiment with the LPRINT command (SHIFT-S). LPRINT works exactly the same way as PRINT, except that it prints on the printer instead of the television screen.

## The Computer as Calculator

Now that you know how to use the PRINT statement, you can do anything with the computer that you can do with a pocket calculator. Just enter the PRINT command followed by an expression that tells what calculations you want done. The computer will print the answer. For example, suppose you are balancing your checkbook, and you want to add a deposit and subtract a couple of withdrawals. Here is how you might do it:

```
PRINT 496.23+200-3.95-14.79
```

The computer prints **677.49**, the correct result.

All of the usual operations of arithmetic—addition, subtraction, multiplication, division, and exponents—are available on the TS1000 or ZX81. However, the symbols that represent some of them may be a little different from what you are accustomed to. The symbols for addition (+) and subtraction (−) are just what you would expect. The symbol for division is a slash (/), and the symbol for multiplication is an asterisk (*). Exponents are denoted by a double asterisk (**). Notice that this double asterisk is a single symbol, which you get by shifting the H key. Do not try to type two single asterisks instead; think of ** as a completely separate symbol.

To illustrate the different arithmetic operations that you can do with the TS1000 or ZX81, enter the following lines:

```
PRINT 7+10
```

```
PRINT 1000-1.2
```

```
PRINT 6*12
```

```
PRINT 365/12
```

```
PRINT 8**3
```

The correct answers are 17, 998.8, 72, 30.416667, and 512. Table 3-1 covers all of the standard arithmetic operations.

You can also combine several different operations in a single line, as long as you make sure the computer understands what you mean. Consider the following command:

```
PRINT 15+6/3
```

There are two different ways that you could interpret this command:

| | | | |
|---|---|---|---|
| *a.* | $15 + 6 = 21$ | *b.* | $6 / 3 = 2$ |
| | $21 / 3 = 7$ | | $15 + 2 = 17$ |

It could mean to add 15 and 6, then divide the result by 3. That would give an answer of 7, as shown on the left. It also could mean to divide 6 by 3 (giving 2) and adding the result (2) to 15. In that case you would get a final answer of 17, as shown on the right. How is the computer supposed to know which one of these two you mean?

To solve this problem, the computer assigns a priority to each different type of arithmetic operation. The ** operation has the highest priority, which means that it is done first, before any of the other operations in the command are considered. Next in priority come the * and / operations, followed by + and −. So in the example above, the division 6/3 will be done first, because division has a higher priority than addition. The result of the division (2) is then added to 15, to give 17. Try it and verify that the computer gives 17 as the answer. Table 3-2 shows the priority levels for arithmetic operations.

What if you want things done in the opposite order? Suppose you want the

**Table 3-1. Arithmetic Operators**

| Symbol | Operation |
|--------|-----------|
| + | Addition |
| − | Subtraction |
| * | Multiplication |
| / | Division |
| ** | Exponentiation |

**Table 3-2. Priority of Arithmetic Operations**

| Symbol | Meaning | Priority |
|--------|---------|----------|
| ** | Exponentiation | Highest |
| *,/ | Multiplication, Division | Middle |
| +,− | Addition, Subtraction | Lowest |

computer to add 15 and 6 and then divide the result by 3. You can get it to do this by putting 15+6 in parentheses, like this:

```
PRINT (15+6)/3
```

When the computer sees parentheses in such a command, it calculates whatever is inside the parentheses first, regardless of what priority the operation would otherwise have. Then it takes the result and combines it with the rest of the expression outside the parentheses to get the final answer.

You can even have parentheses inside of parentheses, as many times as you need to. The computer will evaluate the expression inside the innermost set of parentheses first. Then it will combine that result with the numbers in the next set of parentheses, and so on. For example, consider the command

```
PRINT ((15+6)/3)**2
```

The computer first adds 15 and 6 in the innermost parentheses, getting 21. Then it divides 21 by 3, getting 7. Finally, it squares 7 to get the correct answer, 49.

What do you think the computer would print if you left out all the parentheses and just gave the command

```
PRINT 15+6/3**2
```

Use the table of priorities given above to figure out what would happen. Then enter the command and see if you get what you expected.

Incidentally, one of the most common errors that any programmer makes is to lose track of the parentheses in an expression. If you are writing a very long expression, such as

```
PRINT (15+(6/(2-(23**(3/(5+(2+5)
-7))))))
```

it's easy to leave out a "(" or a ")" symbol, or to put in an extra one. Since parentheses always come in pairs, the number of left parentheses must always be the same as the number of right parentheses. If not, the expression just doesn't make sense, and the computer has no way of knowing what you really meant. In that case, it displays its ▤ cursor and gives you a chance to change the expression.

## Using Names for Numbers

Of course, your TS1000 or ZX81 is much more than just a calculator. Even a programmable calculator cannot begin to compete in power and flexibility with a full-fledged computer. One of the most important advantages of a computer over a calculator is the computer's ability to store a great many numbers (or other kinds of information) in its memory. Most calculators have at least one memory location where you can store a number that you have calculated for later use. Some calculators have several such memory locations. The TS1000, even without the added memory expansion, can store several hundred numbers at a time.

The examples in the previous section simply printed the result of a calculation as soon as the calculation was finished. In this section you will learn how to save and recall numbers from computer memory.

The BASIC language makes it very easy to save and use a number in memory, just by giving the number a name. The BASIC command that stores a number and gives it a name at the same time is the word LET. You use it like this:

```
LET MYNUMBER=7
```

This statement tells the computer to store the number 7 and give it the name MYNUMBER. After the computer receives this command, you can use MYNUMBER in exactly the same way you would the number 7 itself. For example, if you now enter the command

```
PRINT MYNUMBER
```

the computer will print 7. If you enter

```
PRINT MYNUMBER+9
```

it will print **16**, and so on.

The name of a number can be any combination of letters and numbers that you want to use, as long as the first one is a letter. For example, you could call a number DRIVERSLICENSENUMBER, or MAY31PAYMENT, or you could use a single letter, like Q or A. The computer will reject a name like 4THOFJULY, however, because it begins with a number instead of a letter.

You can also re-use the same name for a different number, just by writing another LET statement, such as:

```
LET MYNUMBER=365.5
```

If you do this, the old number will be discarded, unless you have saved it by giving it another name.

The "name" of the number is called a *variable*, and the number itself is the *value* of the variable. In the example above, we would say that the variable MYNUMBER has the value 365.5. Think of the variable as if it were a box with the label MYNUMBER on it. You can put any number into the box, and the new number that you put in replaces the number that was there before. The computer's memory would look something like this:

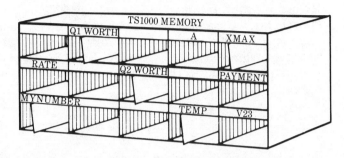

You can have hundreds of different boxes, each with a different name, and you can use the name in a calculation just as you would use the number itself.

The ability to use variables like this provides three important advantages. First, it is possible to store numbers and retrieve them for later use. Second, it is easy to keep track of all the different numbers you may be using, since you can give each number a name that reminds you what the number is being used for. Third, when you use a number more than once, your program will require less memory if you use a variable instead of retyping the number itself.

## AN EXAMPLE OF USING VARIABLES

An example will show how variables can make a calculation easier. Suppose you have $100 invested in a savings account that pays interest at an annual rate of 10%, compounded quarterly. You want to calculate how much will be in the account after half a year (two quarters). To do this calculation, you could begin by defining variables for the principal and the interest rate, like this:

```
LET PRINCIPAL=100

LET RATE=0.10

LET QRATE=RATE/4
```

The computer doesn't care what you call the variables, but it's a good idea to use names, such as PRINCIPAL and RATE, that describe what the variables mean. The third statement also defines a new variable called QRATE, which is the interest rate per quarter.

Now we calculate the interest for the first quarter and add it to the principal, to get the new worth of the account after the first quarter:

```
LET Q1INTEREST=QRATE*PRINCIPAL
LET Q1WORTH=PRINCIPAL+Q1INTEREST
```

By calling the first quarter interest Q1INTEREST and the new worth Q1WORTH, we use the variable names to help us remember what the variables mean. Now we take the new worth, calculate the interest on it for the second quarter, and add it to get Q2WORTH, the total worth at the end of the second quarter. This is the answer we wanted to calculate, and we ask the computer to print it:

```
LET Q2INTEREST=QRATE*Q1WORTH
LET Q2WORTH=Q1WORTH+Q2INTEREST
PRINT Q2WORTH
```

You might like to enter this calculation into the computer, for practice. Enter each of the eight lines in order, exactly as they appear above. Use the single-key entry for the command LET, but type the variable names letter by letter; there are no special single-key entries for variable names. Be very careful to enter the names exactly the same way each time. If you enter the statements without any errors, you will get the answer 105.0625.

### RULES FOR VARIABLES

You must follow three rules in order to use variables correctly:

1. Between LET and the equal sign there must be one variable name, and nothing else.

   For example, both of the following statements are illegal. The computer will report a syntax error (by displaying the ▧ cursor) if you try to enter them:

```
LET A+B=95
LET 17=ABC
```

The first statement is illegal because there is more than one variable name on the left of the equal sign. The second statement is illegal because the number 17 on the left is not a variable. (A variable must begin with a letter, not a number.)

   This rule makes sense if you remember what the LET statement does: it gives a value to the variable that is to the left of the equal sign. Therefore there must be a variable in that position.

2. You have to define a variable before you can use it on the right side of the equal sign, in a PRINT statement, or anywhere else.

Another way of stating this rule is that a variable must appear on the left side of a LET statement at least once before it can appear anywhere else. (Actually, the INPUT statement can define variables, but we will save that for later.)

If you try to use an undefined variable, the computer will print the error code 2 in the lower left-hand corner of the screen and will not proceed with the calculation. There's no way it could go on under those circumstances. Remember that a variable is like a box with a number (its value) in it. When you use a variable on the left side of a LET statement, you are telling the computer what to put into that box. When you use a variable on the right side of a LET statement, you are telling the computer to use the number that is in that box. Using an undefined variable on the right is like asking the computer to use the number from an empty box. Since there is nothing there to use, the computer simply tells you that you made an error and waits for further instructions.

3. Once you have defined a variable, you can change its value as many times as you want, using LET statements. The variable name never goes away unless you unplug the power or execute NEW, LOAD, RUN, or CLEAR.

A LET statement is not the same as an equation in mathematics. At first glance, a LET statement looks very similar to an equation in arithmetic or algebra. For example, the statement

```
LET X = Y + 3
```

looks very much like the equation

$$x = y + 3$$

The two are quite different, however. The LET statement is a command. It tells the computer to perform a specific action: "Take the number that is in box Y and add 3 to it, then put the resulting number in box X." On the other hand, the algebraic equation $x = y + 3$ is not a command at all. It merely states a relationship between x and y, and it doesn't tell anybody to do anything.

BASIC does not use such equations. Every statement of BASIC is a command, telling the computer to do something.

The distinction between mathematical equations and BASIC commands is very important. In mathematics, the equation

$$x = x + 1$$

would have to be a mistake. No number remains the same when you add 1 to it. However, the BASIC command

```
LET X=X+1
```

is perfectly legal. It instructs the computer to take the number that is in the "box" called x, add 1 to it, and put the resulting value back into the "box" called x. Statements like this are very common in BASIC.

To show how such a LET statement might be useful, let's return to the example of a compound interest calculation. Originally, we used a different variable for each quarter's interest and for the new value of the investment at the end of each quarter. The statements to perform the calculation looked like this:

```
LET PRINCIPAL=100
LET RATE=0.10
LET QRATE=RATE/4
LET Q1INTEREST=QRATE*PRINCIPAL
LET Q1WORTH=PRINCIPAL+Q1INTEREST
LET Q2INTEREST=QRATE*Q1WORTH
LET Q2WORTH=Q1WORTH+Q2INTEREST
PRINT Q2WORTH
```

Now we will do the same calculation in a different way, using a single variable, INTEREST, each time we calculate a quarter's interest, and using a single variable, WORTH, to store a running total of the principal plus interest to date. The INTEREST and WORTH from the previous quarter get replaced by the current INTEREST and WORTH. That's all right because by the time we are ready to calculate these values for the next quarter, we are finished with the old values from the previous quarter. Here's how we could do it:

```
LET WORTH=100
LET RATE=0.10
LET QRATE=RATE/4
LET INTEREST=QRATE*WORTH
LET WORTH=WORTH+INTEREST
```

```
LET INTEREST=QRATE*WORTH
LET WORTH=WORTH+INTEREST
PRINT WORTH
```

Again, you might like to try entering these statements. They should give the same answer as the first version, 105.0625.

The second version is simpler and easier to follow than the first version. It also uses fewer variables and therefore takes up less of the computer's memory, but both give exactly the same result. You will see this example program again in Chapter 4, where you will learn how to use some of the other features of BASIC to simplify it even further.

# WRITING AND RUNNING PROGRAMS

The rest of this book is mainly about how to write computer programs for the TS1000 and ZX81. This section tells you more specifically what a computer program is and how to ENTER, EDIT, RUN, and SAVE the programs that you write.

## Commands Versus Programs

Until now, all of the examples in this book have been single-line commands, such as

```
PRINT "THIS IS A SINGLE-LINE COM
MAND"
```

This mode of operation is called *command mode* or *immediate mode*. You ENTER the commands one at a time, and the computer executes each one as soon as you enter it. The computer "remembers" variables you create in this mode (using LET statements), but it "forgets" the commands themselves as soon as it has executed them. In command mode, you cannot tell the computer to back up three commands, for example, and execute one of the previous commands a second time. If you want to do that in command mode, you have to enter the whole command again. Command mode is useful when you just want to do a simple calculation or try out a new kind of BASIC statement to see how it works.

Often, though, you will want to do more than that. You may need to give the computer a list of several commands to remember, so that you can ask it to do all of the commands on the list again, in order, whenever you need them. Also, suppose you make a mistake typing in a command line but fail to notice the mistake until several lines later, when you get a wrong answer or an error message. It would be better if you could keep all the lines there on the screen, go back and change one of them when you need to, and then run the whole set of commands again.

The compound interest example in the previous section illustrates this need. If you made any errors while entering the commands, or if you occasionally lost track of where you were in the sequence of command lines, you will understand some of the limitations of the single-line command mode.

The ability to keep, edit, and rerun a set of commands is a standard feature of the BASIC language. Such a list of commands is a *computer program*, and this mode of operation is called *programmed mode*. Once you have entered a program, you can change parts of it or add more commands to it without having to retype the whole program. You also can list the program on the screen or save it on cassette tape to load back in whenever you want to use it again.

In the following sections, you will learn how to enter programs, edit them, run them, and save and load them on cassette tape. You will also learn some important facts about how computers and computer programs work.

## Entering Programs

Entering a program line is almost exactly like entering a single command. The only difference is that the program has a line number in front of it, like this:

```
10 PRINT "THIS IS THE FIRST LI
NE OF A PROGRAM"
```

Enter the line exactly as it appears above. You don't have to press the SPACE key between 10 and PRINT, or between PRINT and the first quotation mark. The computer will put those spaces in automatically, but you do have to type spaces between the words in quotation marks.

Press the ENTER key, as usual, when you get to the end of the line. The television screen should now look like this:

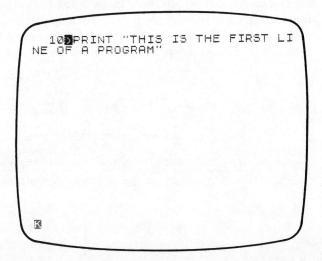

Notice that the computer did not execute the command. Instead, it just wrote the line at the top of the screen and left it there. It did this because the line had a number at the beginning, before the BASIC command word. The line has now become the first line of a program.

Next, enter the command RUN. (The command is on the same key as the letter R. Don't try to type out the word **RUN**.) Now the screen should look like this:

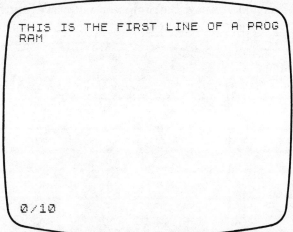

When you enter the RUN command, the TS1000 or ZX81 executes the program that you have entered into its memory. Since this program has only one line, the result is exactly the same as if you had entered the line as a command, without a number. But the program line is still there. Enter the command LIST (on the K key) and you will see it. You can RUN it again, as many times as you like, and the result will always be the same.

Of course, most computer programs have more than one line. To enter a second line, just use a larger line number:

```
 20 PRINT "THIS IS THE LAST LIN
E"
```

Here is how the screen will look after you have entered line 20:

```
   10 PRINT "THIS IS THE FIRST LI
NE OF A PROGRAM"
   20▮PRINT "THIS IS THE LAST LIN
E"




K
```

If you enter RUN now, the computer will first execute line 10, and then line 20. The screen will look like this:

```
THIS IS THE FIRST LINE OF A PROG
RAM
THIS IS THE LAST LINE




0/20
```

Now enter LIST to see the program listing again.

Every program line must have a line number, and there can be only one command per line.

The computer knows which line to execute first. It begins with the one that has the lowest line number, then it executes the next lowest, and so on. (You can also tell it to skip around, but we will save that topic for a later chapter.) It doesn't matter in what order you actually entered the different lines. The computer will use the line numbers to reorder the lines for you. To see how this works, enter the following line:

```
15 PRINT "THIS IS THE MIDDLE L
INE"
```

Although line 15 was entered last, the computer lists the lines in numerical order, with 10 at the top, 15 in the middle, and 20 at the end. If you enter RUN now, the computer will execute the three lines in that order.

It's always a good idea to number your program lines in steps of 10 or more, so that you can go back and insert new lines between them if you want to.

## THE NEW AND CLEAR COMMANDS

Suppose you have entered and run a program, and now you are through with it and ready to enter something new. One way to get rid of the old program would be to delete each of its lines, one at a time, but that would not get rid of the variables that the old program defined. They would still be in memory, using up valuable space. You could unplug and reconnect power, but that is hard on the computer. Fortunately, BASIC provides a command that removes a program and its variables from memory. It is the NEW command, located on the A key. There is also a CLEAR command (on the x key) that gets rid of all the variables without deleting the program.

## THE REM STATEMENT

The REM command tells the computer nothing but to go on to the next line—yet it is one of the most useful commands on the keyboard.

Execute NEW, then enter the line

```
10 REM THIS IS A REMARK
```

Now enter RUN. Nothing special happens.

What the REM statement does is give you a chance to put comments (REMarks) in your program so that you and other people can more easily see and remember how the program works. Putting in REM statements may seem like a waste of time, but the opposite is true. It is a waste of time *not* to put in REM statements, because you will spend so much more time later on, maybe even months later, when you decide you would like to improve the program but can't remember how it works. Get in the habit of using REM statements from the time you begin learning BASIC.

## SLOW AND FAST MODES

By now you have probably noticed that the computer cannot keep up with you if you try to type very fast. Every time you press a key, you have to wait for the computer to display the entire line you were typing, one character at a time, from left to right on the television screen. Every time you press ENTER at the end of a new program line, you have to wait for the computer to redisplay every program line on the screen, from the top down. As your program gets longer, you will notice these effects even more.

The reason the computer's response seems so slow is that it has more to do than just follow what you are doing at the keyboard. It also has to generate the video signal that goes to the television set. Because of the way a television works, the computer cannot just send characters to the screen. In fact, it must keep sending every line of the television picture, from top to bottom, 60 times every second (or in Europe, 50 times every second). This actually takes up a great deal of its time, but the computer still uses the time between video frames to respond to what you are typing or to run your program. The designers of the ZX81 and TS1000 made them this way so that the programs can change the television display while they are running to produce animated effects. Without this capability, most computer games would be rather dull, and the computer would not be nearly as useful in many other ways.

Sometimes you don't really need to see the display all the time, and you would rather have the computer run faster. That's what the FAST command (SHIFT-F) is for. Press FAST, followed by ENTER, and then retype one of the lines you entered above. Now the computer will respond much faster to what you type, but you will not see the individual letters of the line appearing one at a time after each keystroke. Instead, the screen will go blank momentarily when you press a key, and then the entire display, with the new character in it, will reappear all at once.

To reset the computer to the mode it was in before, enter SLOW (SHIFT-D).

When you first plug in the computer, it is in SLOW mode. It goes into FAST mode automatically when you save or load a program from cassette, or when you print on the printer. Then when it finishes, it goes back into SLOW mode again.

You can use FAST and SLOW as single-line commands, or you can use them as program lines. Most people prefer to put the computer into FAST mode when they are entering programs, and to use SLOW mode only when they are running programs that do animation. The first program that you entered in Chapter 2 is an example of animation. If you run it in SLOW mode, you will see the letter I moving in across the screen from the right, and then up the screen from the bottom. If you run the same program in FAST mode, you will not see the letter I move at all. The screen will be blank for a short time, and you will only see the final result, with the I in place at the top of the screen.

## WHEN MEMORY GETS FULL

Without the 16K memory pack, both the TS1000 and the ZX81 have a rather small amount of memory available for storing programs and data. With the ZX81 you can enter about 20 or 30 program lines (depending on what the lines contain) before memory gets full. With the TS1000 you can enter between two and three times that many lines.

As memory gets close to being completely full, the display will begin to behave strangely. Try entering the same line over and over again with different line numbers in order to see what happens. Any one of the lines you entered above will do. (If your system has the 16K memory pack, unplug power and remove the pack first; otherwise you will have to enter hundreds of lines to fill up memory, and the effect on the display will be slightly different.)

The first thing you will notice as memory fills up is that the program listing begins to move up, leaving a blank space at the bottom of the screen. This happens because the screen display also uses up part of the computer's memory, and the computer was designed to take memory away from the display area if necessary in order to make more room for your program. If you keep entering more lines, the display will eventually shrink to nothing, except for maybe a few characters at the very top. The program is still there, however, and you can see it again if you DELETE some of the lines you have entered. (To delete a line, just type its line number, followed by ENTER.)

Other strange things may also happen as the memory gets full. The EDIT key may fail to work. If you try to run a program, it will probably stop before it should. The numeral 4 will appear at the lower left-hand corner of the screen. This number is an *error code* that tells you that you have run out of memory.

There isn't much you can do when memory gets full, except to delete part of the program. You will probably want to delete REM statements first. It also helps to use short names for variables and to use variables instead of numbers whenever you can. Beyond this, the only thing you can do is obtain the 16K memory pack accessory.

## Editing Programs

There are two reasons why you might want to change parts of a computer program. First, you might need to correct a mistake made when you first entered the program. Second, you might decide to make some changes in what the program does. In either case, you will need a way to edit your computer programs.

The TS1000 and ZX81 computers have several special editing keys and other features to help you make changes in your programs. These features include whole-line editing, the DELETE key, the horizontal and vertical arrow keys, and the EDIT key. The following sections describe these features.

## WHOLE-LINE EDITING

You have already learned how to insert a new program line into a program. Just type a line number that corresponds to the place in the program where you want to insert the line, followed by the new line itself. BASIC will automatically insert the line in the right place for you. You can also change an existing line by retyping it with the changes, using the same line number. To illustrate this, first retype the lines given in the section on Entering Programs, earlier in this chapter, so that the television screen looks like this:

```
   10 PRINT "THIS IS THE FIRST LI
NE OF A PROGRAM"
   15 PRINT "THIS IS THE MIDDLE L
INE"
   20 PRINT "THIS IS THE LAST LIN
E"
```

Now enter the following:

```
15 PRINT "NEW MIDDLE LINE"
```

You will see that the new line 15 replaces the old line 15 that you entered before. You can even erase a line entirely by typing just its line number, followed by ENTER. Try this for line 15, and watch the line disappear from the display.

## THE DELETE KEY

The DELETE key (SHIFT-0) deletes the character to the left of the cursor on the screen. Use this key to back up and correct an error any time while you are typing a line. Type a few characters. Then DELETE them to see how the DELETE key works. Notice what happens when you have deleted everything up to the left-hand edge of the screen. The DELETE key now has no further effect. If you want to change something on a previous line in programmed mode, you must either re-enter the whole line or use the EDIT key (explained later in the chapter).

## THE CURSOR LEFT AND CURSOR RIGHT KEYS
## (SHIFT-5 AND SHIFT-8)

Use the ← and → keys to move the cursor backward or forward on the line you are typing. You can insert additional characters anywhere in the line by moving the cursor to the right place and entering the new characters. For example, suppose you have just typed a line that looks like this:

```
15 PRINT "NEW MIDLE LINE"█
```

The █ cursor appears at the right end of the line because you have not yet pressed ENTER. Use the ← key to move the cursor back until the line looks like this:

```
15 PRINT "NEW MID█LE LINE"
```

Now type the second D, followed by ENTER. The corrected line will appear in the program listing. Notice that you can use ENTER at any time, regardless of where the cursor is within the line.

To delete a character in the middle of a line, use the CURSOR LEFT or RIGHT key to position the █ cursor immediately to the right of the character you want to delete. Then press DELETE. You can move back and forth within a line as many times as you like, inserting and deleting characters. The ← and → keys are especially useful for correcting errors that the computer detects and marks with the █ cursor.

## THE EDIT AND CURSOR UP AND CURSOR DOWN KEYS

The editing techniques in the last two sections apply only within a single line, before you press ENTER. To edit a line that is already entered, you first have to select which line to edit. You may have noticed that the symbol █ often appears on one of the program lines, between the line number and the command word. This symbol is the *edit cursor*. You use it to select a line for editing.

To use this editing method, first make sure the screen looks like this:

```
10 PRINT "THIS IS THE FIRST LINE
   OF A PROGRAM"
15█PRINT "NEW MIDDLE LINE"
20 PRINT "THIS IS THE LAST LINE"
```

The edit cursor may be on line 10 or line 20 instead of line 15, depending on which line you entered last, but everything else should be the way it looks above. If it is not, re-enter the line or lines that are different.

Now use the ↑ and ↓ keys (SHIFT-7 and SHIFT-6) to move the █ cursor up and down on the screen. Move it to line 10 and press EDIT (SHIFT-1). A copy of line 10 will appear at the bottom of the screen, where new lines ordinarily appear as you type them. Now use the ← and → keys to move back and forth in the line, inserting or deleting characters just as you would when entering a brand new line. To illustrate this editing method, change the copy of line 10 at the bottom of your program so that it reads:

```
10 PRINT "NEW FIRST LINE"
```

The original line 10 at the top of the screen remains unchanged until you press ENTER. Then the edited line at the bottom disappears, and a copy of it replaces the old line 10 at the top. Now the screen looks like this:

```
10 PRINT "NEW FIRST LINE"
15 PRINT "NEW MIDDLE LINE"
20 PRINT "THIS IS THE LAST LINE"
```

If your program is too large to fit on the screen, you can still use the ↑ or ↓ key to move to any line. The computer will scroll the screen up or down as the ▓ reaches the top or the bottom of the screen. However, if the computer's memory is so full that the television display begins to show less than a full screen, the EDIT key may not work. If this happens, you can still change the line by re-entering it.

You can also move the ▓ cursor up or down with the LIST command, followed by the number of the line where you want the edit cursor. Enter

```
LIST 15
```

and watch the ▓ cursor move to line 15. Use this method with very long programs, when it would take too long to move the cursor from one end of the program to the other with the ↑ or the ↓ key.

Table 3-3 contains a summary of the special editing keys.

## Error Codes

You have probably noticed that a pair of numbers appears at the lower left-hand corner of the screen every time the computer executes a command or runs a program. This pair of numbers, separated by a slash (0/10, for

Table 3-3. Editing Keys

| Keys | Purpose |
| --- | --- |
| DELETE | Delete character to left of cursor |
| ← and → | Move cursor left or right within current line |
| ↑ and ↓ | Move cursor up or down |
| EDIT | Bring the line marked by ▓ to the bottom for editing |

example) is called a *report code* or an *error code*. It contains useful information about what happened while the command or program was executing. Always look at the report code after you run a program.

The number to the right of the slash is the line number of the last line that the computer executed. A zero in this position means that the line was a single-line command, which has no line number at all. The number to the left of the slash tells you whether the computer detected any errors when it tried to obey the program instructions. A zero in this position means that no errors were detected. Other numbers usually mean that some kind of error occurred. The number to the right of the slash shows which line the computer was executing when it detected the error. You will learn more about the different kinds of errors and what to do about them in the following chapters. Appendix B lists all the possible error numbers and their meanings.

## Saving Programs on Tape

In Chapter 2 you learned how to load a prerecorded program from a cassette into your computer. This section will tell you how to save a program of your own onto a cassette, so that you can load it back into the computer and execute it at a later time. You might want to go back and review the cassette section of Chapter 2, to make sure you remember everything that you learned there.

First you need a program to save on tape. You can use the compound interest program that was given a few pages back, the introductory program from Chapter 2, or some other program that you have loaded from tape. Any program will do. With a program entered in the computer, use the jacks to connect the MIC plug on the computer (Figure 2-7) to the MIC or MICROPHONE plug on your cassette recorder. If the cable to the EAR plugs is still connected, unplug it in case your recorder is the kind that will not work correctly with both plugs occupied. Place a blank cassette (or one whose contents you don't want to keep) in the recorder.

Now type in the following command at the keyboard (use the s key for SAVE), but don't press the ENTER key yet:

```
SAVE "PROGRAM1"
```

You can use any name you want between the quotes, instead of PROGRAM1, but you must put a name of some kind there. Otherwise, the computer will refuse the command. The name you use is stored with the program. You will use it with the LOAD command later, when you are ready to read the program, to tell the computer which program to search for on the tape.

Start the cassette recorder in RECORD mode (the instruction manual for the recorder tells you how to do this). Wait until the tape has unwound past the leader and onto the recording surface. If you can't see the leader clearly, just wait about ten seconds after starting the tape.

Next, press ENTER on the computer keyboard, and watch the television display. The picture should go blank for five seconds. Then you will see a pattern of black and white lines, somewhat like the picture in Figure 3-1. This pattern means that the computer is recording your program. After a few seconds (the longer the program, the longer it takes), the screen will return to normal and the report code 0/0 will appear in the lower left-hand corner of the screen. Now stop the recorder.

If this is the first time you have saved a program on a cassette with the TS1000, you should listen to the tape to make sure that the volume was at the right level, and that the recorded program is free of excessive noise. To do this, unplug the jacks from the cassette unit, rewind the tape, turn down the volume (to protect your ears), and play the tape. You should first hear a low hum, then five seconds of silence, and then a screeching noise that corresponds to the program itself. Turn up the volume until the noise is unpleasantly loud. Then rewind to the silent spot and make sure there is no significant background noise where the silence should be. If there is, adjust the settings of the volume and tone controls while saving (if your cassette recorder has these controls).

When you are satisfied with the quality of the recording, reconnect the EAR cable to the computer and load the program back in, following the instructions of Chapter 2. Enter the LIST command. The program listing on the screen should now look exactly the same as it did before you recorded it,

Figure 3-1. Screen pattern while the cassette records a program.

proving that you have found the right settings for the tone and volume controls. Mark the position of the controls on the dials so that you can find them again easily.

You can record as many programs as you have room for on a single tape, one after the other. If you use a different name when you SAVE each one, you can LOAD any one of them back in by name without having to remember exactly where it is on the tape. If you ever forget the name of a program, use the command

```
LOAD ""
```

with no name between the quotation marks. This command simply loads the next program on the tape, regardless of its name.

If your cassette unit has a program counter, use it to keep track of where each program is on the tape. Use the FAST FORWARD mode of the cassette unit to go directly to the program you want, instead of waiting for the computer to search the whole tape. In order for this technique to work, you must remember to reset the counter each time you insert and rewind a different tape, whether to SAVE or to LOAD. When you SAVE a program, write the counter reading on the cassette label, beside the name of the program.

## Interrupting a Program

Sometimes you may want to stop a program earlier than it would normally stop. For example, you might discover an error in your program and decide to stop it immediately instead of waiting for it to finish. Alternatively, the cassette unit might malfunction while loading or saving a program.

The BREAK key stops the program and restores the ▓ cursor immediately. The BREAK key is the same as the SPACE key. If you press it while you are entering a program, it inserts a space. If you press it while a program is running, however, it terminates the program and displays the ▓ cursor.

# HOW PROGRAMS WORK

In the previous sections you have learned what a computer program is. You have seen how to enter program lines and how to edit, run, and save BASIC programs using your TS1000 or ZX81 computer. You have also learned how to use some of the individual programming commands of the BASIC language. Table 3-4 summarizes the commands you have used up to now.

In Chapters 4 and 5, you will meet quite a few more BASIC commands. Now that you have learned enough BASIC to work with, and before we delve further into the specifics of the language, it's time to think more carefully

**Table 3-4. BASIC Commands**

| Command | Meaning |
|---------|---------|
| PRINT | Print numbers or text on the video screen |
| LPRINT | Print numbers or text on the printer |
| LET | Create a variable and give it a value |
| LIST | List program lines on the video screen |
| LLIST | List program lines on the printer |
| COPY | Copy the television screen to the printer |
| RUN | Run the program |
| SAVE | Save a program on cassette tape |
| LOAD | Read a program from cassette tape |
| SLOW | Maintain the display while programs run |
| FAST | Run faster by letting the display go blank during program execution |
| NEW | Delete the program and its variables |
| CLEAR | Delete all variables, but keep the program |
| BREAK | Interrupt the program that is running |

about what a computer can do, about what a computer can't do, and about how it proceeds through a computer program.

## The Obedient, Stupid Servant

The single most important fact to remember about computers is this: computers do exactly what their programs tell them to do. You often hear news reports about so-called "computer errors"—when a computer sends out an incorrect bill, for example, or almost fires a missile by mistake. In practically every case, however, these errors are really human errors. They happen because a programmer gave wrong instructions to the computer. Only very rarely does a computer fail to execute its program correctly, due to a breakdown in one of its electronic circuits.

In one sense, computers are stupid. They have no idea what you want to do or why you want to do it. They simply do exactly as they are told, regardless of the consequences. Even the very best programmers sometimes discover, to their dismay, that what they *told* the computer to do was different from what they *meant* for it to do.

Imagine that you have a servant who obeys every command you give him, perfectly and without fail. Unfortunately, this servant is also very stupid. As a result, you have to be extremely careful about how you phrase your commands. If you tell him to "dust everything in the house," you may come back in a few minutes to find him dusting the pudding or the cat. What will he do if you tell him to dust the roses? Will he sprinkle insecticide on them, or will he get out the feather duster again? With such a servant, you would not want to say, "Could you bring me the hammer?" He would probably answer, "Yes, I could," and then stand there waiting for your next command.

Programming a computer is somewhat like giving orders to our stupid servant. It's sometimes difficult to tell a computer exactly what we mean because we are used to dealing with people who know what we mean from the context, even if we aren't completely precise in the way we say it.

Computer languages, however, deliberately rule out the kind of ambiguity that occurs in an English word like *dust*. If you accidentally type the letter O instead of 0, or the number 1 instead of the letter I, the computer will not guess what you really meant. If you forget to tell the computer to print the answer at the end of a long calculation, the computer will not print it. It can't look at the program and understand your purpose in writing it. All the computer can do is obey the instructions, one at a time.

Computers are becoming easier for people to program and use. The BASIC language is much more "user friendly" than the first computer languages were. Computer scientists are working toward even friendlier ones. It will be a long time, however, before computers really begin to understand our ordinary ways of expressing ourselves. Until then, people who want to write programs for computers must learn to use special computer languages like BASIC, and to be completely clear and explicit in the instructions they give.

## Programs that Make Choices

If computers are really stupid, you may wonder how they can design factories, manage finances, play chess, and do all the other kinds of things that computers do. Part of the answer is that complicated programs for tasks like these are constructed from smaller, simpler units. The kinds of tasks that computers can do well are ones that reduce to simple, individual procedures for performing a single calculation or making a single decision. You have seen how to program your TS1000 or ZX81 to perform calculations and to print numbers and text. Now you will learn some of the ways of programming the computer to make choices.

The kinds of choices that the computer can make are very simple ones. For example, it can compare two numbers to see if they are equal, or to see which is larger. It can also choose one action or another, depending on the result of the comparison. Chapter 6 will describe in detail the kinds of comparisons the computer can make. The present section gives only an overview of this decision-making capability.

The following shows how the TS1000 or ZX81 makes choices. Enter NEW (SHIFT-A) to erase any previous programs. Then enter the following program lines:

```
70 LET TEST=1
80 IF TEST=1 THEN PRINT "UNITY
"
```

```
  90 IF TEST=2 THEN PRINT "DUALI
TY"
```

Don't type out the words **IF** and **THEN**. Use the u key and SHIFT-3 instead.
Now enter RUN and observe what happens. The screen should look like this:

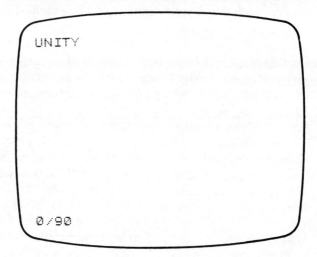

The computer prints **UNITY** because TEST is equal to one, and it ignores
the PRINT command in line 90 because TEST is not equal to two. Now change
line 70 to read

```
  70 LET TEST=2
```

and RUN the program again. This time the screen looks like this:

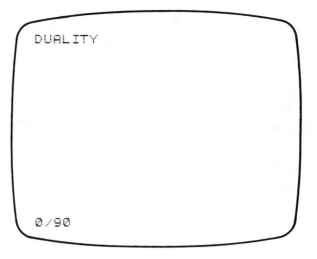

What do you suppose will happen if you give TEST a different value, such as three? Try it and see.

This decision program is not very useful, but it illustrates an important aspect of computer programming. A larger program might have you enter the value of TEST from the keyboard each time you run it. In this way, the program could give you the choice of doing many different things, depending on the value you entered for TEST. Another program might first calculate the value of TEST, and then use it many lines later. In this way, you can get the computer to "remember" what happened earlier in the program.

Numbers and Text

# Chapter Four

**T**his chapter describes how the computer stores and displays its two major types of data: numbers and text. It tells you how to use BASIC commands to create and manipulate both kinds of data and how to use the computer's special *functions* that make such manipulations easier and more powerful.

## HOW TO USE NUMBERS

Chapter 3 introduced the five arithmetic operations that the TS1000 and ZX81 recognize. These operations are summarized in Table 4-1. Chapter 3 also described how to combine these operations with numbers to produce new numbers. Now you will learn more about the rules for combining numbers and about the different ways of entering numbers into the computer.

Table 4-1. Arithmetic Operations

| Symbol | Operation |
| --- | --- |
| + | Addition |
| − | Subtraction |
| * | Multiplication |
| / | Division |
| ** | Exponentiation (powers) |

## Priority in Numeric Operations

Recall that each operation has its own *priority*. The priority determines which operation the computer does first when you combine different operations.

Our previous list of arithmetic operations and their priorities is not quite complete, however, because the minus symbol (–) actually has two possible meanings. It normally occurs between two numbers and means subtraction, but it can also occur with a single number, such as −2. The minus sign here cannot mean subtraction, because there is nothing on the left side of the sign to subtract from. This is a *unary* minus sign, which simply specifies a negative number. It is a unary operator because it goes with only *one* number. The other kind of minus sign (which means subtraction) is a *binary* operator because it goes with *two* numbers. The operators +, *, /, and ** are also binary operators.

The unary minus sign belongs in second place in the table of priorities, after exponentiation but before multiplication and division. A complete arithmetic priority chart is shown in Table 4-2.

Because of these priorities, you can multiply and divide negative numbers without parentheses, like this:

```
PRINT 6*-8
```

The result is −48.

You must be careful, though, if you want to take a negative number to a power. If you have studied algebra, you know that the square of a negative number is always positive. However, since exponentiation has a higher priority than the unary minus, if you give the following command, you will get −9 instead of the positive 9 that you might expect:

```
PRINT -3**2
```

Because ** has higher priority, the computer evaluates 3**2 first, to get 9. Then it applies the unary minus sign to get −9.

You might try to force a positive result by using parentheses, like this:

```
PRINT (-3)**2
```

However, when you execute this command, the computer just prints report code A (illegal argument).

Since the computer is unable to perform exponential functions on negative numbers correctly, you will need to detect the polarity (+/−) in your programs and make the corrections yourself.

**Table 4-2. Priority of Arithmetic Operations**

| Symbol | Meaning | Priority |
|---|---|---|
| ** | Exponentiation | Highest |
| − | Unary minus (negation) | Second highest |
| * and / | Multiplication and Division | Lower |
| + and − | Addition and Subtraction | Lowest |

## Numeric Expressions

A *numeric expression* simply specifies some numbers and how to combine them. Some examples of numeric expressions are

```
PRINT 496.23+200-3.95-14.79

PRINT ((15+6)/3)**2
```

The command PRINT is not part of the expression. It is used in these examples because it tells the computer to evaluate the expression and display the result. As the results you get indicate, when the computer evaluates a numeric expression, the result is always another number.

A numeric expression can be used wherever you can use a number in a BASIC statement, except at the beginning of the line as a line number. If you try to enter an expression for a line number, like this:

```
2+3 PRINT "DO NOT TRY THIS"
```

the computer displays the ▤ cursor and refuses to accept the line.

You can use variables as well as numbers in numeric expressions, as long as you have defined each variable (that is, given it a value) beforehand. For example, if you have entered the command

```
LET VARIABLE1=5
```

then you can use VARIABLE1 in an expression, like this:

```
PRINT VARIABLE1-2
```

## Variables and Constants

The computer recognizes two different ways of specifying a number in an expression: the number itself, or a variable that has that number as its value. The number itself is a *constant*. Unlike a variable, it can never take on a different value. Table 4-3 lists examples of numeric constants and numeric variables, showing the differences.

Remember that the name of a numeric variable must begin with a letter. After that, it can contain any mixture of letters and numbers. It cannot contain symbols, such as $, %, or ", however.

A constant must begin with a digit, a decimal point, or a minus sign. If a number has no decimal part (for example, the number 7) the decimal point is optional. The computer treats the constants 7.0, 7, and 7. exactly alike.

Constants generally look and act just like ordinary numbers, with two exceptions. First, the computer will not understand a number with commas in it, such as 32,768. You must use 32768 instead. Second, the computer will not accept a constant with a plus sign in front of it, such as +4.6, at the beginning of an expression.

## Scientific Notation

Look at the number 1.67E−5 in Table 4-3. The name for this way of writing a constant is *scientific notation*. Scientific notation provides a convenient way of entering very large or very small constants. Suppose you wanted to enter a large constant, such as

$$7300000000000000$$

Using ordinary notation, you could easily enter the wrong number of zeros by mistake. Scientific notation provides a better way of writing it. To use scientific notation, first move the decimal point so it is immediately to the right of the first (leftmost) nonzero digit. Remove all of the zeros after it. Then put an E after the number, followed by the number of places that you moved the decimal point.

Using this procedure, 7300000000000000 would become

$$7.3E+15$$

Table 4-3. Examples of Constants
and Variables

| Constants | Variables |
|-----------|-----------|
| 7 | MYNUMBER |
| 3.1415927 | MINCEMEAT |
| −44.1 | MAY31PAYMENT |
| .25 | VARIABLE1 |
| 1.67E−5 | D2K |

In other words, 7.3E+15 means 73 followed by 14 zeros. The E serves as a separator between the first part (7.3), which tells what the nonzero digits of the number are, and the second part (+15), which tells where the decimal point should be. The part before the E is the *mantissa*, and the part after the E is the *exponent*.

Scientific notation works equally well for very small numbers. For example,

$$.000000000423$$

would become, in scientific notation,

$$4.23E-10$$

The minus sign after the E shows that you moved the decimal point from left to right.

Table 4-4 compares scientific and ordinary notation.

Scientific notation can be used wherever you can use an ordinary constant in a BASIC program, except in line numbers. It works for any constant of any size—even an ordinary one like 2E0, although 2 is obviously a simpler and easier notation.

The computer's PRINT command displays numbers in scientific notation if they are larger than 1E+13 or smaller than 1E-6. The way the computer stores the numbers internally, however, does not change; it just displays them differently.

Try entering some numbers into PRINT statements using scientific notation, like this:

```
PRINT 1.492E+3
```

If you choose numbers that are not too large or too small, the computer will print them in ordinary notation. Doing this, you can compare the two notations to make sure you understand how to convert numbers from one to the other.

**Table 4-4. Examples of Scientific and Ordinary Notation**

| Ordinary | Scientific |
|---|---|
| .005 | 5E-3 |
| .0057 | 5.7E-3 |
| .01 | 1E-2 |
| .8 | 8E-1 |
| 3 | 3E0 |
| 56 | 5.6E1 |
| 608 | 6.08E2 |

## Size of Numbers and Rounding

The TS1000 and ZX81 store and use numbers in an internal format called floating point. The term *floating point* means that the decimal point can be located anywhere it needs to be in order to express numbers of different sizes. You do not need to know many details about how floating point format works, just that BASIC automatically translates your numbers into floating point format when you enter them.

The computer can handle very large and very small numbers precisely, but it does have some limits. The TS1000 and ZX81 can store numbers between 1E+38 and 4E−39. If you try to use a number that is too large, the computer will display error code 6 (the "arithmetic overflow error") at the lower left-hand corner of the screen. If you try to use a number that is too small, the computer will simply convert the number to zero and continue the calculation without reporting an error.

To demonstrate these limits, enter the following commands:

```
PRINT 2*1E+38

PRINT 1E-39
```

The first command gives the report code 6/0 and does not print an answer. The second command prints the answer **0** and gives the report code 0/0, which means no error.

Numbers in the TS1000 and ZX81 have a maximum of nine digits. The PRINT command rounds off after eight digits. To see how this works, enter the following command:

```
PRINT 123456789
```

Observe that the computer rounds off to 123456790. Similarly, it rounds off the fractional number 0.123456789 to 0.12345679. The only time this rounding error is likely to cause problems is when you subtract two numbers that are very close together. For example, the following command should give an answer of 5, but it gives 0 instead:

```
PRINT 1E12+5-1E12
```

The number 1E12 is so big compared to 5 that the 5 disappears in the rounding error. This is a rather unusual calculation because it uses a mixture of very large and small numbers. For the kind of programs you will ordinarily write, you will probably never need to worry about rounding error.

# STRINGS AND STRING EXPRESSIONS

The TS1000 and ZX81 can store and manipulate two kinds of data: numbers and strings. A *string* is any data that should be treated as text. You already know how to use text in a print command, like this:

```
PRINT "GOOD MORNING"
```

The text "GOOD MORNING" is a string. To specify a string, just put its characters between quotation marks. Some examples of strings are

```
"FOURSCORE AND SEVEN YEARS AGO"
```

```
"ADDRESS OF CUSTOMER"
"123-45-6789"
"CINCO DE MAYO"
"$K<+=<>*/$S"
"          "
"TIMEX-SINCLAIR 1000"
""
```

The last example is the *empty string*, which contains no characters at all. Another name for it is the *null string*. It is the only string whose length is zero.

A string can be as long or as short as you like. It can contain graphics characters, reverse video characters, and any of the other characters on the keyboard, except the quote character (") itself. If strings could contain the quote character, the computer would not be able to tell which of the quote characters were part of the string and which were the markers at the ends of the string. Instead, the keyboard contains a special symbol called the *quote image* (SHIFT-Q) that takes the place of the quote character inside strings. The quote image looks like two quote characters in a row, but it acts like a single character. When you use the quote image in a string, it produces a single quote symbol in the display. For example, the command

```
PRINT "I SAID ""BE CAREFUL"" TWI
CE"
```

will print the line

```
I SAID "BE CAREFUL" TWICE
```

Do not confuse the quote image with the expression for the null string. They look exactly alike on the screen, but they are different. The null string is a pair of single quote symbols (SHIFT-P's), and it means a string with no characters in it. The quote image is a single symbol (SHIFT-Q), and it stands for a quote symbol inside a string.

## String Constants, String Variables

Notice that the PRINT commands for strings are very similar to PRINT commands for numbers, like this one:

```
PRINT 5
```

This illustrates the fact that the computer handles numbers and strings in very much the same way. It provides for string constants and string variables, just as it provides for numeric constants and numeric variables. You can also combine strings in string expressions, just as you can combine numbers in numeric expressions.

All of the strings just listed are *string constants*. Like numeric constants, they always have the same value. You have to type them in again, character by character, every time you want to use them. The TS1000 and ZX81 also allow you to use *string variables*. A string variable works the same way as a numeric variable, except that it represents a string instead of a number. The following example shows how to define and use a string variable:

```
LET V$="MODEL NUMBER"
PRINT V$
```

Unlike a numeric variable, the name of a string variable must be exactly two characters long. The first character of the name must be a single letter, and the second character must be a dollar sign. The dollar sign distinguishes string variables from numeric variables. The differences between the names of string variables and numeric variables are shown in Table 4-5.

**Table 4-5. Differences Between Names
of String and Numeric Variables**

| String Variable Names | Numeric Variable Names |
| --- | --- |
| Begin with a letter | Begin with a letter |
| End with a dollar sign | End with any letter or number |
| Exactly two characters long | As long as you like |

Use a string variable whenever you need the same string more than once to avoid having to type it in again each time. A variable saves space in the computer because the computer only has to store the variable once, no matter how many times you use it. A string variable also helps you avoid misspelling the string when you use it over and over. That might not be a problem for a string like "GOOD MORNING", but it could be very important if you had to enter a text that repeated one of the following strings several times:

```
CHAUGOGGAGOGMANCHAUGGAGOGCHABBUN
AGUNGAMUAG

FEVERVERSICHERUNGSGESELLSCHAFT

HUMMINGBIRD-ON-THE-LEFT
```

With a variable, you only have to enter such a string correctly once. After that, it will be correct every time you use the variable.

## String Expressions

A string expression combines strings in much the same way that a numeric expression combines numbers. When the computer evaluates a numeric expression, the result is a number. When it evaluates a string expression, the result is a string. The operations in a numeric expression are just the familiar arithmetic operations, such as addition, subtraction, multiplication, division, and exponentiation. The operations in a string expression are probably not familiar to you unless you already know BASIC. Even then, some of the string operations on the TS1000 and ZX81 are different from the ones on other computers. However, they are all easy to understand and use, and they do exactly the kinds of things you will need to do with strings: connect two strings together into one, extract parts of strings to make new strings, and change parts of strings.

### STRING CONCATENATION

To *concatenate* strings means to join them together. The symbol for string concatenation is the plus sign (+). Although it is also the symbol for numeric addition, it means something entirely different with strings. For example, enter the following line:

```
PRINT "APRIL"+" "+"25"
```

The computer takes the three strings in the command, "APRIL", " ", and "25", and joins them into a single string that prints as

```
APRIL 25
```

The space could also be part of one of the other strings, like this:

```
PRINT "APRIL "+"25"
```

String concatenation works the same way in assigning values to variables as it does in PRINT statements, as you can see from the following:

```
LET B$="APRIL "+"25"
PRINT B$
```

Each of these alternatives prints the same line on the screen, namely:

```
APRIL 25
```

Use the + operator any time you want to join two or more strings together into one. Do not try to use it, though, with a mixture of numbers and strings. For example, if you enter the command

```
PRINT "APRIL"+25
```

the computer will refuse the line and display the ▓ cursor, indicating a syntax error. Remember that the + symbol can represent two totally different operations. One refers to numbers and tells the computer to add them. The other refers to strings and tells the computer to concatenate them. A + symbol with a string on one side and a number on the other side just doesn't make sense.

String concatenation can be useful in many ways. For example, suppose you were trying to decide on a name for your newborn daughter. You might have a list of 20 or 30 possible first names and just as many middle names, and you might want to look at all the different combinations of these with each other and with your last name. To do this, you would need a program to concatenate the names in all possible combinations and list them. Such a program would require some features of BASIC that you have not learned yet, but it gives you an idea of how string concatenation could be useful.

The other arithmetic operators (−, *, /, and **) have no meaning for strings. You will get a syntax error report (the ▓ cursor) if you try to use them.

## SUBSTRINGS

Another useful operation on strings is one that extracts part of a string to make a new string. The name for such a part of a string is a *substring*, and the operation that extracts it is called *slicing*. To choose the part of the string you want, you must specify its first and last characters by their locations in the string. For example, suppose you have a string that gives the part number of some item in your business inventory, and you want to use just the third through the fifth characters (or digits) in the part number. Enter the part number into the computer like this:

```
LET P$="A3923476329"
```

Then, to extract the third through fifth characters in this string, use the following command:

```
LET G$=P$(3 TO 5)
```

(The symbol TO is SHIFT-4, not the separate letters T and O.) This command tells the computer to take a substring of string P$, from the third to the fifth character, and make that into a new string with the name G$. Now when you enter the command

```
PRINT G$
```

the computer prints **923**. Of course, you could easily look at a single inventory number like this and extract the section you want by yourself. However, if you had hundreds or thousands of such numbers in your inventory, a computer program to do it for you would save a great deal of work.

A slicing command can extract any part of a string in this way, as long as the numbers on either side of the TO symbol correspond to actual locations in the string. If the second number in the command is larger than the number of characters in the string, the computer will report error code 3, "subscript out of range." The computer will use the null string if the number on the left is larger than the one on the right, as in the following command:

```
PRINT P$(5 TO 3)
```

The numbers on either side of TO in the slicing command are optional. If you omit the first number, the computer assumes that it is 1. If you omit the last number, the computer assumes that it is the number of the last character in the string. So for the string P$="A3923476329" in the example just used, the command

```
PRINT P$(TO 6)
```

gives exactly the same result as the command

```
PRINT P$(1 TO 6)
```

Because the example string contains 11 characters, the command

```
PRINT P$(4 TO)
```

gives the same result as

```
PRINT P$(4 TO 11)
```

To extract just one character from the string (the fifth character, for example), you can replace the full notation

```
PRINT P$(5 TO 5)
```

with the abbreviated notation:

```
PRINT P$(5)
```

Finally, the command

```
PRINT P$( TO )
```

specifies the entire string P$, because the numbers that go with TO will *default* to the first and last characters in the string—that is, the first and last characters will be used in the absence of other instructions.

Most of these examples use the PRINT command to make it easier to see how the slicing works. String slicing works the same way in a LET statement, however, as you can see from the following:

```
LET X$=P$(4 TO 5)
```

In fact, a sliced string can be used anywhere in a BASIC program wherever any other kind of string can be used.

The following example illustrates string slicing. Suppose you had a long list of geographical place names, each one stored in a string. You want the computer to print out just the ones that begin with the word NEW. A short program to do this is the following:

```
10 REM DEFINE SOME STRINGS
20 LET A$="SOUTH AMERICA"
30 LET B$="NEW YORK"
40 LET C$="NEWFOUNDLAND"
50 REM NOW TEST THEM
60 IF A$(1 TO 3)="NEW" THEN P
RINT A$
70 IF B$(1 TO 3)="NEW" THEN P
RINT B$
80 IF C$(1 TO 3)="NEW" THEN P
RINT C$
```

In Chapter 5 you will learn how to use *loops* to make such programs neater and easier to write, even for very long lists of names. For now, just observe how the string slicing works. Run this program, and the computer will print these two lines on the screen:

```
NEW YORK
NEWFOUNDLAND
```

To select only those strings that begin with NEW as a separate word, simply specify the slice (1 TO 4) and the substring "NEW " with a space at the end. Then lines 60, 70, and 80 of the program become

```
   60 IF A$(1 TO 4)="NEW " THEN P
RINT A$
   70 IF B$(1 TO 4)="NEW " THEN P
RINT B$
   80 IF C$(1 TO 4)="NEW " THEN P
RINT C$
```

After you run the program the screen looks like this:

```
NEW YORK
```

### STRING INSERTION

Now you know how to extract any part of a string to make a new, shorter string. The computer also has a similar command, the *substitution* command, that does just the opposite: It takes a shorter string and replaces part of a longer string with it. For example, define a string by executing the following command:

```
LET A$="JUNE 5, 1723"
```

Then execute the substitution command

```
LET A$(1 TO 4)="JULY"
```

and ask the computer to print the result, using the command

```
PRINT A$
```

The computer now prints this revised line:

```
JULY 5, 1723
```

The command

```
LET A$(1 TO 4)="JULY"
```

told the computer to substitute the substring "JULY" for characters 1 through 4 of the string A$. If the new substring is shorter than the original one, the computer fills in with blanks. Thus, the commands

```
LET A$="JUNE 5, 1723"
LET A$(1 TO 4)="MAY"
PRINT A$
```

will print the result with two spaces between May and 5, as follows:

```
MAY 5,   1723
```

On the other hand, if the new substring is too large for the space that you specify, the computer will throw away the extra characters. The commands

```
LET A$="JUNE 5, 1723"
LET A$(1 TO 4)="AUGUST"
PRINT A$
```

will print the line with "August" abbreviated, as follows:

```
AUGU 5, 1723
```

Clearly, you may get strange-looking results if you are not careful. Nevertheless, substring substitution is a very powerful tool for manipulating text and graphics.

## COMBINING STRING OPERATIONS

Recall that each operation in a numeric expression has its own priority, and that the computer always does the operation of highest priority first unless parentheses indicate a different order. The same is true for string expressions. Slicing has a higher priority than concatenation, so it always comes first. For example, the following commands

```
PRINT "STRING "+"EXPRESSIONS"(1
TO 8)
```

will print the string

```
STRING EXPRESSI
```

because the slicing operation (1 to 8) applies first to the string "EXPRESSIONS". The resulting string, "EXPRESSI", combines with "STRING ".

If you want the computer to perform these two operations in the opposite order, you must use parentheses to specify the order of operations. For example, to concatenate "STRING " and "EXPRESSIONS" and then slice out and display the first eight characters of the concatenated string, enter the following command:

```
PRINT ("STRING "+"EXPRESSIONS")(
1 TO 8)
```

This command concatenates "STRING " and "EXPRESSIONS" first because they are enclosed together in parentheses. Then it slices out characters 1 to 8 of the concatenated string to give

```
STRING E
```

Otherwise unneeded parentheses thus have the same function in string expressions as they do in numeric expressions. They tell the computer to perform the operations inside them first.

# FUNCTIONS

You have seen how to combine numbers or strings into an expression that the computer evaluates to produce a new number or string. In addition to this, the computer can evaluate mathematical *functions*. These functions can appear in expressions, just as numbers or strings do.

## Numeric Functions

An example will help to explain what a function is. The *absolute value* is a numeric function. The symbol for absolute value is ABS, at the bottom of the G key. Recall that the way to enter a function (or anything printed below a white key-square on the keyboard) is to press FUNCTION (SHIFT-ENTER) and then the key that has the function name under it. To enter the function ABS, press SHIFT-ENTER and then the G key. The ▤ cursor appears when you press SHIFT-ENTER, reminding you that the computer will interpret the next key-stroke as a function.

Enter the following line:

```
PRINT ABS -6
```

Observe that the computer prints the answer **6**. The ABS function takes the number to its right, discards the minus sign if the number is negative, and uses the resulting number. The number on the right is the *argument* of the function, and the result is called the *value* of the function. If the argument of the ABS function is a positive number or zero, then the value is the same as the argument. If the argument of the ABS function is a negative number, then the value is a positive number of the same magnitude. Enter some more commands like the one above, but with different numbers in the place of $-6$, and observe how the ABS function works.

The argument of a function like ABS can also be a numeric expression instead of a single number. (Recall that you can use a numeric expression wherever you can use a number, except for line numbers.) For example, the command

```
PRINT ABS (12/2-10)
```

tells the computer to divide 12 by 2 (to get 6), then subtract 10 (to get −4), and finally to take the absolute value and print it. The absolute value of −4 is 4, and that is what the computer prints.

Notice that the argument (12/2−10) has parentheses around it. Whenever you use an expression as the argument of a function, you must enclose the expression in parentheses. Otherwise, the computer will use only the first number of the expression as the argument of the function. In other words, functions have a higher priority than the arithmetic operations +, −, /, *, and **. If you enter the same command but without the parentheses, like this:

```
PRINT ABS 12/2-10
```

the computer will first take the absolute value of 12. It then divides the result, also 12, by 2 to get 6, and finally subtracts 10 to get the answer −4. To make this easier to visualize, we can draw brackets under the commands to show which operations occur first:

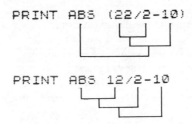

Extra parentheses never do any harm, as long as they are in pairs. If you are ever uncertain about whether you need parentheses, put them in. The computer will always do the operations inside the parentheses first, then combine the result with whatever is outside the parentheses.

Absolute value is thus one example of a function. It has one argument, which can be a numeric constant, variable, or expression. The ABS function itself can also appear as part of an expression, just as if it were a variable. The argument of a function can even be an expression that has a function in it, like the following:

```
PRINT 7-ABS (12/2-ABS (-3*5))
```

The only restriction is that the ABS function takes only numeric arguments. If you try to enter a command like

```
PRINT ABS "GOOD MORNING"
```

the computer will report a syntax error by displaying the ⊟ cursor. The value of the ABS function is also a number, and so you cannot use it in places where the computer expects a string.

The TS1000 and ZX81 keyboard contains a number of different functions. Each function appears beneath one of the white key-squares. (A few of the symbols beneath the key-squares, such as TAB and AT, are not functions.) Do not be concerned if some of these functions are unfamiliar. For example, if you have never studied trigonometry, the trigonometric functions will seem obscure. In that case, you probably will not need them in your programs anyway. The important thing is to understand how functions work and how to use the ones you need.

Table 4-6 describes all the functions on the keyboard that involve only numbers, not strings. Functions that involve strings are explained later in this chapter.

**Table 4-6. Functions Not Involving Strings**

| Function | Value |
|---|---|
| ABS | The absolute value of the argument. Equal to the argument if it is positive or zero. Equal in magnitude but with positive sign if the argument is negative. |
| ACS | The trigonometric arc cosine of the argument. |
| ASN | The trigonometric arc sine of the argument. |
| ATN | The trigonometric arc tangent of the argument. |
| COS | The trigonometric cosine of the argument. |
| EXP | The exponential of the argument. Equals the number $e$ (2.7182818; the base of the system of natural logarithms) raised to the power of the argument. |
| INT | The integer part of the argument. Equals the largest integer that is smaller than or equal to the argument. |
| LN | The natural logarithm (base $e$) of the argument. To convert a natural logarithm to a common logarithm (base 10), divide the natural logarithm by LN 10. |
| PEEK | The contents of the memory location specified by the argument (see Chapter 7). |
| PI | 3.1415927, the ratio of the circumference of a circle to its diameter. |
| RND | A random number between zero and one. |
| SGN | The signum of the argument. Equals one if the argument is positive; zero if the argument is zero; and minus one if the argument is negative. |
| SIN | The trigonometric sine of the argument. |
| SQR | The square root of the argument. |
| TAN | The trigonometric tangent of the argument. |
| USR | This function calls the machine language subroutine that begins at the memory location specified by the argument. The value is taken from the BC register pair (see Chapter 8). |

All the numeric functions have one thing in common: Each one converts its argument into a new number (its value) that is in some way related to the number that was the argument. The particular relationship between arguments and values is different for each function.

## INT AND ROUNDING

INT gives the first whole number (integer) that is smaller than or equal to the argument, as shown in the examples in Table 4-7.

A function that rounds off to the nearest integer would be more useful for ordinary arithmetic. Although the TS1000 and ZX81 do not have such a function, you can get the same result by first adding .5 to the argument and then using INT. The following program rounds off the value of X and prints the result:

```
10 LET X=4.9
20 PRINT INT (X+.5)
```

Run this program several times, editing line 10 each time to change the value of X. Some typical results are shown in Table 4-8.

Because of the way the computer calculates numbers, INT sometimes gives incorrect results for arguments that should be exact integers. The following program illustrates the problem:

```
10 LET A=5*.4
20 PRINT A
30 PRINT INT A
```

Instead of printing 2 twice, as it should, the computer prints 2 the first time and 1 the second time. This happens because the computer's internal representation of 5*.4 is not exactly 2.

Check your programs for these errors. If they show up, you can correct them by testing the results of the program and correcting the math as necessary.

Table 4-7. Examples of INT Rounding

| Argument | Value of INT |
|---|---|
| 3 | 3 |
| −3 | −3 |
| 8.2 | 8 |
| −8.2 | −9 |

Table 4-8. INT Rounding with X + .5

| Before Rounding | After Rounding |
| --- | --- |
| 4.9 | 5 |
| 8.2 | −8 |
| 10 | 10 |
| 549.23 | 549 |
| −8.2 | −8 |
| −8.8 | −9 |

## NUMERIC FUNCTIONS WITH NO ARGUMENT

Most of the functions in Table 4-6 have a single argument. Two of them, however, have no argument. These are PI and RND. The first of these, PI, is an example of a *constant function*. That is, the function's value is always the same, namely 3.1415927. This number, which expresses the relationship of the diameter of a circle to its circumference, occurs frequently in many kinds of mathematical formulas. The TS1000 and ZX81 provide it just to save you the trouble of typing in this number when you need it.

The function RND also has no argument, but it is not a constant function. In fact, it is useful precisely because you cannot predict what its value will be. The RND function is a *random number generator;* its value is a randomly chosen number between zero and one.

To see how it works, first execute the command

```
RAND
```

Do not confuse this RAND with RND. RAND is a command, located on the T key, while RND is a function, located below the same key. Whenever you execute RAND, the computer resets the random number generator so that it will not produce the same sequence of random numbers it did the previous time you ran the program. (If you *want* the same sequence each time, put a number after RAND. As long as this number remains the same, the computer will produce exactly the same sequence of numbers every time.)

Now execute the command

```
PRINT RND
```

several times in a row and notice what kind of numbers you get. They will all be between zero and one. If you execute the command enough times, they will cover the whole range between zero and one fairly evenly.

Random numbers are important in many computer programs. Computers are designed to be very predictable. That is, if you give a computer the same commands today that you gave it yesterday, it is supposed to do exactly the same thing it did then. However, some computer programs need to be unpredictable in some way. Many computer games contain a built-in element of chance. For example, the computer might simulate a roll of the dice or provide a one-in-ten chance that one spaceship will blow up another spaceship when it fires its weapons. Even in a game like chess, the computer's moves should be a little bit unpredictable so that a player can try the same opening several times and get a different game each time.

You can use the RND function to simulate the roll of a die—that is, to display a random integer between one and six—by means of the following program:

```
  30 REM GET A NUMBER BETWEEN 0
AND 1
  40 LET A=RND
  50 REM CONVERT TO NUMBER BETWE
EN 1 AND 7
  60 LET A=6*A+1
  70 REM THROW AWAY THE DECIMAL
PART
  80 LET A=INT A
  90 REM PRINT THE RESULT
 100 PRINT A
```

Observe how line 60 converts a number between zero and one into a number between one and seven. First it multiplies the original number by six to get a number between zero and six. Then it adds one to produce a number between one and seven. However, this number is not an integer; it has digits to the right of the decimal point. Line 80 uses the INT function to throw away the fractional part and leave just the whole number that was to the left of the decimal point. The result is an integer between one and six.

Run the program 20 or 30 times, keeping track of how many times you see each digit. If you run the program enough times, it will print each of the six digits about the same number of times. Any program that played a game involving dice would probably contain a routine like this one.

If you don't understand completely how the program works, insert the following lines and run it again:

```
 45 PRINT A
 65 PRINT A
```

Now the program shows what happens at each stage of the calculation. It prints the initial random number, which is between zero and one. On the next line it prints the "shifted" random number, which is between one and seven. On the third line it prints the final result without the decimal part.

Whenever you are uncertain about how a program works, try inserting PRINT statements like these to display what happens after each step. This is also a good technique for finding and fixing errors in your own programs.

The die program uses three separate LET statements:

```
40 LET A=RND
60 LET A=6*A+1
80 LET A=INT A
```

A program that uses several short, fairly simple statements is easier for people to understand. The program will run faster and take up less of the computer's memory, however, if these operations are condensed into one LET statement:

```
LET A=INT (6*RND+1)
```

This single statement does exactly the same thing as the three statements.

### TRIGONOMETRIC FUNCTIONS

If you have studied trigonometry and want to use the trigonometric functions, you will need the following information: The argument of the functions SIN, COS, and TAN must be in radians. The values of the inverse trigonometric functions ACS, ASN, and ATN are also in radians. If you prefer degrees instead, use the formula: Degrees $\times (\pi/180) =$ Radians. The following example takes an angle B in degrees, converts it to radians, computes its sine, and stores the result as the variable A:

```
LET A=SIN ((PI/180)*B)
```

Similarly, the following command computes the arc tangent of Y in radians, converts the result to degrees, and stores it as X:

```
LET X=(180/PI)*ATN Y
```

Be aware that some functions produce "illegal" answers. This is generally caused by a function calculation that results in a division by zero or an answer that is too large or too small for the computer's range of numbers.

## Other Numeric Functions

Some of the other numeric functions have special properties that you may need to know. The argument of the natural logarithm function, LN, must be positive or the computer will report error A. It reports the same error ("invalid argument") if you try to use the SQR (square root) function with a negative argument. Like most of the limits mentioned about the trigonometric functions, these restrictions are not imposed by the computer itself. They are mathematical properties of the functions LN and SQR.

# Functions Involving Strings

All of the above functions have numbers as their arguments and numbers as their values. Several other functions on the TS1000 or ZX81 keyboard have arguments that are strings instead of numbers, and some of them represent strings instead of numbers.

The name of a function shows whether it represents a number or a string. If the name ends with the symbol $, the function represents a string. If it ends with a letter, the function represents a number. The names of string functions look very similar to the names of string variables. Both end with $. A function name, however, contains more than one letter.

Table 4-9 summarizes the TS1000 and ZX81 functions that involve strings.

## THE INKEY$ FUNCTION

The simplest string function is INKEY$. This function does not have an argument. Its contents are determined by whether or not you are pressing a key on the keyboard at the time the computer executes INKEY$. If a key is pressed, then INKEY$ will contain a one-character string consisting of the character on the pressed key. If no key is pressed at the time, then INKEY$ will contain the empty string (" "). The following program illustrates how INKEY$ works:

```
10 SLOW
20 REM THE NEXT STATEMENT JUST
WASTES TIME
30 LET DUMMY=(SQR 2)*(SQR 2)
40 LET Z$=INKEY$
```

Table 4-9. Functions Involving Strings

| Function | Value |
| --- | --- |
| CHR$ | A string consisting of the character in the character code that the numeric argument represents. |
| CODE | The number in the character code that represents the first character in the string. |
| INKEY$ | A string consisting of the character for the key that is pressed on the keyboard. If no key is pressed, the value is the null string (" "). |
| LEN | The number of characters in the string. |
| STR$ | The string you would see on the screen if you asked the computer to PRINT the argument. |
| VAL | If the argument string is a numeric expression, the value of VAL is the number you get when you evaluate the expression. If the argument string is not a numeric expression, the computer reports an error. |

```
50 PRINT Z$
60 IF Z$="" THEN PRINT "YOU DI
D NOT PRESS A KEY"
```

Remember to use SHIFT-P for the " " symbols in line 60. Do not use SHIFT-Q.

The first three statements produce a delay, which gives you time to enter RUN and remove your finger from the ENTER key before the computer gets to the INKEY$ function in line 40. Run the program, remove your finger from ENTER, and quickly press another key (such as A). Hold it down until you see the letter **A** appear on the screen. When the computer executes line 40, it checks the keyboard and finds that the A key is pressed, so it assigns "A" to the Z$ variable in the program. It does not print the final message when it reaches line 60, because Z$ does not contain the empty string. Now run the program again, but do not touch the keyboard while the program is running. This time when the computer executes line 40, it assigns the empty string " " to Z$ because no key was pressed. Then when it gets to line 60, it prints the message

```
YOU DID NOT PRESS A KEY.
```

INKEY$ reads the keyboard while a program is running, without stopping and waiting for input. It is especially useful for games and other kinds of interactive graphics. The program can check the keyboard and decide what to do next, depending on which key the user presses, all without interrupting the action on the screen. INKEY$ will correctly detect any of the letters, numbers, symbols, and even the editing functions such as EDIT, DELETE, and the arrow keys. However, it will interpret the SPACE key as BREAK instead of SPACE, stopping the program with report code D.

### THE LEN FUNCTION

The argument of the LEN function is a string, and its value is a number. The value is simply the number of characters in the string argument. In other words, LEN counts the number of characters in the string. To demonstrate it, enter the following commands:

```
PRINT LEN "ABCDEFGH"

PRINT LEN ""

PRINT LEN "+"

LET U$="TESTSTRING"

PRINT U$(LEN U$-2 TO LEN U$)
```

The correct answers are 8, 0, 1, and ING. The last example shows how to use the LEN function to slice out characters at the end of a string. Observe how the

LEN function appears in the slice specification. You can use it just as you would use a constant or a numeric variable.

## STR$ AND VAL

The argument of the STR$ function is a numeric expression. The STR$ function converts this number into a string that looks exactly like what you would see if you told the computer to print the number on the screen. The following program shows how it works:

```
   10 REM DEFINE A NUMERIC VARIAB
LE
   20 LET Y=SQR 3
   30 REM MAKE A STRING FROM IT
   40 LET A$=STR$ Y
   50 REM PRINT EACH OF THEM
   60 PRINT Y
   70 PRINT A$
```

The computer prints exactly the same thing for A$ as it does for Y, although A$ is a string and Y is a number.

Use STR$ when you want your program to calculate a number and then determine some special property of the number, such as how many characters it will take to print the number. To illustrate the method, first suppose you have in some way calculated a variable called Y. The following statement produces a value for Y:

```
   10 LET Y=SQR 3
```

If you wanted to print no more than five characters, for example, you could use the following program:

```
   20 REM CONVERT Y TO A STRING
   30 LET Z$=STR$ Y
   40 REM DETERMINE THE LENGTH OF
 Z$
   50 LET LENGTH=LEN Z$
   60 REM PRINT IF IT IS NOT TOO
LONG
   70 IF LENGTH < 6 THEN PRINT Y
   80 REM OTHERWISE, PRINT FIRST
5 CHARACTERS
   90 IF LENGTH > 5  THEN PRINT Z
$(1 TO 5)
```

The STR$ function gives you a way of determining how many characters it would take to print the number.

The function VAL does just the opposite of STR$. That is, VAL converts a string such as Z$, which resembles the way the computer would print out a number, into a numeric variable. For example:

```
10 LET B$="2040"
20 LET C=VAL B$
30 LET D=C/2
40 PRINT D
```

The computer prints **1020** when you run this program.

If you need to do arithmetic with a string that looks like a number (or a numeric expression), first use the VAL function to convert the string to a numeric variable. This function also provides a way of dealing with errors that the people who use your program might make in the process of typing in their data. Instead of reading data as numbers, you can read each piece of data as a string and check it to make sure it has no errors. If it has errors, the program can print an error message and ask for the number again. If it has no errors, use VAL to turn the string into a number and proceed with the calculation.

Of course, the argument of VAL cannot be just any string. It must be a string (or a string expression that evaluates to a string) that looks exactly like a valid numeric expression. For example, the following command is "legal," as long as the variable X has been defined:

```
PRINT VAL "INT X + 2"
```

## CODE AND CHR$

In order to understand the final two string functions explained in this chapter, you need to know how the computer stores strings in its memory. Internally, the computer can only deal with numbers. Therefore, it uses numbers to represent characters. Each character has its own unique number. The list of characters and their numbers is the *character code*. Every computer that handles text uses a character code of some kind, but the details of the code may be different on different computers. For example, some computers use the number 1 to represent the letter A, while others use 65 or 38 or some other number to represent A. The TS1000 and ZX81 use their own special character codes. You will find a complete list of the characters and their corresponding numbers in Appendix C.

Inside the computer, a string is just a list of numbers. When you ask the computer to print a string, it takes the string's numbers one at a time, looks each one up in a table in read-only memory (ROM), and displays the corresponding characters on the screen. You usually do not need to think about the character code at all, because the computer takes care of the conversion for you.

However, you may sometimes need to deal directly with the character codes. The computer provides two functions for this purpose. The CODE function takes a string argument and returns as its value the character code of the first character in the string. For example, the following command prints the number 41 on the screen:

```
PRINT CODE "D"
```

Look up the character D in Appendix C, which confirms that its character code is 41. The argument of CODE can be any string expression. The function CODE simply evaluates the expression and uses the character code of the first character as its value.

The function CHR$ does just the opposite of CODE. The argument of CHR$ is a number (or a numeric expression), and its value is the character that the number represents in the character code. Use CHR$ just as you would use a string with one character in it. For example, if you give the command

```
PRINT CHR$ 41
```

the computer prints the letter **D** on the screen, just as if you had given the command

```
PRINT "D"
```

Incidentally, besides the letters, numbers, punctuation, and graphics symbols, the character code in Appendix C contains a number for each of the BASIC commands and functions. It also has quite a few numbers that do not correspond to any character. For example, the following command:

```
PRINT CHR$ 210
```

prints the function named PEEK because 210 goes with PEEK in Appendix C. If you use PRINT CHR$ with a number like 75, which does not correspond to any character, the computer will simply print a question mark.

Input and Output

# Chapter Five

nput is information you put into your computer's memory. Output is information the computer sends to other devices, such as the television screen or printer. The principal output commands on the TS1000 and ZX81 are PRINT and LPRINT, which display numbers and strings on the television and printer, respectively. Chapter 4 introduced one of the primary input capabilities, INKEY$, which examines the keyboard while a program is running. This chapter presents another way of giving your computer information, the INPUT command. The chapter then explains some further capabilities of the PRINT command and introduces several other commands for controlling the display.

## THE INPUT COMMAND

The INPUT command, like the LET command, gives a value to a variable. Use LET to specify the value of a variable in command mode or while you are writing a program, like this:

```
LET QVAR=93.4
```

Use INPUT instead if you want to stop the program until you enter a value. This value, which can be string or numeric, is called the *input variable*. For a numeric variable, use an INPUT statement like this:

```
230 INPUT QVAR
```

Given this command, the computer displays the ▤ cursor and waits. When you enter the value of QVAR, followed by ENTER, it continues with the next line of the program. The input variable to the right of INPUT must be a single variable, not a constant or a compound expression.

If the INPUT variable is a string variable instead, as in

```
10 INPUT E$
```

the computer displays the ▤ cursor with quotation marks around it, like this:

```
"▤"
```

The quotation marks show that the computer expects a string.

If an INPUT statement uses a numeric variable, you must enter a number, or else the computer will report error code 2 at the lower left-hand corner of the screen. If an INPUT statement uses a string variable, you may enter any combination of letters, numbers, graphics, and other symbols. However, if you delete the quotation marks around the ▤ cursor, the computer will display the ▤ cursor when you try to enter the string. Re-enter the quotation marks at the beginning and end of the string, and the computer will accept it.

Unlike most BASIC commands, the INPUT command does not terminate when you press the BREAK key. Since the BREAK key is the same as the SPACE key, INPUT interprets it as a space in the input rather than a break. For numeric variables, INPUT simply ignores spaces. For string variables. it treats a space as part of the string. To terminate a program that is waiting for numeric input, simply enter a letter instead of a number. The computer reports error code 2 and stops. If the computer is waiting for string input, delete the quotation marks and enter STOP (SHIFT-A) to terminate the program.

A good program should print a message before the INPUT command to explain what kind of data it expects, especially if it uses INPUT several different times for different variables. The following program illustrates this technique. It asks for the radius of a circle and then calculates and prints the circle's area:

```
10 REM GET VALUE OF RADIUS
20 PRINT "ENTER RADIUS"
30 INPUT R
40 REM CALCULATE AND PRINT ARE
A
50 LET AREA=PI*R**2
60 PRINT AREA
```

The INPUT statement can be used only in programmed mode. An INPUT in command mode, without a statement number, produces error code 8. All other BASIC commands can be used in either programmed or command mode, although some of them, such as STOP, FOR, NEXT, and RETURN, are useless in command mode.

## FORMATTING PRINTED OUTPUT

All the examples of the PRINT and LPRINT commands so far have printed only one string or number per line. Now you will learn how to print several such items on a single screen line and how to specify the arrangement of items on the screen.

### Using Commas

One way of printing several items with one command is to separate them with commas, like this:

```
PRINT 1,2,3,4,5
```

Execute this command and observe how the computer arranges the numbers on the screen. The numbers appear in the same order as in the PRINT statement, but arranged in columns, two numbers per line, like this:

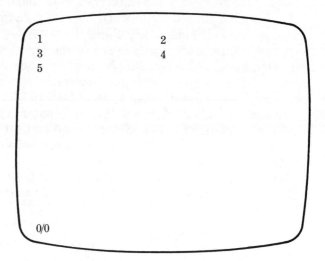

If your system includes the Timex or Sinclair printer, you can also try an LPRINT statement with commas:

```
LPRINT 1,2,3,4,5
```

With either PRINT or LPRINT, the computer displays two items per line. The first item in each pair starts at the beginning of the line and the second starts 16 columns to the right. Since each line contains 32 character positions, the second item begins in the middle of the line. Thus, you can use this form of the

PRINT or LPRINT statement to print a table of numbers or strings lined up in columns. The leftmost character of each item lines up with the ones above it, in the first column or in the 17th column.

If one of the items is longer than 15 characters, the computer skips to the next vacant starting position (that is, the first or 17th column). Therefore, a PRINT statement using commas may print one or two items per line, depending on the items' lengths. Try the following example:

```
PRINT "ABCDEFGHIJKLMNOPQRSTUVWXY
Z", "ABC", "ABCDE"
```

After you press ENTER, the screen looks like this:

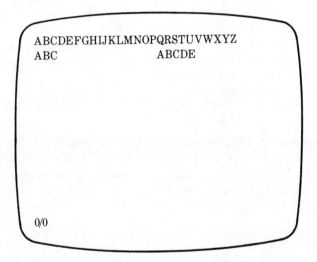

This format can cause problems if you don't know in advance how long each printed item will be. In such cases, you can better control the display by using other forms of the PRINT and LPRINT statements, described in the sections that follow.

## Using Semicolons

A semicolon in a PRINT or LPRINT statement causes the computer to print the next item immediately after the previous one, with no extra spaces at all between them. The command

```
PRINT "JOHN"; "MARY"; "LUCINDA"
```

produces the line

```
JOHNMARYLUCINDA
```

You may also include spaces between the items as part of the names or as separate strings. The following example illustrates both methods:

```
PRINT "JOHN ";"MARY";" ";"LUCIND
A"
```

It prints this line:

```
JOHN MARY LUCINDA
```

If the combined items to be printed are longer than a single line on the screen, the computer just goes on to the beginning of the next line when it reaches the end of the current one.

The semicolon in a PRINT statement is similar in some ways to the string concatenation operator (+). For example, this command produces the same display line as the previous one:

```
PRINT "JOHN "+"MARY"+" "+"LUCIND
A"
```

However, the semicolon can be used only in a PRINT or LPRINT statement. It cannot be used in a LET statement, for example, where the + symbol is "legal." Its one major advantage over the + operator is that the semicolon works for numbers as well as for strings. You can even mix numbers and strings in a single PRINT statement, with semicolons between them, as follows:

```
PRINT "GLADIATORS ";6;", LIONS "
;0
```

Enter this command carefully, with all the spaces and punctuation marks in the right places, and the computer will print the following:

```
GLADIATORS 6, LIONS 0
```

The semicolon does exactly the same thing regardless of whether the items it separates are in a single PRINT statement or separate ones. The computer will print the same line as before when you enter and run the following program:

```
10 PRINT "GLADIATORS ";
20 PRINT 6;
30 PRINT ", LIONS ";
40 PRINT 0
```

The computer "remembers" whether the previous PRINT statement ended with a semicolon. If it did, the computer begins the next PRINT statement where the last one ended. The location on the screen where the next PRINT statement will begin is called the *print position*. A PRINT statement ordinarily moves the print position to the beginning of the next line, but if the previous PRINT statement ended with a semicolon, the print position remains where it was.

Use the semicolon to display a piece of explanatory text beside the result of a calculation. With this feature, the program to calculate the area of a circle can be made clearer as follows:

```
10 REM GET VALUE OF RADIUS
20 PRINT "ENTER RADIUS"
30 INPUT R
40 REM CALCULATE AND PRINT ARE
A
50 LET AREA=PI*R**2
60 PRINT "THE AREA IS ";AREA
```

## Using TAB

The PRINT items TAB and AT provide still more ways of controlling the print position. The TAB is below the P key, and AT is below the C key. Although they are not functions, you enter them exactly as you would enter a function, by first pressing the FUNCTION key to activate the ▦ cursor.

In a PRINT statement, TAB and AT look like variables or constants for printing. However, they do not actually print anything themselves. Instead, they change the print position for the next item in the PRINT statement, as in the following example:

```
10 PRINT SQR 7;TAB 10;"IS THE
SQUARE ROOT OF 7"
20 PRINT SQR 4;TAB 10;"IS THE
SQUARE ROOT OF 4"
```

After you enter the commands just given, the screen should display this:

```
2.6457513 IS THE SQUARE ROOT OF
7
2         IS THE SQUARE ROOT OF
4
```

Like the tab key on a typewriter, TAB moves the print position forward to the specified column. In the above example, TAB 10 moves the print position to column 10. If the print position is already past that column, TAB does not go backward. Instead, it moves to that column on the next line. Thus, TAB is similar to the comma separator but more powerful. While the comma always moves the print position to the first or the middle column, TAB moves the print position to any column you specify.

Using TAB in an LPRINT command controls the printer in the same way. If your system has a Timex or Sinclair printer, run the previous program with LPRINT substituted for PRINT in both lines.

Each line on the display or the printer contains 32 columns, numbered from 0 to 31 rather than from 1 to 32. Therefore, TAB 0 puts the print position at the leftmost column on the screen, and TAB 31 puts it at the rightmost column. Given a TAB column larger than 31, the computer simply ignores the extra columns. For example, TAB 32 does the same thing as TAB 0, and TAB 33 does the same thing as TAB 1.

Use TAB to make different items line up neatly in columns. You can use it as many times as you like in a single PRINT statement, but make sure that none of the printed items is longer than the space between TAB positions. Remember to use a semicolon after the TAB column number. Otherwise, the print position will change again before the computer prints the next item.

## Using AT

The print item AT provides the most complete control possible over the print position. It specifies both the line and the column where the next item will appear. While TAB only moves the print position forward from its present location until it reaches the specified column, AT moves forward, backward, up, or down if necessary to reach the specified location, regardless of where the print position was previously.

An example is the following:

```
PRINT AT 10,5;"BLINK"
```

The first number after AT specifies the line, and the second number specifies the column. The screen contains 22 lines. The top line is line 0 and the bottom line is line 21. (Actually, there are two more lines below line 21, but you cannot print on them. The computer uses them for its EDIT line and error messages.) The line number for AT must be between 0 and 21, and the column number must be between 0 and 31, just like the column number for TAB. Unlike TAB, however, AT will not disregard the extra lines or columns if the numbers exceed this range. Instead, it will report an error.

To understand how AT works, imagine that the display screen is divided into separate squares, one for each possible character position, as shown in Figure 5-1. The numbers down the left side of the drawing correspond to the 22 screen lines, and the numbers across the top correspond to the 32 columns. To design a complicated screen display, refer to this figure or make a similar drawing of your own and fill in the squares with the characters you want in

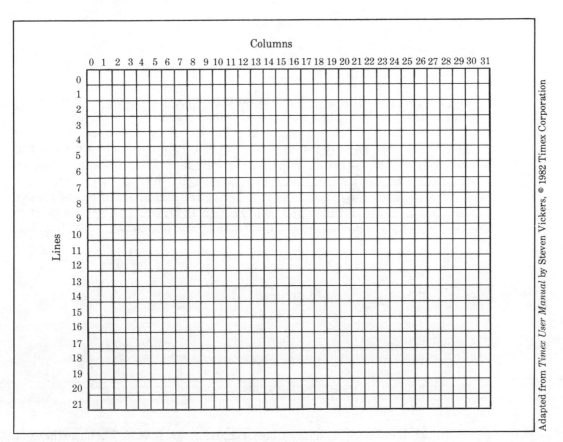

Figure 5-1. Character positions on the television display

the positions where you want them. Then read the line and column numbers from the drawing and use them in PRINT AT statements.

With LPRINT, AT is not very useful because the printer paper is a continuous roll with no top or bottom line. Thus the line number in an LPRINT AT command has no meaning, and the computer simply ignores it and moves to the specified column in the current printer line. An LPRINT AT command must still have a line number smaller than 22, however, to avoid a syntax error.

For graphics and animation, AT is very useful because it ignores anything that may already be on the screen at the new print position. It simply replaces the old text with new, as the following program demonstrates:

```
10 SLOW
20 PRINT AT 0,5;"BLINK"
30 PRINT AT 0,5;"BLINK"
```

Adapted from *Timex User Manual* by Steven Vickers, © 1982 Timex Corporation

```
40 PRINT AT 0,5;"B█INK"
50 PRINT AT 0,5;"BL█NK"
60 PRINT AT 0,5;"BLI█K"
70 PRINT AT 0,5;"BLIN█"
80 PRINT AT 0,5;"BLINK"
```

Remember to use the GRAPHICS key (SHIFT-9) before the reversed video characters and to press it again after each one to restore the █ cursor.

Watch closely as this program runs. The reversed video appears to move across the word rapidly from left to right. The computer actually prints the word **BLINK** seven times, with the reversed character in different positions, but it does this so fast that your eye sees a smooth movement across the word.

To slow down the motion, insert a do-nothing statement after each PRINT statement to waste time. The SQR function is a good choice because it is relatively slow. The following will slow the program down:

```
10 SLOW
20 PRINT AT 0,5;"BLINK"
25 LET A=SQR 2
30 PRINT AT 0,5;"█LINK"
35 LET A=SQR 2
40 PRINT AT 0,5;"B█INK"
45 LET A=SQR 2
50 PRINT AT 0,5;"BL█NK"
55 LET A=SQR 2
60 PRINT AT 0,5;"BLI█K"
65 LET A=SQR 2
70 PRINT AT 0,5;"BLIN█"
75 LET A=SQR 2
80 PRINT AT 0,5;"BLINK"
```

To avoid typing in each new line, first just insert line 25. Then use the EDIT key to bring line 25 down to the bottom of the screen, delete the line number, type the new line number 35, and press ENTER. The result is exactly the same as if you had typed in line 35. Now EDIT line 35 to make line 45, and so on. The revised program runs so slowly that you can see each individual letter being reversed and then restored to normal video.

Try replacing SQR with different functions, such as RND, SIN, or VAL (with the appropriate kind of argument for each one), and observe the resulting difference in the rate of movement.


## Delaying with PAUSE

The PAUSE command delays a program in a more controlled way than a function like SQR does. For example, the following command instructs the computer to wait exactly one second before going on to the next line:

```
PAUSE 60
```

To get a timed pause, just multiply the number of seconds you want to pause by 60 and put the resulting number after PAUSE. (For the British model of the ZX81, multiply by 50 instead.) Change each of the delay statements in the previous "blink" program to PAUSE 30, run the program, and observe the result. Unfortunately, PAUSE produces a flicker on the screen. However, it is the only means of animation in fast mode, since the display disappears from the screen while any other statement executes. Enter and run the following example:

```
10 FAST
20 PRINT "DEMO";
30 PAUSE 120
40 PRINT "NSTRATION"
```

The computer displays **DEMO** for two seconds and then completes the word. An advantage of PAUSE is that the pause ends and the computer goes on immediately to the next line whenever you press any key on the keyboard. Furthermore, if the number after PAUSE is larger than 32767, the pause does not terminate at all unless you press a key. Thus, like INKEY$, this feature makes interactive keyboard input easy. The following example, which runs correctly in either slow or fast mode, makes the computer act like a typewriter:

```
10 PAUSE 40000
20 PRINT INKEY$;
30 GOTO 10
```

The GOTO command in line 30 causes the computer to go back to line 10 and repeat the PAUSE and PRINT commands over and over, until you press BREAK. You will learn more about GOTO in Chapter 6.

Incidentally, some of the first ZX81's (and the 8K ZX80's) had a mistake in the PAUSE command. If your computer is one of these, you must follow every PAUSE command with this command:

```
POKE 16437,255
```

Without this POKE command the computer may go completely blank later in the program, after PAUSE has been executed. To determine whether your ZX81 is one that requires this extra command, enter the following lines:

```
PRINT 0.25**2
PRINT PEEK 54
```

The first command should give **0.0625** and the second should give **136**. If your result is different for either of these, remember to include the POKE command after every PAUSE.

## GRAPHING WITH PLOT AND UNPLOT

The PRINT AT command is ideal for animated text, but plotting and pictorial graphing often require higher-resolution graphics. For this purpose, the TS1000 and ZX81 divide each character space on the display into four portions (called *picture elements* or *pixels*) like this:

In the above drawing, the large square represents one character on the display, and each of the four smaller squares represents one pixel. Each pixel can be made black or white to form pictures or graphs on the screen.

The special graphics characters on the keys 1, 2, 3, 4, 5, 6, 7, 8, Q, W, E, R, T, Y, and SPACE provide all the different combinations of black and white pixels that a character can have. For example, the following program uses the symbol on the Y key to draw a diagonal line across the screen:

```
10 SLOW
20 FOR P=0 TO 21
30 PRINT AT P,P;"◥"
40 NEXT P
```

The commands PLOT and UNPLOT let you specify each pixel individually, instead of specifying them four at a time as graphics characters. The PLOT command makes the specified pixel black, and UNPLOT makes it white. The following program uses these two commands to draw a diagonal line from the top left and then erase it:

```
10 SLOW
20 FOR P=0 TO 43
30 PLOT P,P
40 NEXT P
50 FOR P=0 TO 43
60 UNPLOT P,P
70 NEXT P
```

The PRINT command and the PLOT and UNPLOT commands are equally capable of producing any combination of black and white pixels on the display. However, some patterns are easier to program with one kind of command than with the other. Programs that draw pictures usually use PRINT; programs that draw line graphs usually use PLOT and UNPLOT. (Chapter 7 explains how to plot graphs on the TS1000 or ZX81.)

The major differences between PRINT AT and PLOT/UNPLOT are shown pictorially in Figure 5-2. These differences are

· Pixels are only half as wide as characters. The screen has 64 pixel coordinates (numbered 0–63) from left to right and 44 pixel coordinates (numbered 0–43) from bottom to top. For character input, the screen has 32 columns and 22 lines.

· Character positions begin with (0,0) at the *upper* left corner of the TV screen. Pixel coordinates also begin with (0,0), but at the *lower* left corner.

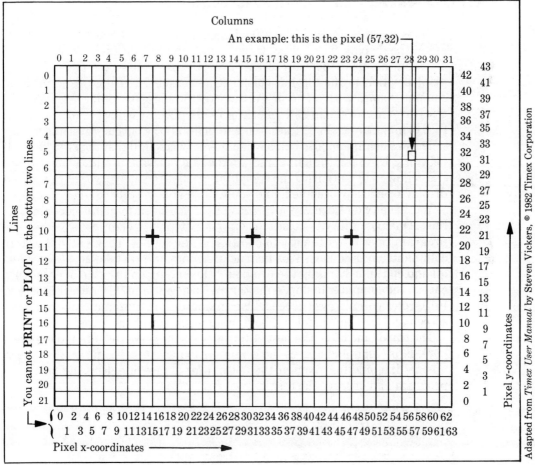

Figure 5-2. Differences between PRINT AT (character)
and PLOT/UNPLOT (pixel) input

- The PRINT AT command specifies the vertical position (the line number), followed by a comma and the horizontal position (the column number). The PLOT and UNPLOT commands specify the horizontal coordinate first, followed by a comma and the vertical coordinate.

- The print position moves to the next display line when a PRINT AT command is finished, unless the command ends with a semicolon. After a PLOT or UNPLOT command, however, the print position moves to the first pixel location after the changed pixel. Semicolons cannot be used in PLOT and UNPLOT commands.

## SCREEN CONTROL: CLS, CONT, AND SCROLL

Three more commands that you will generally use in connection with PRINT affect the display. The first of these is CLS, which stands for "clear screen." This command (on the v key) erases everything on the screen and moves the print position to the top left corner. One reason for using CLS is that the computer stops with an error message (error code 5) whenever a program tries to print more than 21 lines on the TV display. By using CLS in a program that prints more than 21 lines, you can print all the output without errors.

The CLS command also helps when memory is so full that the EDIT key will not work. First put the edit cursor on the line you want to edit. Then execute CLS, followed by EDIT. Now the computer can use the memory that the screen display previously occupied, and you will be able to edit the line.

You have two alternatives besides CLS if you need to print more than 21 lines. One possibility is to let the computer stop with error code 5 when the program tries to write past the bottom of the screen. Then enter the CONT command (on the c key). This instructs the computer to take up where it left off and continue running the program. Depending on the kind of error that caused the computer to stop, it may or may not continue. After error 5 (screen full), CONT will always succeed. The computer will automatically clear the screen and continue printing, beginning at the top of the screen.

The third (and often the best) alternative is the SCROLL command (on the B key). This command causes the computer to move everything on the screen up one line, making room at the bottom for a new line. Run the following program and observe the result:

```
 5 SLOW
10 PRINT AT 3,0;"SCROLL DEMONS
TRATION"
20 SCROLL
30 PRINT SQR 2
40 SCROLL
50 PRINT SQR 3
60 SCROLL
```

```
70 PRINT SQR 4
80 SCROLL
90 PRINT SQR 5
```

At the first SCROLL command (line 20), the print position moves to the bottom of the display. Thereafter, everything on the screen moves up one line each time SCROLL is executed. At line 80, the title line disappears off the top of the screen.

Obviously, you should use SCROLL only in slow mode or with PAUSE. Otherwise, you will never see the lines that scroll off the top, since in fast mode the computer does not show the display until the program pauses or is finished.

Table 5-1 summarizes the TS1000 and ZX81 input and output features.

### Table 5-1. Input and Output Summary

| Symbol | Description |
| --- | --- |
| INPUT | A command that reads the value of a variable from the keyboard. |
| INKEY$ | A function whose value is the character on the key that is pressed when INKEY$ is executed. If no key is pressed, the value is the empty string. |
| PRINT | A command that displays numbers or strings on the television screen. |
| LPRINT | A command that displays numbers or strings on the printer. |
| , | An item in a PRINT or LPRINT statement that moves the print position to the left side or middle of the screen, whichever comes next. |
| ; | An item in a PRINT or LPRINT statement that causes the print position to stay at the end of the last character printed instead of going to the next line. |
| TAB | An item in a PRINT or LPRINT statement that moves the print position forward to a specified column. |
| AT | An item in a PRINT or LPRINT statement that moves the print position forward or backward to a specified column and to a specified line for a PRINT statement (the line number is ignored in an LPRINT statement). |
| PLOT | A command that darkens a pixel (one-fourth of a character square) at a specified location. |
| UNPLOT | A command that whitens a pixel at a specified location. |
| PAUSE | A command that waits a specified period of time before going on to the next line of the program. The display is visible during the pause, even in fast mode. |
| CLS | A command that clears the screen. |
| CONT | A command that tells the computer to continue after an error and is used to see more output after the screen fills up. |
| SCROLL | A command that moves the entire display up one line to make room for a new line at the bottom. The top line disappears. |
| LIST | A command that displays the current program on the television screen. |
| LLIST | A command that displays the current program on the printer. |
| COPY | A command that copies the television screen display to the printer. |

# DRAWING PICTURES

Table 5-1 includes all the different printing capabilities of the TS1000 and ZX81. These capabilities give you all the tools you need to draw pictures on the screen or printer. Look again at the graphics characters on the top three lines of the keyboard. Recall that you enter a graphics character by first pressing GRAPHICS (SHIFT-9) to turn on the ▤ cursor, which stays on until you press GRAPHICS again. While the ▤ cursor is on, enter any graphics character by shifting the key where the graphics character appears. Enter the reverse video image of any letter by pressing it without SHIFT while the ▤ cursor is on. A shifted key with no graphics character on it produces the reverse video image of its shifted symbol.

The keyboard contains 21 graphics symbols. You can draw a great variety of pictures by using them in PRINT or LPRINT commands, in the same way as for ordinary text. Each graphics symbol uses a space the same size as any other character, and TAB and AT work the same way for graphics characters as for any other printed text. As already explained, the graphics symbols on the keys 1 through 8 and Q, W, E, R, T, and Y divide the character space into four square quarters (pixels). You can make any one of the four quarters black and the rest white, or any one of them white and the rest black, or two of them black and the other two white, just by selecting the appropriate graphics symbol. The remaining graphics symbols, on A, S, D, F, G, and H, provide a grey color for parts of the character space, and the SPACE key produces a solid black character. The PLOT and UNPLOT commands also change the color of individual pixels as already explained.

The best way to learn to draw pictures with the computer is to experiment with it yourself. Imagine how you might use the computer's symbols to draw a picture of a person, animal, or object. A few examples will help you begin. The following one draws the outline of a die with three dots on it:

```
 10 PRINT AT 0,10;"              "
 20 PRINT AT 1,10;"█            █"
 30 PRINT AT 2,10;"█            █"
 40 PRINT AT 3,10;"█            █"
 50 PRINT AT 4,10;"█            █"
 60 PRINT AT 5,10;"█            █"
 70 PRINT AT 6,10;"█            █"
 80 PRINT AT 7,10;"█            █"
 90 PRINT AT 8,10;"              "
100 PRINT AT 2,12;"*";AT 4,14;"
*";AT 6,16;"*"
```

Line 10 uses the graphics symbol on the 6 key. Lines 20 through 80 use the symbols on the 5 key (after the first quotation symbol) and on the 8 key (just before the last quotation symbol). Line 90 uses the symbol on the 7 key. After you run this program, the screen will look like this:

Notice that the PRINT statements themselves form a figure that looks like the figure the program produces when it runs. This is not always so because a PRINT statement may sometimes be too long to fit on one line.

If your system includes a Timex or Sinclair printer, replace the PRINT commands with LPRINT commands to print the figure on the printer. Alternatively, leave them as PRINT commands, run the program, and use the COPY command to transfer the result to the printer. If you have a different printer designed to work with the ZX81 or TS1000, use the commands specified by the printer's manufacturer.

The next program draws a picture of a cat:

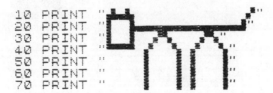

His name is Cheops, and he was a favorite of the builder of the great pyramid:

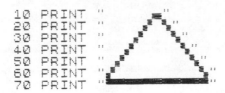

Obviously, you cannot draw a completely realistic picture with this small set of graphics symbols. With a little effort, though, you can represent just about any object you want.

Program Control

# Chapter Six

A computer performs calculations like a calculator and prints text like a typewriter, but it is much more than just a calculator and a typewriter combined. A computer can test the result of a calculation or a keyboard entry and determine what it should do next. It can repeat the same section of a program over and over until a specified condition is satisfied, or it can skip one part of a program to execute another part. This chapter tells you how to use these decision-making capabilities in your programs. It also describes how to organize large amounts of data in tables and similar groupings, called *arrays*, to make the best use of these powerful capabilities.

## SKIPPING AROUND WITH GOTO

Up to this point this book's programs have simply been lists of commands for the computer to execute in exactly the same order as they are numbered. The line numbers tell the computer that these commands are part of a program, and specify their order of execution. Such a program could be diagrammed like this:

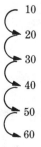

10
20
30
40
50
60

In many cases, however, a program needs to perform one operation over and over with few or no changes. Alternatively, it may need to perform different operations, depending on what is input from the keyboard, or depending on the results of calculations. The simplest BASIC command that changes the flow of a program is the GOTO command. It instructs the computer to skip forward or backward to a specified line number, like this:

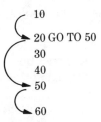

```
10
20 GO TO 50
30
40
50
60
```

Thus the line numbers perform an added function: They not only specify the order of statements in the program, but also serve as addresses for GOTO commands. A GOTO statement *branches* or *jumps* to a new line number. These terms simply mean that instead of proceeding to the next program line after GOTO, the computer skips to the new line number specified in the GOTO command and resumes execution there. The new line number can be a constant, a variable, or a mathematical computation. If there is no line with that number, the computer jumps to the nearest existing line number that is higher than the specified number.

Programs use the GOTO statement for two purposes: to repeat an operation, or to skip sections of a program. The following sections describe these two uses of GOTO.

## Repeating a Program Section

To repeat a section of a program, insert a GOTO statement at the end of the section. The GOTO statement must specify the number of the line at the beginning of the section to be repeated. An example is the following program to calculate square roots:

```
 5 SLOW
10 REM DEFINE A STARTING VALUE
20 LET A=1
30 REM THE REPEATED SECTION BE
GINS HERE
40 REM PRINT THE SQUARE ROOT
50 PRINT "THE SQUARE ROOT OF "
;A;" IS ";SQR A
60 REM INCREASE THE NUMBER BY
ONE
```

```
70 LET A=A+1
80 REM NOW REPEAT
90 GOTO 50
```

This program prints the square root of each integer, starting with one, until the screen fills up and the computer stops with error code 5. If you now enter CONT, the computer clears the screen and fills it again with the square roots of the next integers. You can use the BREAK key (the same as the SPACE key) to stop the computer at any point, and you can use CONT to resume from that point.

A repeated program section is called a *loop*. In the above example, the program *loops* between lines 50 and 90. Loops are extremely useful in computer programming, and you will encounter them often in the pages that follow.

Since the computer ignores REM statements, you could use GOTO 30 or GOTO 40 in line 90, instead of GOTO 50. However, because a REM statement takes up time, the program will run faster if you use GOTO 50.

The following example repeatedly simulates the throw of a die until the screen is full:

```
2 SLOW
5 RAND
10 PRINT INT (6*RND+1)
20 GOTO 10
```

With this form of the program, you can easily generate a large number of throws without having to run the program over and over. To get even more throw results per screenful, you can modify the program to PRINT several numbers per line, like this:

```
2 SLOW
5 RAND
10 PRINT INT (6*RND+1);" ";
20 GOTO 10
```

Now the screen fills with 16 numbers per line instead of only one. You can print more or fewer numbers per line by changing the length of the blank string at the end of line 10. Try it with no spaces and then with two, three, or four spaces. Since each line has 32 columns, the numbers will not line up directly under each other unless the combined length of the random number, plus the spaces after it, divides evenly into 32.

The next example of a loop converts the "blink" animation program from Chapter 4 into a display like a flashing billboard:

```
10 SLOW
20 PRINT AT 0,5;"BLINK"
30 PRINT AT 0,5;"BLINK"
40 PRINT AT 0,5;"BLINK"
```

```
50 PRINT AT 0,5;"BLINK"
60 PRINT AT 0,5;"BLINK"
70 PRINT AT 0,5;"BLINK"
80 GOTO 20
```

Since this program keeps printing in the same spot, it never fills the screen, and so will continue looping until you press the BREAK key. Use this kind of animation to call attention to a particular part of the information displayed on the screen. For example, it could highlight a prompt that tells the user what input the computer expects next from the keyboard.

## Skipping Part of a Program

A program may need to do different things, depending on the result of a calculation or input it receives from the keyboard. Chapter 3 introduced the IF and THEN keywords for testing whether two numbers or numeric expressions are equal. This section will explain how to combine this test with the GOTO statement so that your programs can make choices.

As an example of program control employing IF, THEN, and GOTO, consider a program that requests two numbers as input, divides the first by the second, and prints the result. Without any added control statements, the program is as follows:

```
10 REM GET NUMBERS FROM KEYBOA
RD
20 PRINT "ENTER FIRST NUMBER"
30 INPUT NUM1
40 PRINT "ENTER SECOND NUMBER"
50 INPUT NUM2
60 REM DIVIDE AND PRINT RESULT
70 PRINT "THE QUOTIENT IS ";NU
M1/NUM2
```

Run this program several times, entering different numbers to see how it works. Then enter zero for NUM2. The computer stops at line 70, reports error code 6, and does not print a quotient. Since the rules of arithmetic make it impossible to divide by zero, a good program should test the divisor to prevent such errors. The following improved program tests NUM2 first. If it is zero, the program prints an explanatory error message and omits the division:

```
10 REM GET NUMBERS FROM KEYBOA
RD
20 PRINT "ENTER FIRST NUMBER"
30 INPUT NUM1
40 PRINT "ENTER SECOND NUMBER"
50 INPUT NUM2
60 IF NUM2=0 THEN GOTO 120
```

```
  70 REM DIVIDE AND PRINT RESULT
  80 PRINT "THE QUOTIENT IS ";NU
M1/NUM2
  90 REM SKIP ERROR MESSAGE
 100 GOTO 130
 110 REM PREVENT DIVISION BY ZER
O
 120 PRINT "YOU CANNOT DIVIDE BY
 ZERO"
 130 REM
```

Run the improved program, entering some nonzero numbers to verify that it still works as it did before. Then enter zero for NUM2 and observe how it handles the problem.

## THE STOP COMMAND

Another command for controlling the flow of your programs is the STOP command (SHIFT-A). It makes the computer stop the program and display the ▧ cursor. You can also stop a program by pressing the BREAK key, but the STOP command assures that you will stop at a specific line. To see one use of STOP, modify the blinking billboard program as follows to check for a pressed key and stop if one is not pressed:

```
10 SLOW
20 PRINT AT 0,5;"BLINK"
30 PRINT AT 0,5;"BLINK"
40 PRINT AT 0,5;"BLINK"
50 PRINT AT 0,5;"BLINK"
60 PRINT AT 0,5;"BLINK"
70 PRINT AT 0,5;"BLINK"
75 IF INKEY$="" THEN STOP
80 GOTO 20
```

When you enter RUN for this program, keep your finger on the ENTER key so that the computer will find a key pressed when it reaches line 75. In this way, INKEY$ will receive the ENTER code instead of the empty string, and the program will loop back to line 20. When you remove your finger, the new value of INKEY$ will be the empty string. The program will stop with the last letter of BLINK in reverse video. By moving the IF statement to other places in the program, you can make it stop with a different letter reversed, or with none of them reversed.

## COMPARISONS AND DECISIONS

The IF-THEN statement is the principal decision-making statement in BASIC. Between the words IF and THEN is a *condition* for the computer to test. After the word THEN is another BASIC command for the computer to execute if the condition is true. If the condition is false, the computer ignores the command after THEN and goes directly to the next line of the program.

Some examples of the IF-THEN statement from previous sections are:

```
IF INKEY$="" THEN STOP

IF NUM2=0 THEN GOTO 110

IF TEST=1 THEN PRINT "UNITY"
```

The command to the right of THEN can be any other BASIC command. If it is a GOTO statement, and the "if" condition is true, the computer will skip to the line number specified after GOTO and execute that section of the program. If the command to the right of THEN is not a GOTO statement, then the computer will always execute the lines directly below, and the condition only determines whether the computer will execute or skip the one command to the right of THEN.

All of the examples above use the same type of conditional test. They test a variable to determine whether it is equal to a particular value. The symbol they use for equality is =, the same symbol that the LET statement uses to give a value to a variable. These two uses of the = symbol are really very different, however. The computer chooses the correct meaning by examining the first keyword in the command. If the keyword is LET, the computer must give a value to a variable. If the keyword is IF, it must compare a variable to a specified value.

## Relational Tests

The TS1000 and ZX81 recognize six different kinds of *relational tests*. The "equality" test just discussed is one of these six. The computer can also determine which of two numbers is larger. It can even understand such combined relationships as "not equal" and "greater than or equal to." The different relationships between variables that the computer can test, and the symbols for these relationships, are shown in Table 6-1. Each of these comparison symbols is a single symbol, located on a single key. For example, <= is a shifted symbol on the R key. Do not type two separate symbols, < and =, instead.

Use each of these symbols in the same way you use the = comparison. For example, the following program prints the string BUY IT if the value of the variable PRICE is smaller than the value of the variable LIMIT:

```
10 INPUT PRICE
20 INPUT LIMIT
30 IF PRICE<LIMIT THEN PRINT "
BUY IT"
```

**Table 6-1. Relational Operators**

| Operator | Meaning |
|----------|---------|
| = | Equal |
| < | Less than |
| > | Greater than |
| <= | Less than or equal to |
| >= | Greater than or equal to |
| <> | Not equal to (means the same as "less than or greater than") |

The computer can perform relational tests on strings as well as on numbers. For numbers, the meaning of such comparisons as "equal," "larger," and "smaller" is obvious. For strings, however, these words do not have a familiar meaning. To explain them, we begin with the concept of string equality. Two strings are equal if they have exactly the same characters in the same order; in other words, they are equal if they are exactly alike. Obviously, then, two strings of different lengths cannot possibly be equal. Some examples of string equality and inequality are shown in Table 6-2. The last pair of strings is unequal because they have different numbers of spaces between the words PERSONAL and COMPUTER.

Two strings can even look exactly alike on the screen and still not be equal. For example, one of them could have an extra space at the end, or one could use a special BASIC word while the other spelled out the same word with letters. To demonstrate the second possibility, enter the following program. Use SHIFT-S for the string LPRINT in line 10, and type out the individual letters of **LPRINT** in line 20:

```
10 LET A$=" LPRINT "
20 LET B$=" LPRINT "
30 IF A$=B$ THEN PRINT "EQUAL"
40 IF A$<>B$ THEN PRINT "NOT E
QUAL"
```

The computer prints NOT EQUAL because the two strings have different representations inside the computer, even though they look alike on the screen. The first string consists of the single character code 225, which represents the command word LPRINT (see Appendix C). The second string consists of the character codes for the individual letters in the same word.

**Table 6-2. String Equality**

| First String | Second String | Are They Equal? |
|--------------|---------------|-----------------|
| MASSACHUSETTS | MASSACHUSETTS | Yes |
| BACON AND EGGS | BACON AND EGG | No |
| PERSONAL  COMPUTER | PERSONAL COMPUTER | No |

You can test the result of an INPUT statement to determine whether the person running your program entered a particular string. The following program will either divide or multiply two numbers, depending upon the input:

```
10 REM GET TWO NUMBERS
20 PRINT "ENTER FIRST NUMBER"
30 INPUT NUM1
40 PRINT "ENTER SECOND NUMBER"
50 INPUT NUM2
60 REM DETERMINE WHAT TO DO
70 PRINT "DO YOU WANT TO MULTI
PLY?"
80 INPUT D$
90 IF D$="YES" THEN GOTO 130
100 REM DO WHAT WAS SPECIFIED
110 LET ANS=NUM1/NUM2
120 GOTO 170
130 LET ANS=NUM1*NUM2
160 REM PRINT THE ANSWER
170 PRINT "THE ANSWER IS ";ANS
```

This program asks a question in line 70 and uses the = comparison on strings to analyze the answer. If you enter **YES**, then the command GOTO **130** in 90 is executed. The computer skips the division in line 110 and performs the multiplication in line 130. If you enter anything other than YES, the computer skips the command GOTO 130 in line 90 and performs the division in line 110. Then line 120 branches to line 170, skipping the multiplication.

Unfortunately, this program is not very tolerant of mistakes. If you mistype the string YES, it will assume that you meant NO. We will fix this later.

In BASIC, the "smaller" of two strings is simply the one that comes first in alphabetical order. For example, observe what happens when you execute the following command:

```
IF"FRED"<"JIM" THEN PRINT "LESS
"
```

The computer prints **LESS** because FRED comes before JIM in alphabetical order. Notice that the < and > comparisons for strings have nothing to do with the length of the strings. A shorter string can come either before or after a longer string in alphabetical order. In BASIC's string < and > comparisons, only the alphabetical order matters. Try the following program, which reads two strings from the keyboard and prints them in alphabetical order:

```
10 INPUT A$
20 INPUT B$
30 IF B$<A$ THEN GOTO 70
40 PRINT A$
50 PRINT B$
```

```
60 STOP
70 PRINT B$
80 PRINT A$
```

## Logical Expressions

Recall that numeric variables and constants combine with numeric operators like +, −, *, /, and ** to produce numeric expressions, and that strings combine with various operators to produce string expressions. In the same way, relational tests combine with *logical* operators to produce new tests. Such combinations are called *logical expressions*. The operators that appear in logical expressions are AND, OR, and NOT. The following program illustrates the AND operator:

```
10  INPUT A
20  INPUT B
30  INPUT C
40  INPUT D
50  IF A=B AND C=D THEN PRINT "
BOTH PAIRS ARE EQUAL"
```

Run the program several times, entering different numbers for A, B, C, and D. The computer prints BOTH PAIRS ARE EQUAL only if A is equal to B and C is equal to D.

To illustrate the OR operator, modify line 50 in the previous program so that the program becomes

```
10  INPUT A
20  INPUT B
30  INPUT C
40  INPUT D
50  IF A=B OR C=D THEN PRINT "A
T LEAST ONE PAIR IS EQUAL"
```

The computer will print its message if A is equal to B or if C is equal to D. It will also print the message if both equalities are true.

The operator NOT is slightly different from OR and AND because it refers to just one relational test instead of two. The following program illustrates the NOT operator:

```
10  INPUT A
20  INPUT B
30  IF NOT A=B THEN PRINT "NOT
EQUAL"
```

Notice that NOT goes in front of the expression to which it applies. Think of NOT as a function that takes a relational expression as its argument, evaluates it as true or false, and uses the opposite of the result as its value. Every logical expression employing NOT has another, equivalent form without NOT. For example, the following line does exactly the same thing as line 30 above, but without using NOT:

```
 30 IF A<>B THEN PRINT "NOT EQU
AL"
```

Use NOT whenever it makes logical expressions easier for you to write or understand.

The logical operators AND, OR, and NOT have their own relative priorities, just as the different numerical and string operators do. The highest of the three is NOT, followed by AND and OR in that order. For example, the following command will cause the computer to stop if A is not greater than B or if C is equal to D:

```
IF NOT A>B OR C=D THEN STOP
```

You can use parentheses to specify different priorities, just as you can with numeric and string expressions. The following command does exactly the same thing as the previous one:

```
IF (NOT A>B) OR C=D THEN STOP
```

The next command causes the computer to stop if either "A is greater than B" or "C is equal to D" is false:

```
IF NOT (A>B OR C=D) THEN STOP
```

In simple expressions, the logical operators generally mean just what you would expect the English words AND, OR, and NOT to mean. However, in compound expressions, spoken English takes shortcuts that the computer will not understand. For example, the English sentence "X is larger than Y or Z" actually means that two things are true: "X is larger than Y" and "X is larger than Z." In BASIC you must express this idea as two relations joined by AND, like this:

```
X>Y AND X>Z
```

If you tried to copy the English sentence directly, you would write

```
X>Y OR Z
```

In BASIC this last expression can only mean "X is larger than Y, or Z is true," which is quite different from the original sentence.

The logical operators AND, OR, and NOT are also called *Boolean operators*, in honor of a mathematician named Boole who studied their properties in detail. These operators make it much easier to tell the computer what you want and to keep track of what you have told it. For example, we can improve the program that selects either division or multiplication by comparing the input string to NO as well as to YES, and printing an error message if it is not one of these two. The new test uses the OR operator, as follows:

```
10 REM GET TWO NUMBERS
20 PRINT "ENTER FIRST NUMBER"
30 INPUT NUM1
40 PRINT "ENTER SECOND NUMBER"
50 INPUT NUM2
60 REM DETERMINE WHAT TO DO
70 PRINT "DO YOU WANT TO MULTI
PLY?"
80 INPUT D$
82 IF D$="YES"  OR D$="NO" THE
N GOTO 90
84 PRINT "ENTER YES OR NO"
86 GOTO 70
90 IF D$="YES" THEN GOTO 130
100 REM DO WHAT WAS SPECIFIED
110 LET ANS=NUM1/NUM2
120 GOTO 170
130 LET ANS=NUM1*NUM2
160 REM PRINT THE ANSWER
170 PRINT "THE ANSWER IS ";ANS
```

# FOR-NEXT LOOPS

A *loop* is just a section of a program that the computer repeats. When a GOTO statement branches back to an earlier part of the program, it produces a simple loop. Some loops use a relational test to determine when to quit looping. The blinking billboard program that you used before is an example of such a loop:

```
10 SLOW
20 PRINT AT 0,5;"BLINK"
30 PRINT AT 0,5;"BLINK"
40 PRINT AT 0,5;"BLINK"
50 PRINT AT 0,5;"BLINK"
60 PRINT AT 0,5;"BLINK"
70 PRINT AT 0,5;"BLINK"
75 IF INKEY$="" THEN STOP
80 GOTO 20
```

Loops can terminate in several different ways. In many cases, the programmer specifies exactly how many times a loop will be executed. Such a loop requires an additional variable, called a *control variable* or a *counter*, to keep a running count of the number of passes through the loop. For example, the following program moves a reverse-video character through a word 15 times:

```
10 SLOW
12 LET C=1
20 PRINT AT 0,5;"BLINK"
```

```
30 PRINT AT 0,5; "BLINK"
40 PRINT AT 0,5; "BLINK"
50 PRINT AT 0,5; "BLINK"
60 PRINT AT 0,5; "BLINK"
70 PRINT AT 0,5; "BLINK"
75 LET C=C+1
80 IF C<=15 THEN GOTO 20
```

Line 12 *initializes* the control variable C. That is, it defines C as a variable and gives it its starting value. Each time the computer goes through the loop, it encounters line 75 and increases the value of C by 1. Then line 80 sends it back to line 20 to repeat the loop. After the fifteenth pass, C will be equal to 16 and the GOTO in line 80 will not get executed. Thus the computer does the loop exactly 15 times and then goes on to the next line of the program.

Counting loops are so common that BASIC provides two special commands for writing them: the FOR statement and the NEXT statement. The FOR statement always goes at the beginning of the loop, and the NEXT statement always goes at the end of the loop. You can use these commands to simplify the blinking billboard program in the following way:

```
10 SLOW
12 FOR C=1 TO 15 STEP 1
20 PRINT AT 0,5; "BLINK"
30 PRINT AT 0,5; "BLINK"
40 PRINT AT 0,5; "BLINK"
50 PRINT AT 0,5; "BLINK"
60 PRINT AT 0,5; "BLINK"
70 PRINT AT 0,5; "BLINK"
80 NEXT C
```

The FOR statement instructs the computer to begin a loop, using a specified control variable (called C in the above program) as the counter. It also initializes C to 1 and specifies that the loop terminate and the computer go on to the rest of the program when C becomes greater than 15. The number 1 after STEP tells the computer to add one to C each time it gets to the end of the loop. Thus the FOR statement does almost all of the work required to create a loop.

The NEXT statement in line 80 simply marks the end of the loop, the place where the program loops backward or moves forward, depending on the current value of the control variable.

The name of the control variable of a FOR-NEXT loop must be just a single letter. The number after STEP can be any numeric expression. It specifies the change in the control variable at the end of each loop. If you omit STEP and the number after it, the computer assumes a STEP of one. For example, the following two FOR statements will do exactly the same thing:

```
FOR C=1 TO 15 STEP 1
FOR C=1 TO 15
```

The STEP size can also be negative, in which case the number after TO must be smaller than the number before TO. The STEP can even be a fraction. The loop will terminate as soon as the counter passes the value specified in the FOR statement, whether it hits the value exactly or not.

The next example of a FOR-NEXT loop uses a program from Chapter 3 that calculates compound interest for two quarters. The original program was the following:

```
10 LET WORTH=100
20 LET RATE=0.10
30 LET QRATE=RATE/4
40 LET INTEREST=QRATE*WORTH
50 LET WORTH=WORTH+INTEREST
60 LET INTEREST=QRATE*WORTH
70 LET WORTH=WORTH+INTEREST
80 PRINT WORTH
```

Observe that lines 60 and 70 are identical to lines 40 and 50. To calculate the value of the investment after, say, 20 quarters, you would have to duplicate this pair of lines in the program 20 times. With a FOR-NEXT loop, however, you can repeat this pair of commands any number of times without retyping them, and you can read in the number of quarters as a variable. The following improved program works equally well for any number of quarters:

```
2 PRINT "HOW MANY QUARTERS?"
5 INPUT NQUARTS
10 LET WORTH=100
20 LET RATE=0.10
30 LET QRATE=RATE/4
40 FOR I=1 TO NQUARTS
60 LET INTEREST=QRATE*WORTH
70 LET WORTH=WORTH+INTEREST
75 NEXT I
80 PRINT WORTH
```

## USING THE CONTROL VARIABLE

The control variable of a FOR-NEXT loop is more than just a counter. You can also use it inside the loop to determine which pass through the loop is in progress. For example, to print out the number of each quarter together with the worth at the end of that quarter, insert the following line in the previous program:

```
72 PRINT "WORTH AFTER QUARTER
";I;" IS ";WORTH
```

There are two things you must never do with the control variable, however. Never try to change its value with a LET or INPUT statement inside the loop, and never use GOTO to branch into the middle of a FOR-NEXT loop without executing the FOR statement. After such a branch, the computer would be in the middle of the loop without having defined the control variable.

To understand other uses of the control variable of a FOR-NEXT loop, begin with the original version of the blinking billboard program, without any loops:

```
10 SLOW
20 PRINT AT 0,5;"BLINK"
30 PRINT AT 0,5;"BLINK"
40 PRINT AT 0,5;"BLINK"
50 PRINT AT 0,5;"BLINK"
60 PRINT AT 0,5;"BLINK"
70 PRINT AT 0,5;"BLINK"
```

Observe that lines 30 through 70 are identical, except that each line has a different character in reverse video. For a longer word than BLINK, it would be inconvenient to use a separate program line for each character position in the word. A much simpler program would use a FOR-NEXT loop to go through the word one character at a time, reversing that one character, printing the resulting string, and then unreversing the character to prepare the string for the next pass through the loop. Such a revised program follows:

```
10 SLOW
20 LET A$="BLINK"
30 PRINT AT 0,5;A$
40 FOR K=1 TO LEN A$
50 LET A$(K)=CHR$ (CODE A$(K)+
128)
60 PRINT AT 0,5;A$
70 LET A$(K)=CHR$ (CODE A$(K)-
128)
80 NEXT K
```

Line 20 defines a variable A$ in order to avoid re-entering the word BLINK several times. Line 30 prints the string with no reverse-video characters. Then line 40 begins a loop that is executed once for each character in the string.

Lines 50 and 70 do most of the work. To understand them, first find the character code for the letter B in Appendix C. Its number is 39. Now add 128 to 39 to get 167, and look up that character in Appendix C. You will find that it is ▉, the reverse-video version of character number 39. Look down the list and observe that each of the single characters (codes 0 to 63) and its reverse-video counterpart differ by exactly 128. Line 50 in the above program simply

1. Takes the character code for the character (CODE A$(K)).
2. Adds 128 to obtain the character code for the corresponding reverse-video character.

3. Uses the CHR$ function to convert the result to the reverse-video character itself.

4. Uses string substitution to replace the original character with the reversed one.

Line 60 prints the string with the reversed character in it, and line 70 undoes what line 50 did, to leave the string the way it was originally.

Run the program to verify that it does the same thing the original program did, only more slowly. It should move the reverse-video character through the word BLINK once, from left to right, leaving the ▣ reversed.

This latest version of the blinking billboard program is not actually much shorter or simpler than the original version. With a longer string in the place of BLINK, however, the original version would require an additional line for each added letter. The new version of the program needs no more program lines, regardless of how long the string is. In fact, its biggest advantage is that it will work for any string at all. To prove it, replace line 20 with the following:

```
20 LET A$="THIS IS A LONGER ST
RING"
```

Now run the program and watch the reverse video move across this longer string. Replace the string in line 20 with your name, or with any other string you want to use.

Thus, a well-designed loop makes a program more general, eliminating any dependence on the particular piece of data it uses. To make the program even more general, replace line 20 with an input statement that lets you choose the string each time you run the program, like this:

```
20 INPUT A$
```

## Loops Within Loops

To make the blinking billboard program repeat the motion across the string several times, as it did before, simply add another set of FOR-NEXT statements. The resulting program has two loops, shown with brackets in the following illustration:

```
      10 SLOW
      20 INPUT A$
   ┌─ 25 FOR C=1 TO 15
   │  30 PRINT AT 0,5;A$
   │┌─ 40 FOR K=1 TO LEN A$
   ││  50 LET A$(K)=CHR$ (CODE A$(K)+128)
   ││  60 PRINT AT 0,5,A$
   ││  70 LET A$(K)=CHR$ (CODE A$(K)+128)
   │└─ 80 NEXT K
   └─ 90 NEXT C
```

This program is an example of *nested* loops, which just means one loop inside another. The brackets at the left side of the listing show you where each loop begins and ends. The outside bracket connects the FOR and NEXT statements that use C as their control variable, and the inside bracket connects the FOR and NEXT statements that use K as their control variable. The INPUT statement (Line 20) comes before both loops, because you only want to read the string once.

Observe that the loop with control variable K is completely inside the loop with control variable C. This illustrates a very important rule for nested loops: They must not overlap. In other words, if you drew the connecting brackets from the beginning to the end of each loop, they must not cross each other. Draw such brackets when you are designing nested loops to make sure they obey this rule. A program can have any number of separate loops, one after the other, and it can have many loops inside each other, as long as no brackets cross. The following example shows an "illegal" loop:

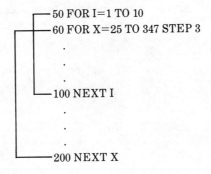

```
50 FOR I=1 TO 10
60 FOR X=25 TO 347 STEP 3
    .
    .
    .
100 NEXT I
    .
    .
    .
200 NEXT X
```

## Loops That Go Backward

Previous examples of loops have added one to the control variable each time through the loop. You can specify a different amount of change in the control variable by including STEP in the FOR statement. For example, if you switch the first and last values of the control variable and make the step negative, the loop will run "backward." In the blinking billboard program, such changes in the inner loop will cause the reverse-video character to move across the line from right to left, instead of from left to right. Run the following modified program and watch the animation go in the opposite direction:

```
10 SLOW
20 INPUT A$
25 FOR C=1 TO 15
30 PRINT AT 0,5;A$
40 FOR K=LEN A$ TO 1 STEP -1
```

```
   50 LET A$(K)=CHR$ (CODE A$(K)+
128)
   60 PRINT AT 0,5;A$
   70 LET A$(K)=CHR$ (CODE A$(K)-
128)
   80 NEXT K
   90 NEXT C
```

A similar change in the outer loop (the one with control variable C) would not change what the program does because the program never uses C for anything inside the loop.

To illustrate the effect of STEP in another way, substitute the following for line 40:

```
   40 FOR K=LEN A$ TO 1  STEP -2
```

Now only every second character in the string will get reversed. The control variable that chooses the characters to be reversed by line 50 is now changing by two each time through the loop, and the loop only runs half as many times as it did before. Try different values of STEP until you are sure you understand it.

When writing loops, you must make sure that the step changes the control variable in the right direction. The following program, which prints the numbers from 5 to 10, clearly shows what the different parts of the FOR statement do:

```
   10 FOR G=5 TO 10
   20 PRINT G
   30 NEXT G
```

Interchange the 5 and the 10, changing STEP to −1 at the same time, and the program will print the same numbers backward, starting with 10 and going to 5. To see this, run the following program:

```
   10 FOR G=10 TO 5 STEP -1
   20 PRINT G
   30 NEXT G
```

However, if you switch 5 and 10 without changing STEP, or if you make STEP negative without switching 5 and 10, the program will not print anything at all. Try the next two programs:

```
   10 FOR G=10 TO 5
   20 PRINT G
   30 NEXT G
```

or

```
   10 FOR G=5 TO 10 STEP -1
   20 PRINT G
   30 NEXT G
```

**Table 6-3. Rules for FOR-NEXT Loops**

1. The control variable name must be a single letter.
2. The NEXT statement must use the same control variable as the FOR statement.
3. The FOR statement must be executed before the NEXT statement.
4. GOTO cannot be used to jump into the middle of a FOR–NEXT loop.
5. The value of the control variable cannot be changed with LET or INPUT while inside the loop.
6. Multiple loops can be separate or nested, but they cannot overlap.
7. If the final value of the control variable is larger than the starting value, then STEP must be positive.
8. If the final value of the control variable is smaller than the starting value, then STEP must be negative.

You cannot go from 10 to 5 in steps of 1 because you're already past 5 when you start. Similarly, you cannot go from 5 to 10 in steps of $-1$ because you're already past 10 (that is, smaller than 10) when you start. The computer knows that a negative STEP means going to smaller values of the control variable. If the starting value is already past the limit, it will just ignore the loop entirely.

The rules for FOR-NEXT loops are summarized in Table 6-3.

# ARRAYS

Arrays are a systematic way of naming a large number of variables. If you do not already understand what arrays are, or how to use them, then read on. The information that follows will be very important to your programming efforts.

Arrays are a useful shorthand means of describing a large number of related variables. Consider, for example, a table of 200 numbers. How would you like to assign a unique variable name to each of the 200 numbers? It would be far simpler to give the entire table one name and identify individual numbers in the table by their location within the table. This is precisely what an array does for you.

When you have two or more data items, instead of giving each data item a separate variable name, you can give the collection of data items a single name. The collection is called an *array*, and its name is an *array name*. The individual data items in the array are called *array elements* or *members* of the array. The elements in an array are numbered. In this way you can select an individual item using its position number, which is referred to as its *index*.

As an example of array usage, consider how you might keep track of individual scores in a bowling tournament. You could use a separate variable name for each bowler, like this:

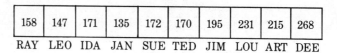

| 158 | 147 | 171 | 135 | 172 | 170 | 195 | 231 | 215 | 268 |
|-----|-----|-----|-----|-----|-----|-----|-----|-----|-----|
| RAY | LEO | IDA | JAN | SUE | TED | JIM | LOU | ART | DEE |

But what do you do at the next tournament, where the bowlers have different names?

How about keeping the scores in an array, like this?

| 158 | 147 | 171 | 135 | 172 | 170 | 195 | 231 | 215 | 268 |
|-----|-----|-----|-----|-----|-----|-----|-----|-----|-----|
| B(1) | B(2) | B(3) | B(4) | B(5) | B(6) | B(7) | B(8) | B(9) | B(10) |

The array name is B. (The name of an array must be a single letter.) Each element in this array will be one bowler's score. An index (enclosed in parentheses) follows the array name. Thus a specific data item (that is, one bowler's score) is identified by an array name and an index. For example, B(3) has the score for bowler number 3.

The TS1000 and ZX81 also provide for arrays of strings as well as arrays of numbers. Thus, if you wanted to, you could have two arrays: one array of numbers for the bowlers' scores and one array of strings (call it N$) for the bowlers' names, like this:

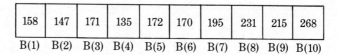

| 158 | 147 | 171 | 135 | 172 | 170 | 195 | 231 | 215 | 268 |
|-----|-----|-----|-----|-----|-----|-----|-----|-----|-----|
| B(1) | B(2) | B(3) | B(4) | B(5) | B(6) | B(7) | B(8) | B(9) | B(10) |

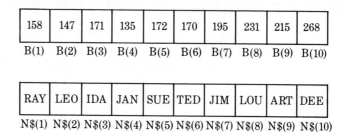

| RAY | LEO | IDA | JAN | SUE | TED | JIM | LOU | ART | DEE |
|-----|-----|-----|-----|-----|-----|-----|-----|-----|-----|
| N$(1) | N$(2) | N$(3) | N$(4) | N$(5) | N$(6) | N$(7) | N$(8) | N$(9) | N$(10) |

## Dimensioning Arrays

To illustrate how to use arrays, begin with just one array, an array of numbers. First, you must tell the computer that B is an array, and how many elements B has. You do this with a DIM statement; DIM stands for *dimension*, which means the size of the array. Suppose that the program may have to store scores for as many as ten bowlers. Before you can use the array, you must have the computer execute the following DIM statement:

```
DIM B(10)
```

This DIM statement creates ten variables. The first one is B(1), the second one is B(2), and so on up to B(10). The DIM statement also gives the value zero to each of the ten variables in the array. (Most BASIC computers would also create a variable B(0). The TS1000 and ZX81 do not.)

You can have both a single variable called B and an array called B if you want to, as long as you don't get them confused. The computer will keep them straight because it knows that numeric array elements must include an array index in parentheses.

## Putting Data into Arrays

You can use a FOR-NEXT loop to enter the bowlers' scores into an array, and another FOR-NEXT loop to print them. The program to do all of this follows:

```
 1 DIM B(10)
 5 FOR I=1 TO 10
10 INPUT B(I)
12 NEXT I
50 FOR K=1 TO 10
60 PRINT B(K)
70 NEXT K
```

Notice that variables (or even more complicated numeric expressions) can be used as the array index. This makes it easy to use arrays with FOR-NEXT loops.

Enter the following ten numbers to use as input to this program. Then RUN the above program and type in these numbers, following each by ENTER:

```
158
147
171
135
172
170
195
231
215
268
```

After you enter the tenth number, the program simply prints out the list of numbers in the same order in which you entered them.

This program isn't particularly exciting, but it provides a good example of how arrays work. Once the numbers are stored in an array, you can do many other things with them besides just printing them. For example, you could arrange the bowling scores in numerical order and print them out that way, from the lowest to the highest. Arranging data items in order is called *sorting*.

## Sorting Array Elements

If you haven't done so already, enter the entire bowling score program (lines 1-70), run it, and enter the sample data. You can now use the data in array B to illustrate a sorting program. Besides being useful in its own right, the sorting program will show you more about how to use arrays.

This program will work in a very simple way. It will go through the array of numbers, one at a time, comparing each number in turn with the one that follows it. If the second number is smaller than the one before it, the program will switch the two numbers so that the smaller one comes first. After it does this once, the numbers will be closer to being in order than they were to begin with, although they may still not be in perfect order. If we repeat this process enough times, the numbers will eventually be sorted perfectly.

We begin with a program to go through the array just one time, switching adjacent pairs of numbers that are out of order. It is like the previous program, but with lines 20 through 45 added:

```
 1 DIM B(10)
 5 FOR I=1 TO 10
10 INPUT B(I)
12 NEXT I
20 FOR J=1 TO 9
25 IF B(J)<=B(J+1) THEN GOTO 45
30 LET TEMP=B(J)
35 LET B(J)=B(J+1)
40 LET B(J+1)=TEMP
45 NEXT J
50 FOR K=1 TO 10
60 PRINT B(K)
70 NEXT K
```

Notice how lines 30 through 40 use a temporary variable to contain the old value of B(J). Otherwise, there would be no way to get it back after line 35. Statement 25 skips the switching statements if the pair of numbers is already in the correct order.

If you have already entered the ten numbers into B, use GOTO 20 instead of RUN to start the program. If not, use RUN and enter the numbers as given above. In either case, the program will print the same numbers you originally entered, but in a different order, as shown in Table 6-4.

The program switched the first and second numbers, the third and fourth

**Table 6-4. Results of a Simple Array Program**

| Original Order | New Order |
|:---:|:---:|
| 158 | 147 |
| 147 | 158 |
| 171 | 135 |
| 135 | 171 |
| 172 | 170 |
| 170 | 172 |
| 195 | 195 |
| 231 | 215 |
| 215 | 231 |
| 268 | 268 |

numbers, and several other adjacent pairs. The new list is closer to being in order than the original one was, but it isn't perfect yet.

The numbers are still stored in the array B, but in the new order. Enter GOTO **20** again, and the program will switch some pairs again to produce a still better order. Finally, enter GOTO **20** one more time and you will see a perfectly ordered list, from the smallest to the largest.

To make the sorting completely automatic, you can put it inside another loop that does what you did when you ran the program several times. This extra loop will keep repeating the sorting procedure until the entire list is in order:

```
 1 DIM B(10)
 5 FOR I=1 TO 10
10 INPUT B(I)
12 NEXT I
15 LET SWITCH=0
20 FOR J=1 TO 9
25 IF B(J)<=B(J+1) THEN GOTO 4
   5
27 LET SWITCH=SWITCH+1
30 LET TEMP=B(J)
35 LET B(J)=B(J+1)
40 LET B(J+1)=TEMP
45 NEXT J
47 IF SWITCH<>0 THEN GOTO 15
50 FOR K=1 TO 10
60 PRINT B(K)
70 NEXT K
```

Statement 47 keeps branching back to statement 15 until the numbers are all ordered. Of course, the program has to have some way of knowing whether the ordering is finished at the end of each loop. To do this, the program uses a variable called SWITCH. At the beginning of each pass through the list of numbers, statement 15 gives SWITCH the value zero. If the list is not perfectly ordered, line 27 will get executed at least once. At the end of the pass, at statement 47, SWITCH will no longer be zero, and the computer will branch back for another pass. When the ordering is complete, statement 27 will not be executed any more. SWITCH will still be zero when line 47 is executed, and the computer will quit branching and print the results.

To use this program, enter RUN and re-enter the list of numbers in the original order, or any ten numbers you want to try. The computer will print them in order.

## Multi-Dimensional Arrays

Array B in the sorting program has only one index, so it is called a *one-dimensional* array. The TS1000 and ZX81 can handle arrays of any number of dimensions, provided enough memory is available. A one-dimensional array is a table with just one row of numbers. The bowling scores just discussed are an example:

| 158 | 147 | 171 | 135 | 172 | 170 | 195 | 231 | 215 | 268 |
|------|------|------|------|------|------|------|------|------|------|
| B(1) | B(2) | B(3) | B(4) | B(5) | B(6) | B(7) | B(8) | B(9) | B(10) |

The index identifies a number within the single row. An array with two dimensions is like an ordinary table of numbers with rows and columns: one index identifies the row and the other index identifies the column.

Let's extend the bowling tournament example to two dimensions. Suppose there are four teams, each with ten bowlers. The tournament could be represented by one two-dimensional array, like this:

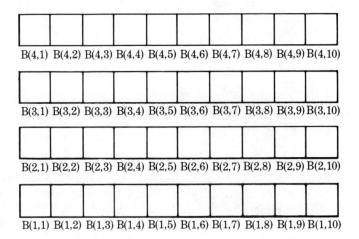

| | | | | | | | | | |
|---|---|---|---|---|---|---|---|---|---|
| B(4,1) | B(4,2) | B(4,3) | B(4,4) | B(4,5) | B(4,6) | B(4,7) | B(4,8) | B(4,9) | B(4,10) |

| | | | | | | | | | |
|---|---|---|---|---|---|---|---|---|---|
| B(3,1) | B(3,2) | B(3,3) | B(3,4) | B(3,5) | B(3,6) | B(3,7) | B(3,8) | B(3,9) | B(3,10) |

| | | | | | | | | | |
|---|---|---|---|---|---|---|---|---|---|
| B(2,1) | B(2,2) | B(2,3) | B(2,4) | B(2,5) | B(2,6) | B(2,7) | B(2,8) | B(2,9) | B(2,10) |

| | | | | | | | | | |
|---|---|---|---|---|---|---|---|---|---|
| B(1,1) | B(1,2) | B(1,3) | B(1,4) | B(1,5) | B(1,6) | B(1,7) | B(1,8) | B(1,9) | B(1,10) |

The first index of the two-dimensional array is the team number and the second is the bowler number on that team. So B(3,2) would be the score of bowler 2 on team 3. To create such an array, you would use a DIM statement like this:

```
DIM B(4,10)
```

## String Arrays

The TS1000 and ZX81 can also work with arrays of strings. In fact, a string is already very much like an array of characters, except that it does not require a dimension statement. Recall that a statement like

```
PRINT A$(2)
```

is a short form of a more complete expression that uses string slicing:

```
PRINT A$(2 TO 2)
```

These two statements do exactly the same thing. Each of them prints the second character in the string A$. A one-character slice out of a string is just like an element of an array. Of course, you can also take slices of more than one character from strings, using a statement like the following:

```
PRINT A$(2 TO 5)
```

There are no corresponding operations for numeric arrays, however. The following statement will give only a syntax error:

```
PRINT B(2 TO 5)
```

What we have here are really two notations for different situations. One is the slicing notation for parts of strings, and one is the array element notation for members of arrays. In just one case, the one-character slice, these two notations are identical.

Although you don't have to dimension an ordinary string, you still must remember that it has a finite length. The length is determined when you define the string with a LET or INPUT statement. You will get a syntax error if you try to use a string element that doesn't exist, like this:

```
LET D$="ABC"
PRINT D$(4)
```

The effect is the same as if you had tried to reference a nonexistent element of a numeric array:

```
DIM F(3)
PRINT F(4)
```

You can also have string arrays of more than one dimension. In fact, string arrays can have as many dimensions as you want, just as numeric arrays can, as long as your system has enough memory to contain them. To define a two-dimensional string array, for example, you would use a statement like the following:

```
DIM H$(4,7)
```

This DIM statement creates an array of four strings, each of which is seven characters long. The last dimension of a string array always tells how many characters each individual string contains. This means that all of the strings in a string array must be the same length, although some of the characters may be blank spaces.

You don't specify the last index, the length of the string, when you use an element of a string array. The computer will treat such an expression just like an ordinary string. For example, if you enter the following commands, the PRINT statement will print the five-character string APRIL:

```
DIM G$(3,5)
LET G$(2)="APRIL"
PRINT G$(2)
```

You can refer to individual characters in a string if you wish, by specifying the last index. After you enter the above statements, for example, the following command will print the letter R:

```
PRINT G$(2,3)
```

You can even use any of the forms of the slicing operations that you learned earlier, but only for the *last* index of the array. Either of the following two commands will print the substring PRI from the APRIL array just defined:

```
PRINT G$(2,2 TO 4)
```

or

```
PRINT G$(2)(2 TO 4)
```

The next commands, which change the letters assigned to four characters, or elements in the array, will print CHILL:

```
LET G$(2,1 TO 4)="CHIL"
PRINT G$(2)
```

Just remember that you can only apply slicing to the last index of a string array, and that it works the same way there as it does for a single string.

String arrays can be used to write a program that arranges a list of strings in alphabetical order. The strings themselves might be the names of bowlers in a bowling tournament, names of cities, or any other kind of string. The following statements set up an array of ten strings, each a maximum of 12 characters long, and let you enter the ten strings from the keyboard:

```
1 DIM X$(10,12)
5 FOR I=1 TO 10
10 INPUT X$(I)
12 NEXT I
```

Recall that the symbols < and > for strings refer to alphabetical order. One string is "smaller" or "less" than another if it comes before it in alphabetical order. This means we can use the same technique for alphabetizing strings that we used for sorting numbers. All we have to do is modify our earlier sorting program to use string arrays instead of numeric arrays:

```
1 DIM X$(10,12)
5 FOR I=1 TO 10
10 INPUT X$(I)
12 NEXT I
15 LET SWITCH=0
20 FOR J=1 TO 9
25 IF X$(J)<=X$(J+1) THEN GOTO
45
27 LET SWITCH=SWITCH+1
30 LET T$=X$(J)
35 LET X$(J)=X$(J+1)
40 LET X$(J+1)=T$
45 NEXT J
47 IF SWITCH<>0 THEN GOTO 15
50 FOR K=1 TO 10
60 PRINT X$(K)
70 NEXT K
```

Enter the program, including lines 1-12. Then run it and enter any ten strings you like, as long as each of them is no longer than 12 characters. The program will print your 12 strings, rearranged in alphabetical order.

Consider how hard it would be to do the same thing without arrays. You would need a different variable name for each string, and you would not be able to use loops. Even if you could write a program to alphabetize ten strings without using arrays, it would be much longer because it would have to deal with each pair of strings separately, by name. Worst of all, it would only work for exactly ten strings. The above program will work for any number of strings if you just change the 10 in lines 1, 5, and 50, and the 9 in line 20.

Can you see how to write a more general program that would first accept the number of strings from the keyboard, and then accept that same number of strings and print them out in alphabetical order?

# SUBROUTINES

As the computer programs you write get longer, you will frequently find that you need to tell the computer to do the same thing at several different places in a program. For example, you might want to display different blinking messages at different times. You might want to test several different keyboard entries to make sure that each is a valid number. Or you might want to calculate compound interest for several different interest rates.

One way to have the computer do the same task more than once in a program is to put the commands you want repeated inside a loop. However, in many situations that isn't good enough. You might want to display a blinking message or test an input at several different places that won't fit together in a single loop.

Another solution is simply to duplicate the same code in different parts of the program:

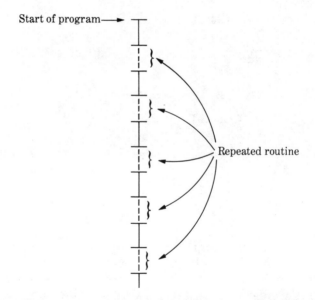

For example, if you wanted to display two different flashing messages, you could do it like this:

```
10 SLOW
15 REM DISPLAY FIRST LINE
20 LET A$="COMPUTER"
30 PRINT AT 0,5;A$
40 FOR K=1 TO LEN A$
50 LET A$(K)=CHR$ (CODE A$(K) +
128)
60 PRINT AT 0,5;A$
```

```
   70 LET A$(K)=CHR$ (CODE A$(K)-
128)
   80 NEXT K
   85 REM DISLAY SECOND LINE
   90 LET A$="PROGRAMMING"
  100 PRINT AT 0,5;A$
  110 FOR K=1 TO LEN A$
  120 LET A$(K)=CHR$ (CODE A$(K)+
128)
  130 PRINT AT 0,5;A$
  140 LET A$(K)=CHR$ (CODE A$(K)-
128)
  150 NEXT K
```

Lines 30 through 80 are identical to lines 100 through 150. Although this approach works, it wastes valuable space in the computer. The more times you repeat the routine, the more wasteful it becomes. A well-written, useful computer routine is a valuable thing, and you ought to be able to use it whenever you want to, without all that trouble.

A third way you might try to solve this problem is by putting in the repeated routine just once and inserting a GOTO statement each time you want to use it:

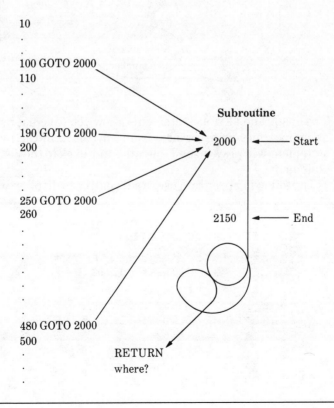

The problem with this method is that when you finish the routine, you need to go back to the next line after the GOTO that you used to get to the routine. Since there are several GOTOs in the program, you need a command that acts like GOTO, but that also remembers where you were in the program when you executed it and goes back there when the repeated routine is finished.

The BASIC language provides exactly this capability. The statement that acts like GOTO, but remembers where it came from, is called GOSUB. The section of the program that you access in this way, from different parts of a program, is a *subroutine*. We say that the program *calls* the subroutine. This just means that the program uses GOSUB to branch to the subroutine. At the end of the subroutine is a RETURN statement, which tells the computer to go back to the next statement after the GOSUB command that called the subroutine:

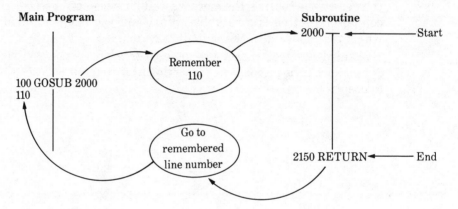

The GOSUB and RETURN statements allow you to re-use a part of your program as many times as necessary, from any place in the program. The RETURN statement will always send the computer back to the next line after the GOSUB statement.

The following program uses a subroutine to display two flashing messages:

```
10 SLOW
15 REM DISPLAY FIRST LINE
20 LET A$="COMPUTER"
30 GOSUB 100
40 REM DISPLAY SECOND LINE
50 LET A$="PROGRAMMING"
60 GOSUB 100
70 STOP
80 REM
90 REM THE SUBROUTINE STARTS H
ERE
100 PRINT AT 0,5;A$
110 FOR K=1 TO LEN A$
120 LET A$(K)=CHR$ (CODE A$(K)+
128)
```

```
130 PRINT AT 0,5;A$
140 LET A$(K)=CHR$ (CODE A$(K)-
128)
150 NEXT K
160 RETURN
```

When you run this program, the reverse video moves through the word COMPUTER once. Then the word PROGRAMMING takes its place and the reverse video moves through this word once. Then the program stops.

The STOP command in line 70 is there to prevent the computer from running the subroutine a third time. Take it out and run the program again, and the word PROGRAMMING will flash across the screen twice. This happens because A$ is still equal to PROGRAMMING when the computer gets to line 100 for the third time. There is nothing special at the beginning of the subroutine to tell the computer, "A subroutine starts here."

If you make the mistake of letting the computer go into a subroutine directly, instead of with a GOSUB statement, the computer doesn't know that you meant for that part of the program to be a subroutine. Then when it reaches the RETURN statement, it doesn't know where to go. This is why the program without line 70 gives error code 7, "No corresponding GOSUB for a RETURN statement." Make sure any subroutine you write can only be entered by using GOSUB. Sometimes you might be able to make a program a little shorter by letting the computer go into a subroutine directly from the previous line or by jumping into the middle of a subroutine with GOTO, but such tricks make your program messy and difficult to follow. You will make fewer mistakes if you treat each subroutine as a separate program unit and access it only with GOSUB.

The main part of the program (lines 10 through 70) passes information to the subroutine by means of the variable A$. The subroutine can use any of the variables the main program uses. Thus, a subroutine may do something slightly different each time it is called, because the values of the variables it shares with the main program may have changed. In the above program, A$ is the only shared variable. If you wanted to have each word appear on a different line, for example, you could do it by making the line number in the PRINT AT command a shared variable also, like this:

```
10 SLOW
15 REM DISPLAY FIRST LINE
20 LET A$="COMPUTER"
25 LET LINE=0
30 GOSUB 100
40 REM DISPLAY SECOND LINE
50 LET A$="PROGRAMMING"
55 LET LINE=2
60 GOSUB 100
70 STOP
80 REM
90 REM THE SUBROUTINE STARTS H
ERE
```

```
100 PRINT AT LINE 5;A$
110 FOR K=1 TO LEN A$
120 LET A$(K)=CHR$ (CODE A$(K)+
128)
130 PRINT AT LINE 5;A$
140 LET A$(K)=CHR$ (CODE A$(K)-
128)
150 NEXT K
160 RETURN
```

Be careful, though, not to use the same variable name in the subroutine and the main program unintentionally. Your program may do strange things if the subroutine changes the value of a variable when the main program does not "expect" that particular variable to change.

It's perfectly all right for one subroutine to call another subroutine, for that subroutine to call still another, and so on. That's called *nesting* of subroutines. The computer still remembers where each one was called and goes back to the right place each time it executes RETURN. However, you should not try to have a subroutine call itself or call a subroutine that called it. Although careful, experienced programmers may sometimes do this in BASIC, the language is not really designed for it.

# Advanced Programming in BASIC

# Chapter Seven

Now that you have learned the fundamental commands and functions of TS1000/ZX81 BASIC, you are ready to explore some special topics that go beyond fundamentals. Since these are advanced functions, you will probably find some of them more useful than others, depending on the kinds of programs you write.

## OPTIMIZING PROGRAMS

Ideally, a good computer program should (a) occupy as little space in the computer as possible, (b) execute quickly, and (c) be easy for other programmers to read and understand. Unfortunately, in practice, an improvement in one of these qualities often detracts from the others. As a programmer, you must find a suitable compromise among these three goals. Their relative importance may be different for different programs. For example, a game program using animated graphics must run fast enough to be fun for the players. On the other hand, if the program you are writing becomes too large to fit in the available memory, your top priority may be to redesign the program to use less space.

### Optimizing Clarity

Make your program as clear and understandable as space and running time permit. The following suggestions will help you:

- Use remarks (REM statements) liberally (but don't clutter your programs with unnecessary ones). Remarks should explain how the program works, not merely restate a program line in words. For example,

```
REM DONT TRANSPOSE IF PAIR ALREA
DY IN ORDER

IF B(J)<=B(J+1) THEN GOTO 45
```

is much better than

```
REM GO TO 45 IF B(J) IS SMALLER
```

The second example does not tell you how the command fits into the design of the program. Remarks are especially important at the beginnings of subroutines, explaining their purposes and listing all of the variables they share with other routines.

- Choose variable names that describe the variable's function in the program. Names like LOCATION or LOC are likely to be more helpful than names like X and B3. (Unfortunately, the names of arrays and strings cannot be more than one letter.)

- Use subroutines to organize your programs. Divide long or difficult tasks into simple, manageable parts, using a separate subroutine to do each part. Test each subroutine separately, and then incorporate the subroutines into the larger program. It is faster to write a short testing program for each subroutine than it is to test a larger program, because if the larger program fails to do what it should, it will be much harder to determine which part of the program contains the error.

- Use GOTO sparingly. Too many GOTOs branching in different directions can really complicate your programs.

- Except for loops, avoid jumping backward in your programs.

## Optimizing Speed

Techniques for making your programs run faster can conflict with the principles for writing readable programs. Therefore, use techniques like those that follow only when speed is important:

- Never jump to a REM statement with GOTO or GOSUB; jump to the next statement instead. Place REM statements before or after loops, rather than inside them. If you need still more speed, delete all REM statements —each one takes time to execute. Keep a copy of the old program with the remarks in it for reference, however.

- Put subroutines near the beginning of your program, not at the end. The computer will find them more quickly there because it starts looking for them at the beginning of the program each time it executes a GOSUB command. Use a single GOTO statement at the beginning of your program to jump over the subroutines and begin the main program.

- Avoid unnecessary subroutines. If the program calls a subroutine from only one place, replace the GOSUB command with its subroutine.

- Perform as many calculations as possible before the beginnings of animation or other time-critical parts of the program. If a program calculates the same number several times, modify it to calculate the number only once and store it in a variable. If a loop contains a calculation that gives the same result each time, put the calculation before the beginning of the loop so that the computer will only have to do it once.

- Whenever possible, replace several short strings in a PRINT statement with a single long string. Don't use a loop, for example, to print a string of repeated characters, like this:

```
FOR I=1 TO 20
PRINT "▄";
NEXT I
```

Use a single quoted string instead, like this:

```
PRINT "▄▄▄▄▄▄▄▄▄▄▄▄▄▄▄▄▄▄▄▄"
```

- Insert the following command after each SCROLL command:[5]

```
PRINT AT 21,31;AT 21,0;
```

This will make a big difference if the next PRINT statement is long or the program has arrays with large dimensions.

## Optimizing Size

The following suggestions will shorten your programs so that they use less memory. Some of them may make your programs less readable, however, so use them only if space is important.

---

[5]Oliger, John, *Syntax Z80* (The Harvard Group, Bolton Road, Harvard, Mass. 01451: April 1982).

- Remove any REM statements. Each character in a REM statement occupies one byte of memory. Keep a copy of the old program with the remarks in it for reference.

- Eliminate repeated sections of code that are longer than two or three lines by making them into subroutines. Avoid short subroutines, however, because GOSUB and RETURN also use memory space.

- Use short variable names. Every character in a variable name uses one byte of memory each time it appears in the program. If the program has several successive loops (not nested loops), use the same name for the loop counter in all of them. Re-use other variable names whenever you can.

- If the program uses the same constant more than once, use LET or INPUT to create a variable with that value and use it instead of the constant. Do this for both numeric and string constants. The reason for this is that in addition to the characters that you see on the display, each constant occupies five more undisplayed bytes every time it is used.

- Shorten the prompts and other string constants. One way to do this is to use keywords (such as PRINT and STOP) in quoted strings, instead of typing out the words. The keywords will be printed just as if you typed them letter-by-letter. Each typed character uses one byte.

- Clear the display screen often with CLS.

- Avoid unnecessary parentheses in expressions. Take advantage of the priorities of numeric, string, and logical operators. For example, the expression

```
LET A=-(B+C)
```

means the same as the shorter expression

```
LET A=-B-C
```

- If a program has many LET statements, enter them in command mode instead. The variables will keep their values when you SAVE and LOAD the program from a cassette, and you will save the memory that the LET statements occupied. (If you use this method, you must use GOTO instead of RUN when you start the program, to avoid erasing the variables.)

## STORING DATA ON CASSETTES

Unlike many personal computers, the TS1000 and ZX81 do not provide a method of storing data files on cassette tapes. The only practical way to store data is to put it into variables and save the program with the variables. If you know in advance what the data should be, you can enter it as an array, using an INPUT loop, the first time you run the program. After that, the data will remain in the program when you save and load the program from cassette. But you must remember not to execute CLEAR or RUN, because these commands erase all the program's variables.

The following program illustrates cassette data storage. It reads ten numbers from the keyboard into array B and prints them on the television screen display.

```
 1 DIM B(10)
 5 FOR I=1 TO 10
10 INPUT B(I)
12 NEXT I
50 FOR K=1 TO 10
60 PRINT B(K)
70 NEXT K
```

RUN the program and enter any ten numbers. Then delete lines 1-12. Use SAVE to record the program on cassette, and read it back with LOAD. Use GOTO 50 to start the program. Array B will still be there with the numbers you entered.

Remember, though, that if you want to keep the numbers stored in B, you must always use GOTO 50 instead of RUN to start the program. In addition, you should write down the variable names and their dimensions in case you want to modify the program later.

## BAR AND LINE GRAPHS

A graph can display data in a clear, direct way that is easier to comprehend than a table or a list of numbers. A program that draws a graph must first *scale* the data. That is, it must determine how each data item will relate to the overall size of the graph on the television screen. For example, for a bar graph that will be 30 dots (pixels) wide, the program must multiply the numbers to be represented by a *scaling factor* that gives 30 for the largest number in the list.

The following subroutine finds the largest member of an array of numbers, scales it to 30 pixels, and draws a bar graph of the numbers in the array:

```
1000 REM B IS THE ARRAY OF NUMBE
RS
1010 REM N TELLS HOW MANY NUMBER
S THERE ARE
1015 REM FIRST SCALE THE NUMBERS
1020 LET MAX=B(1)
1030 FOR I=2 TO N
```

```
1040 IF B(I)>MAX THEN LET MAX=B(
I)
1050 NEXT I
1060 LET SCALE=30/MAX
1070 REM PLOT THE NUMBERS
1080 FOR I=1 TO N
1090 FOR J=1 TO B(I)*SCALE
1100 PLOT J,42-4*I
1110 NEXT J
1120 NEXT I
1130 RETURN
```

To use this subroutine, you will also need to write a master program that reads in the numbers and calls the subroutine as follows:

```
10 INPUT N
20 DIM B(N)
30 FOR I=1 TO N
40 INPUT B(I)
50 NEXT I
60 GOSUB 1000
70 STOP
```

Enter the program and subroutine. To see how they work, enter 5 for N and 5, 10, 15, 20, 10 for the elements of B. The program will then produce the following bar graph on the display:

You can improve the bar graph routine by adding a title, labels along the left side, and a scale across the bottom. Your master program should print the title, since you may use the same subroutine for many different graphs. For the labels, you can add an array of N strings, each five characters long. The master program will define these strings, and the subroutine will print them beside the corresponding bars. The subroutine will also print the scale. (If your system is the ZX81 without memory expansion, delete the REM statements to save memory space before making these changes.) The complete program is as follows:

```
 5 PRINT "MILLIONS OF SALES PE
R YEAR"
10 INPUT N
20 DIM B(N)
25 DIM L$(N,5)
30 FOR I=1 TO N
```

```
  35  INPUT L$(I)
  40  INPUT B(I)
  50  NEXT I
  60  GOSUB 1000
  70  STOP
1000  REM B IS THE ARRAY OF NUMBE
RS
1010  REM N TELLS HOW MANY NUMBER
S THERE ARE
1015  REM FIRST SCALE THE NUMBERS
1020  LET MAX=B(1)
1030  FOR I=2 TO N
1040  IF B(I)>MAX THEN LET MAX=B(
I)
1050  NEXT I
1060  LET SCALE=30/MAX
1070  REM PLOT THE NUMBERS
1080  FOR I=1 TO N
1085  PRINT AT 2*I,0;L$(I)
1090  FOR J=1 TO B(I)*SCALE
1100  PLOT J+8,42-4*I
1110  NEXT J
1120  NEXT I
1130  PRINT AT 2*N+2,4;
1140  FOR I=1 TO 6
1150  PRINT ". ";
1155  NEXT I
1160  PRINT AT 2*N+3,4;"0";AT 2*N
+3,19;MAX
1170  RETURN
```

Run this program using 5 for N again and enter the following array values:

| I | L$(I) | B(I) |
|---|-------|------|
| 1 | 1978  | 5    |
| 2 | 1979  | 10   |
| 3 | 1980  | 15   |
| 4 | 1981  | 20   |
| 5 | 1982  | 10   |

The resulting display is

```
MILLIONS OF SALES PER YEAR
1978 ▬▬
1979 ▬▬▬▬
1980 ▬▬▬▬▬▬
1981 ▬▬▬▬▬▬▬▬
1982 ▬▬▬▬
     .  .  .  .  .  .
     0              20
```

Bar graphs like the ones above are ideal for comparing a fairly small set of numbers. Line graphs, on the other hand, are usually better for displaying mathematical functions, or information whose general shape and trend is more important than the detailed values of the points. A line graph is like a bar graph, but only the last pixel of the bar is plotted. In addition, while bar graphs may be either horizontal or vertical, a line graph always has the function plotted vertically.

The following program draws a graph of the SIN function between zero and $2*PI$. The subroutine that it calls will plot any set of points whose coordinates are given by the arrays X and Y. (For the ZX81 without the memory expansion unit, change the value of N from 63 to 9.)

```
   5 LET N=63
  10 DIM X(N)
  20 DIM Y(N)
  30 FOR I=1 TO N
  40 LET X(I)=PI*(I-1)*2/(N-1)
  50 LET Y(I)=SIN X(I)
  60 NEXT I
  70 GOSUB 1000
  80 STOP
1000 LET MINX=X(1)
1010 LET MAXX=X(1)
1020 LET MINY=Y(1)
1030 LET MAXY=Y(1)
1040 FOR I=2 TO N
1050 IF X(I)<MINX THEN LET MINX=
X(I)
1060 IF X(I)>MAXX THEN LET MAXX=
X(I)
1070 IF Y(I)<MINY THEN LET MINY=
Y(I)
1080 IF Y(I)>MAXY THEN LET MAXY=
Y(I)
1090 NEXT I
1100 LET XB=63/(MAXX-MINX)
1110 LET YB=43/(MAXY-MINY)
1120 FOR I=1 TO N
1130 PLOT (X(I)-MINX)*XB,(Y(I)-M
INY)*YB
1140 NEXT I
1150 RETURN
```

## MORE ABOUT LOGICAL EXPRESSIONS

Chapter 6 described the logical operators AND, OR, and NOT and explained how to use them with such comparisons as =, <, and >. These operations are related to each other in regular ways, and you can often simplify your programs and make them clearer by understanding these relationships. In addition, the TS1000 and ZX81 represent the results of such comparisons as ordinary numbers, which you can use to construct more powerful commands for controlling the flow of your programs.

### Opposite and Equivalent Expressions

Each of the six relational operators that your computer recognizes has one of the others as its opposite. Table 7-1 gives the opposite of each one. To put it another way, for each kind of test there is another test using the NOT operator that means exactly the same thing. This is shown in Table 7-2. These relationships are really nothing more than common sense. For example, if A is smaller than B or equal to B, then obviously A cannot be larger than B.

The logical operators AND and OR also combine in special ways with NOT. Consider the following expressions:

```
IF NOT (A=B OR C=D)

IF NOT (A=B AND C=D)
```

As Table 7-3 shows, each such expression has an equivalent form without parentheses.

**Table 7-1. Opposite Pairs of Relational Operators**

| Operator | Meaning | Opposite Operator |
|----------|---------|-------------------|
| = | Equal | <> |
| < | Less than | >= |
| > | Greater than | <= |
| <= | Less than or equal | > |
| >= | Greater than or equal | < |
| <> | Not equal | = |

**Table 7-2. Equivalent Tests Using NOT**

| | |
|-----------|-----------------|
| IF A=B | IF NOT A<>B |
| IF A<B | IF NOT A>=B |
| IF A>B | IF NOT A<=B |
| IF A<=B | IF NOT A>B |
| IF A>=B | IF NOT A<B |
| IF A<>B | IF NOT A=B |

**Table 7-3. Equivalent Expressions**

| Expression | Equivalent Expression |
|------------|----------------------|
| IF NOT (A=B OR C=D) | IF NOT A=B AND NOT C=D |
| IF NOT (A=B AND C=D) | IF NOT A=B OR NOT C=D |

These expressions are examples of a general rule: If NOT comes before an expression in parentheses that uses OR or AND, you can remove the parentheses if you change the operator inside the parentheses and repeat NOT for each part of the expression.

## Logical Operations on Numbers

Chapters 4 and 6 described the three different kinds of expressions in the BASIC language (see Table 7-4 for a summary).

When the computer evaluates an expression of any kind, it stores the result as a number. For strings, it uses a character code (Appendix C) to represent each symbol on the keyboard. The computer also uses numbers to store the result of logical expressions.

You can use conditional tests without knowing how the computer translates the tests into numbers, just as you can use strings without knowing the character code. However, by learning about the numeric representations, you will be able to use them to write even better programs.

**Table 7-4. Types of Expressions**

| Type | Example |
|------|---------|
| Numeric Expressions | A+B |
| String Expression | A$+B$ |
| Logical Expression | A<B OR C=D |

## "TRUE OR FALSE" TESTS

To demonstrate how the computer stores the results of comparisons, enter the following commands:

| Command | What the Computer Prints |
|---------|--------------------------|
| PRINT 1<2 | 1 |
| PRINT 2<1 | 0 |
| PRINT 7=7 | 1 |
| PRINT 7=10 | 0 |

If the condition is true, the computer uses one to represent the result of the test. If the condition is false, the computer uses zero. Thus, a command like

```
LET ANSWER=10<>15
```

may look strange to us, but the computer understands it perfectly. Since the expression 10<>15 is true, the computer gives the variable ANSWER a value of one.

The logical operators AND, OR, and NOT ordinarily apply to expressions like 10<>15. Recall that an expression using AND is true if both conditions are true. For example, the expression (10<>15 AND 5=5) is true. The expression (10<>15 AND 5=6), however, is false because five is not equal to six. As you can see, the computer represents the results of these longer expressions by numbers as well:

| Command | What the Computer Prints |
|---------|--------------------------|
| PRINT (10<>15 AND 5=5) | 1 |
| PRINT (10<>15 AND 5=6) | 0 |

**Table 7-5. AND Operation Truth Table**

The AND operation gives 1 (true) only if both values are 1.

| | |
|---|---|
| 1 AND 1 gives 1 | 1 AND 0 gives 0 |
| 0 AND 1 gives 0 | 0 AND 0 gives 0 |

**Table 7-6. OR Operation Truth Table**

The OR operation gives 1 (true) only if either value is 1.

| | |
|---|---|
| 1 OR 1 gives 1 | 1 OR 0 gives 1 |
| 0 OR 1 gives 1 | 0 OR 0 gives 0 |

**Table 7-7. NOT Operation Truth Table**

The NOT operation gives the opposite of each value.

NOT 1 gives 0
NOT 0 gives 1

Just as before, the computer uses one to represent a true expression and zero to represent a false expression. Table 7-5 shows what happens with the AND operator for all four possible combinations of true and false expressions.

Table 7-5 is called a *truth table*. It tells everything there is to know about the AND operator. Table 7-6 is the truth table for the OR operator.

The last operator is NOT. Its truth table is the simplest because it operates on only one expression (Table 7-7).

Enter the following commands and verify that they give the answers specified by the truth tables:

```
PRINT 1 AND 1
PRINT (5=5 AND 6<=7)
PRINT 0 AND 1
PRINT (10>20 AND 9=9)
PRINT 0 OR 1
PRINT (3=1000 OR 3<4)
PRINT 0 OR 1
PRINT (10<=-1 OR 10>=-2)
PRINT NOT 1
PRINT NOT 0
PRINT NOT 5=5
```

Since one and zero represent true and false, you might expect a syntax error when you use some other number with AND, OR, or NOT. Instead, the computer accepts any numbers with these operators. It does this by treating any number other than zero as true. The following examples show how it evaluates such expressions:

| Command | What the Computer Prints |
|---|---|
| PRINT 10 AND 50 | 10 |
| PRINT 0 AND 50 | 0 |
| PRINT 10 AND 0 | 0 |
| PRINT 0 AND 0 | 0 |

If either of the numbers is zero (false), the overall expression will be false. (That's what AND means.) If neither is zero, the expression is true. Note that when the result is true, the left number of the pair is used to represent that truth.

You can use any number or numeric expression with the OR operator, as well. The following example illustrates how OR works:

| Command | What the Computer Prints |
|---|---|
| PRINT 10 OR 50 | 1 |
| PRINT 0 OR 50 | 1 |
| PRINT 10 OR 0 | 10 |
| PRINT 0 OR 0 | 0 |

The first three results count as "true," and the last one as "false." If the number on the right of OR is not zero, the value of the overall expression is one. If the number on the right is zero, then the value of the overall expression is equal to the number on the left.

The NOT operator simply gives one (true) if its argument is zero (false) and zero (false) if its argument is one (true):

| Command | What the Computer Prints |
|---|---|
| PRINT NOT 0 | 1 |
| PRINT NOT 1 | 0 |
| PRINT NOT 17 | 0 |

## BRANCHING

The following expression will be equal to A, B, or C depending on whether I is equal to 1, 2, or 3:

```
(A AND I=1)+(B AND I=2)+(C AND I
=3)
```

(The expression will be equal to zero if I has a value different from any of these.)

Many programs display a *menu* of options and ask the user to select one of them by entering a special code (such as the first letter of the name of the desired option). Such a program needs to branch to a different line or call a different subroutine, depending on the option selected. The following program shows how to use AND to implement a menu selection:

```
  10 PRINT "SELECT ONE OF THE FO
LLOWING:"
  20 PRINT "      N - START A NEW
GAME"
  30 PRINT "      R - RESUME THE P
REVIOUS GAME"
  40 PRINT "      T - PRINT THE TO
TAL SCORE TO DATE"
  50 PRINT "      F - FORGET ABOUT
 ALL PREVIOUS GAMES"
  60 INPUT A$
  70 GOTO (100 AND A$(1)="N")+(4
76 AND A$(1)="R")+(802 AND A$(1)
="T")+(1000 AND A$(1)="F")
```

This program will branch to statement 100 if you type N, to 476 if you type R, to 802 if you type T, and to 1000 if you type F. Of course, you could accomplish the same result with four conditional statements instead of line 70, as follows:

```
70 IF A$(1)="N" THEN GOTO 100
72 IF A$(1)="R" THEN GOTO 476
74 IF A$(1)="T" THEN GOTO 802
76 IF A$(1)="F" THEN GOTO 1000
```

The second method is more straightforward, but it occupies more memory and runs more slowly than the method using AND.

As a rule, AND works best with addition, and OR works best with multiplication. For example, a department store having a sale might program its computers to use a different discount rate for purchases from different departments. The following commands illustrate one way of writing such a program:

```
300 REM D$ IS THE DEPARTMENT
310 IF D$="HOUSEWARES" THEN LET
PRICE=PRICE*.80
320 IF D$="CLOTHING" THEN LET P
RICE=PRICE*.70
330 IF D$="JEWELRY" THEN LET PR
ICE=PRICE*.85
```

The following program using the special properties of the OR operator, however, will do the same thing more quickly and occupy less memory:

```
300 REM D$ IS THE DEPARTMENT
310 LET PRICE=PRICE*(.80 OR D$<
>"HOUSEWARES")*(.70 OR D$<>"CLOT
HING")*(.85 OR D$<>"JEWELRY")
```

If D$ is equal to one of the quoted strings, the <> relation will be false, and the OR expression will be equal to the corresponding discount rate. Whenever D$ is not equal to the quoted string, the true <> relation will produce a value of one, leaving the price unchanged.

## Logical Operations on Strings

The TS1000 and ZX81 permit only one kind of logical operation on strings. The operator must be AND and the string must be on the left side. The computer evaluates such a logical expression just as it would evaluate the same logical operation on a number:

| Command | What the Computer Prints |
|---|---|
| `PRINT "TEST" AND 50` | `"TEST"` |
| `PRINT "TEST" AND 0` | `""` |

The number on the right of AND can also be any relational expression. You can use logical operations on strings to make commands like the following shorter and faster:

```
30 IF TIME<12 THEN PRINT "GOOD
MORNING"
40 IF TIME>12 THEN PRINT "GOOD
AFTERNOON"
```

An equivalent command using a logical expression is

```
30 PRINT "GOOD ";("MORNING" AN
D TIME<12)+("AFTERNOON" AND TIME
>12)
```

## Priority in Expressions of Mixed Type

Recall that each operation in BASIC has a priority. When the computer evaluates an expression, it does the highest priority operations first, then the ones of next highest priority, and so on. Parentheses override this priority system, forcing the computer to evaluate the part of the expression between the parentheses first.

Priority rules also apply to the two kinds of mixed-type expressions that the TS1000 and ZX81 permit: logical operations on numbers and logical operations on strings. Table 7-8 gives the priority of every kind of operation. Refer to it whenever you need to know which operations the computer will evaluate first. Use parentheses whenever you want the computer to follow a different order.

If an expression contains more than one operation of the same priority, the computer evaluates them from left to right.

# INSIDE BASIC

The purpose of BASIC is to make the computer easy to use. Without BASIC (or a language like it) you would have to learn many complicated details about the inner workings of the computer to make it do what you want. BASIC allows you to use familiar English words like LET, PRINT, and NOT, familiar symbols like =, +, and −, and convenient variable names to write programs easily and quickly. You don't need to know any more about how the computer works, or about how BASIC does what it does, in order to write good BASIC programs. However, if you do learn more about these subjects, you will be

Table 7-8. Priority Table

| Symbol | Operation | Priority |
|---|---|---|
| ( ) | Subscripting and slicing | 12 |
| ABS, CHR$, etc. | Functions (except NOT and unary minus) | 11 |
| ** | Exponentiation | 10 |
| − | Unary minus | 9 |
| *, / | Multiplication and division | 8 |
| +, − | Addition and subtraction | 6 |
| =, <, >, <=, >=, <> | Relational operators | 5 |
| NOT | NOT | 4 |
| AND | AND | 3 |
| OR | OR | 2 |

**SOURCE:** *Timex User Manual* by Steven Vickers, © 1982 by Timex Corporation

able to use more of the features of the TS1000 or ZX81. The remainder of this chapter describes some of the advanced features of BASIC and how to use them in your programs.

## The Organization of Memory

The fundamental unit of memory in most personal computers, including the TS1000 and ZX81, is the *byte*. A byte can contain any number between 0 and 255. A floating point number (like the numeric constants and variables of BASIC) occupies five bytes. The thousands of bytes that make up the computer's memory are numbered consecutively, beginning with byte number 0. These numbers are the *addresses* of the bytes. To find out what number is stored in a byte, or to store a different number in a byte, you must know the byte's address.

The TS1000 and ZX81 computers contain two kinds of memory: read-only memory (ROM) and read/write memory (RAM). The read-only memory is located between addresses 0 and 8191. The numbers in read-only memory are permanent. You cannot change them, and they remain the same even if you unplug and reconnect the power cord. Read-only memory contains the master program that controls the computer and carries out all the commands of BASIC. It also contains other permanent information, such as the list of character codes and the shape of each kind of character for the television display and printer.

Read/write memory begins at address 16384. (The TS1000 and ZX81 do not use the addresses between 8192 and 16383 at all.) Read/write memory contains your program, your variables and their values, and the television display image. BASIC also uses part of the read/write memory for storing variables of its own (the *system variables*), for doing calculations, and for keeping track of nested GOSUB calls, among other things. The blocks of addresses used for various functions are shown in Figure 7-1.

You can read from and write to the contents of read/write memory, but when you disconnect power, everything you stored disappears.

## PEEK and POKE

The PEEK function (on the o key) takes an address as its argument and gives the contents of that address (the number stored in that byte) as its value. For example, to determine the contents of the first ten bytes of read-only memory, run the following program:

```
10 FOR A=0 TO 9
20 PRINT PEEK A
30 NEXT A
```

Address

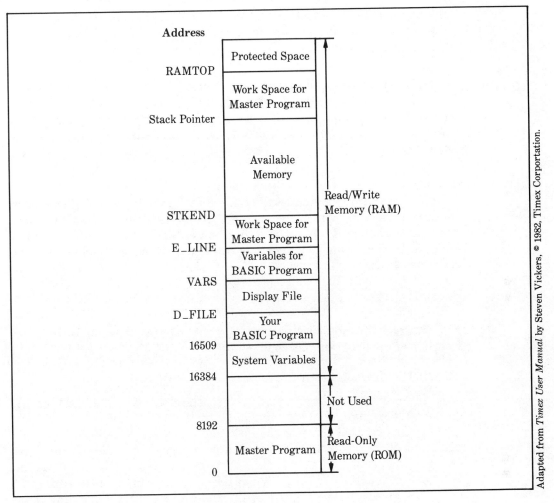

Figure 7-1. The organization of memory

The program prints the following numbers:

```
211
253
1
255
127
195
203
```

```
3

42
22
```

The TS 1000 and ZX 81 do not have any memory between locations 8192 and 16383. You can still PEEK these addresses, but the computer will subtract 8192 from any address you give it in this range. For example, the computer will print the same numbers as before if you replace line 10 above with the following:

```
10 FOR A=8192 TO 8201
```

The POKE command changes the contents of a byte in read/write memory (RAM). To use it, press POKE (on the o key), followed by the address of the byte you want to change, a comma, and the number that you want to store at that address. The following program illustrates POKE. Be sure to include the REM statement exactly as follows:

```
1 REM X
10 POKE 16514,20
```

Run the program and then press ENTER again to see the program listing. The first line of the program has changed to

```
1 REM =
```

When you enter a program, BASIC stores the characters that you type in a section of RAM memory beginning at address 16509 (Figure 7-1). Address 16514 is the byte that contains the first character after REM in line 1 of this program. By POKEing a different character code into this address, you changed the program itself. Look in Appendix C and verify that 20 is the character code of the = symbol. Change the number 20 in line 10 to a different character code, run the program again, and watch the corresponding character from Appendix C appear in the program listing.

POKE is a powerful command and should be used carefully. Although you cannot actually damage the computer by using POKE, you can change any part of your program or the system variables (locations 16384 to 16508) that BASIC uses for its own internal purposes. If you do accidentally POKE the wrong address, you can make the computer stop functioning. For example, if you enter the following command the computer will produce an unusual television display:

```
POKE 16384,49
```

The result is different for systems with different amounts of read/write memory. If your system includes the memory expansion unit, you may want to try this command both with and without the unit. (Remember to unplug power before changing the memory expansion.) Once you have entered this POKE command, you cannot continue without unplugging and reconnecting power.

You cannot POKE read-only memory (addresses 0 to 8191). The computer does not report an error if you try to POKE these locations, but the POKE command will not change the contents of the byte.

## The System Variables

Appendix B lists all of the system variables and their functions. A typical entry in Appendix B looks like this:

ERR_NR 16384    1 less than the report code

The first column gives the name of the variable. This particular variable's name is ERR_NR. These names, however, are not BASIC variable names — in fact, the underscore character (_) that appears in some of them is illegal in BASIC. These variable names thus provide a convenient way of referring to the system variables in system program listings, but the computer does not recognize them. The only way of accessing the system variables is to PEEK or POKE their addresses.

The second column in the list gives the address of the variable in read/write memory. Most of the system variables occupy either one or two bytes.

Use ERR_NR if you want your BASIC program to produce error reports at the lower left corner of the screen for special errors. For example, the following command produces an error report G/O at the lower left corner of the screen:

```
POKE 16384,15
```

If you use this command within a program (that is, if you give it a line number), it will also stop the program at that point. If you POKE a number between 0 and 14, you will produce one of the standard system error codes (1 through 9 and A through F). If you POKE a number between 15 and 34, you will produce one of the letters G through Z. If you POKE a number between 99 and 127, you will produce a graphics symbol or a reverse-video character in the first position of the error report. If you POKE any higher numbers into this address, your program will stop and you will have to pull the plug to restart.

## The Highest Memory Location

The system variable RAMTOP, at addresses 16388 and 16389, keeps track of how much read/write memory the system has. Like many of the system variables, it is larger than 255. Since 255 is the largest number a single byte can contain, RAMTOP requires two bytes. To find the value of such two-byte variables, multiply the contents of the second byte by 256 and add it to the first byte. For example, to find the value of RAMTOP, enter the following command:

```
PRINT PEEK 16388+256*PEEK 16389
```

The result depends on how much read/write memory your system has, because RAMTOP is the variable that BASIC uses to remember how much memory it has available. The TS1000 has 2048 bytes (2K) of read/write memory. Since read/write memory always begins at address 16384, the above command will print **18432** (which is 16384+2048) on a TS1000 without the memory expansion unit. For a ZX81 with 1024 bytes of read/write memory (1K), the command will print **17408**. It will print **32768** on either computer with the 16K memory expansion pack attached. The highest available memory location is actually one less than RAMTOP.

By POKEing a new value into RAMTOP, you can make BASIC act as if it had more or less read/write memory than it actually has. For example, you might want BASIC to ignore a section of read/write memory in order to reserve those addresses for a machine language subroutine (see Chapter 8) or for some other purpose. To change a two-byte variable like RAMTOP, you have to separate it into two numbers between 0 and 255. The following program shows how to change RAMTOP to 16610:

```
10 LET TOP=16610
20 POKE 16389,INT (TOP/256)
30 POKE 16388,TOP-256*PEEK 163
89
40 NEW
```

Line 20 divides TOP by 256 and discards the remainder to get the *more significant byte* of the number TOP. Line 30 calculates the part of TOP that is left over (the *less significant byte*). In two-byte system variables, the less significant byte always comes first in memory, so the program POKEs the less significant byte into memory address 16388 and the more significant byte into location 16389. Follow this procedure whenever you need to change a two-byte system variable.

The NEW command in line 40 is not part of the general procedure for other system variables. It is necessary when you change RAMTOP, in order to force BASIC to rearrange its memory organization to fit the new RAMTOP.

When you run the above program, the program disappears and the ▓ cursor appears at the bottom, just as it always does when you execute NEW.

But now BASIC thinks it has only a few bytes of RAM for storing programs and displaying information. The effect is obvious as soon as you begin to enter a new program. Enter the following line:

```
10 REM 12345
```

When you type 5, the line moves from the bottom to the top of the screen. BASIC reduces the size of the display to make room in read/write memory for the program line. Type more characters, and the display line will actually get shorter as the computer shrinks the display file to make room for the program.

Unplug and reconnect power to restore BASIC to its normal condition.

## The Program Storage Area

BASIC stores your program in read/write memory beginning at address 16509. It stores each program line as shown in Figure 7-2.

The first two bytes give the line number, and the third and fourth bytes give the number of bytes in the line. The number of bytes is stored with the less significant byte first, just like the system variables, but the line number has the more significant byte first.

A BASIC program can use PEEK to examine the program storage area, and it can use POKE to change what is there. Such a program is actually rewriting itself while it runs. Be very careful if you try to write such programs, because any errors or inconsistencies that you produce in the program storage area will probably make BASIC malfunction, and you will have to pull the plug.

The following program shows how to examine the program storage area and extract information from it. It does not change any of the bytes stored there, but it uses PEEK to determine what its own line numbers are. Then it prints a list of the line numbers on the television display.

```
    5 REM CALCULATE DFILE, WHICH
MARKS THE
    7 REM END OF THE PROGRAM STOR
AGE AREA
   10 LET DFILE=PEEK 16396+256*PE
EK 16397
   15 REM FBYTE IS THE FIRST BYTE
 OF THE LINE
   17 REM THE FIRST LINE ALWAYS S
TARTS AT 16509
   20 LET FBYTE=16509
   27 REM CALCULATE LNUM, WHICH I
S THE
   28 REM LINE NUMBER OF THIS PRO
GRAM LINE
   30 LET LNUM=PEEK (FBYTE+1) +256
*PEEK FBYTE
```

```
 40 PRINT LNUM
 45 REM CALCULATE THE FIRST ADD
RESS OF THE NEXT LINE
 50 LET FBYTE=FBYTE+PEEK (FBYTE
+2)+256*PEEK (FBYTE+3)+4
 55 REM LOOP BACK TO DO NEXT LI
NE
 56 REM UNLESS END OF PROGRAM H
AS BEEN REACHED
 60 IF FBYTE<DFILE THEN GOTO 30
```

Line 10 calculates the system variable D—FILE, which marks the end of the program listing in read/write memory (Appendix E). Line 20 initializes the variable FBYTE, the address of the first byte of the next program line. Line 30 uses FBYTE to determine the line number, which is stored with the most significant byte first (see Figure 7-2). Then line 50 uses the next two bytes to calculate the length of the line and adds this length to FBYTE. It also adds four for the four bytes at the beginning. These store the line number and length. The new value of FBYTE is the address of the first byte of the next line in the program. Line 60 compares FBYTE to D—FILE to determine whether there are any more program lines. If so, it branches back to do the next one. Run the program and observe that it prints the correct list of statement numbers.

A program that just prints out a list of line numbers is not very useful. However, now that you understand how to examine the program area, you can also write programs that change what is there. The following program asks for a first line number and an increment between line numbers, and

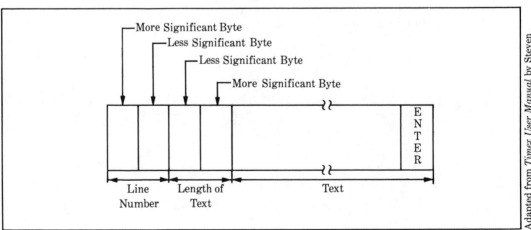

Figure 7-2. A BASIC program line in memory

then renumbers the program lines so that the line numbers are equally spaced:

```
9900 REM RENUMBER PROGRAM
9905 PRINT "FIRST LINE NUMBER?"
9910 INPUT LNUM
9920 PRINT "INCREMENT?"
9930 INPUT INC
9940 LET FBYTE=16509
9950 IF (PEEK (FBYTE+1) +256*PEEK
 FBYTE) >=9900 THEN STOP
9960 POKE FBYTE,INT (LNUM/256)
9970 POKE FBYTE+1,LNUM-256*PEEK
FBYTE
9980 LET LNUM=LNUM+INC
9990 LET FBYTE=FBYTE+PEEK (FBYTE
+2) +256*PEEK (FBYTE+3) +4
9995 GOTO 9950
```

This program will renumber all program lines below 9900. It must not try to renumber its own lines because that would confuse BASIC while the renumbering was going on. Line 9950 makes sure the number of the line it is about to change is smaller than 9900 and stops if it is not.

To demonstrate the RENUMBER program, enter it together with another program for it to renumber. You can use the compound interest program shown earlier in this book. When you have entered both programs, the complete listing should look like this:

```
   2 PRINT "HOW MANY QUARTERS?"
   5 INPUT NQUARTS
  10 LET WORTH=100
  20 LET RATE=0.10
  30 LET QRATE=RATE/4
  40 FOR I=1 TO NQUARTS
  60 LET INTEREST =QRATE*WORTH
  70 LET WORTH=WORTH+INTEREST
  75 NEXT I
  80 PRINT WORTH
  90 STOP
9900 PRINT "FIRST LINE NUMBER?"
9910 INPUT LNUM
9920 PRINT "INCREMENT?"
9930 INPUT INC
9940 LET FBYTE=16509
9950 IF (PEEK (FBYTE+1) +256*PEEK
 FBYTE) >=9900 THEN STOP
9960 POKE FBYTE,INT (LNUM/255)
9970 POKE FBYTE+1,LNUM-256*PEEK
FBYTE
9980 LET LNUM=LNUM+INC
9990 LET FBYTE=FBYTE+PEEK (FBYTE
+2) +256*PEEK (FBYTE+3) +4
9995 GOTO 9950
```

Line 90 separates the two programs and prevents the computer from going on to the second one after it finishes the first. Now enter GOTO **9900** to start the RENUMBER program. Enter **100** for the first line number and **20** for the increment. When the program has finished running, press ENTER again to see the program listing. It should look like this, with the compound interest program neatly renumbered:

```
100 PRINT "HOW MANY QUARTERS?"
120 INPUT NQUARTS
140 LET WORTH=100
160 LET RATE=0.10
180 LET QRATE=RATE/4
200 FOR I=1 TO NQUARTS
220 LET INTEREST=QRATE*WORTH
240 LET WORTH=WORTH+INTEREST
260 NEXT I
280 PRINT WORTH
300 STOP
9900 PRINT "FIRST LINE NUMBER?"
9910 INPUT LNUM
9920 PRINT "INCREMENT?"
9930 INPUT INC
9940 LET FBYTE=16509
9950 IF (PEEK (FBYTE+1)+256*PEEK
 FBYTE))=9900 THEN STOP
9960 POKE FBYTE,INT (LNUM/256)
9970 POKE FBYTE+1,LNUM-256*PEEK
FBYTE
9980 LET LNUM=LNUM+INC
9990 LET FBYTE=FBYTE+PEEK (FBYTE
+2)+256*PEEK (FBYTE+3)+4
9995 GOTO 9950
```

Use the RENUMBER program whenever a program you are writing has its line numbers too closely spaced, preventing you from inserting more lines where you want them. It will save you the trouble of editing all the program lines to change their numbers. If your program is long, the time you save in editing will be worth the extra time it takes to type in the RENUMBER program.

Be careful, though. RENUMBER does not change GOTO or GOSUB statements, so you must still use the editor to make them correspond to the new line numbers.

## The Display File

Directly above the program storage area in read/write memory is the *display file* (Figure 7-1). The system variable D—FILE contains the address of the first byte of the display file, and the system variable VARS gives the starting address of the next region of read/write memory, the *program variables area.* The display file is simply a list of all the characters on the screen, in order, one character per byte. For the end of each line on the screen, the display file includes a byte containing 118, the character code for ENTER. The computer uses the information in the display file to produce the display and to produce a copy of the screen on the printer when you execute the COPY command.

You can change the display by POKEing character codes into the display file, but you must be careful not to change one of the ENTER bytes. To work correctly, the computer requires exactly the right number of ENTER bytes in the display file.

On systems including the 16K memory expansion unit, each blank line on the screen has a full line of blanks in the display file. On systems without the memory expansion, each blank line is represented by a single ENTER byte in the file.

The following program uses PRINT AT to make sure the display file contains a full line of blanks for the top line on the screen. Then it calculates D__FILE using PEEK, and POKES the codes for the letters of the alphabet into the display file bytes for this line, over and over.

```
 1 SLOW
 5 PRINT AT 0,31;
 6 LET DFILE=PEEK 16396+256*PE
EK 16397
10 LET A=38
20 FOR I=0 TO 30
30 POKE DFILE+I+1,A
40 LET A=A+1
50 IF A>63 THEN LET A=38
55 NEXT I
60 GOTO 20
```

Run the program and watch the letters move across the line. To stop the program, press BREAK.

The system variable DF__CC contains the address (in the display file) of the print position, which is the location where the PRINT command will print the next character. You can change the print position by POKEing a new value into DF__CC, as long as the number you choose corresponds to a real character position on the screen, not an ENTER byte. BASIC programs do not ordinarily need to change DF__CC in this way or to POKE numbers into the display file, however, because they can accomplish the same thing with PRINT AT.

Machine Language

# Chapter Eight

The most fundamental language of any computer is its *machine language*. This is the language that the central processor of the computer understands and obeys. When the computer executes a program in BASIC (or any other language), it must first translate the commands into machine language.

The translating program for BASIC is part of the master program in read-only memory (ROM), and it does its job automatically. When you run a BASIC program, you don't have to think about machine language at all. However, a machine language program can use some of the features of the computer that BASIC programs cannot use, and machine language programs run much faster than BASIC programs. For this reason, BASIC includes a function called USR that calls machine language subroutines.

This book will not attempt to teach you how to write machine language programs. That topic really requires a whole book by itself. (Appendix N lists several good books on the subject.) This chapter explains how you can use the machine language routines that appear in published programs without having to learn machine language itself. It includes several machine language subroutines as examples, and Appendix G gives several more. Don't be concerned if you don't understand the details of these routines. Most personal computer users never bother to learn machine language. You can still use the machine language subroutines that other people write, just by following a few simple instructions.

# ENTERING MACHINE LANGUAGE SUBROUTINES

Machine language is very different from a *high-level* language like BASIC. Each machine language instruction is just a number stored in a byte of read/write memory. The machine language programmer uses a small portion of memory to store a machine language subroutine. A BASIC program that calls the machine language subroutine must do two things. First, it must store the machine language instructions in the correct addresses of read/write memory (usually by means of the POKE command). Second, it must execute the USR function to call the subroutine.

The argument of the USR function is the address in memory where the subroutine begins. The machine language programmer determines the value of the USR function for each machine language subroutine. In some cases, the main purpose of the machine language subroutine is to calculate a value for USR. In other cases the value of USR is irrelevant.

A machine language subroutine must occupy a part of memory where it cannot interfere with the activities of the master program. Machine language programmers usually store their routines in one of two places: in a REM statement at the very beginning of the BASIC program or in protected space above RAMTOP.

## Machine Language in a REM Statement

Like any other BASIC statement, a REM statement occupies one byte of read/write memory for each character. BASIC doesn't care what the characters in a REM statement are. It ignores them and goes on to the next line. A REM statement usually contains text that reminds the programmer how the program works, but a machine language programmer can put the bytes of a machine language subroutine into it instead. There the subroutine cannot interfere with the master program, and the SAVE and LOAD commands preserve it on cassette along with the BASIC program.

The following program stores a machine language subroutine in a REM statement: [6]

```
1 REM Y██ :█NOT $TAB █RND█ TAB
█RNDTAN
2 FOR X=16514 TO 16529
3 INPUT I
4 POKE X,I
5 NEXT X
```

The REM statement must be the first statement in the program, in order to make certain that its text begins at address 16514. In this example, the REM

---

[6] Miller, Harold. *Syntax Z80* (The Harvard Group, Bolton Road, Harvard, Mass. 01451: August 1982).

statement has 16 characters because this particular machine language subroutine will have 16 bytes. It doesn't really matter what characters you type when you first enter the REM statement, as long as you type at least 16 of them. The example program uses digits because they are easy to count. The rest of the program is a loop that reads the 16 bytes from the keyboard and POKEs them into the REM statement. Run it and enter the following numbers: [7]

```
62
128
6
4
14
176
215
13
194
136
64
5
194
134
64
201
```

These numbers constitute a machine language subroutine. Don't try to understand what they mean. As a BASIC programmer, you can use other people's machine language subroutines without learning the details of machine language.

Press ENTER again after the last number to see the program listing. If you typed all the numbers correctly, the screen should look like this: [8]

```
    1 REM Y██. :█NOT $TAB ██RND█ TA
B ▚RNDTAN
    2 FOR X=16514 TO 16529
    3 INPUT I
    4 POKE X,I
    5 NEXT X
```

The REM statement now contains the machine language subroutine. The master program, however, still displays it on the television screen as if it

[7] Miller, Harold. *Syntax Z80.*

[8] Miller, Harold. *Syntax Z80.*

contained text. For example, the first byte you entered was 62, and Y is character 62. Therefore, the first character in the REM statement is Y. Machine language subroutines in REM statements always produce a strange-looking display line.

With the machine language subroutine safely stored in the REM statement, delete lines 2-5. To call the subroutine, enter the command

```
RAND USR 16514
```

The USR function is on the L key. Its argument is 16514 because that is the address of the REM statement in read/write memory. Some machine language subroutines return a useful value for the USR function. This one does not. Nevertheless, USR is still a function, so you must use it in a command where a function is legal.

Either of the following commands would also call the routine:

```
LET X=USR 16514
PRINT USR 16514
```

The PRINT command is most suitable when the machine language subroutine returns a value for USR that you want to display on the screen. The LET command is best when you need to save the value for future use. Finally, RAND is best when you don't care what the value is, because RAND doesn't alter the display and it doesn't waste space for an unnecessary variable.

When you execute any of the commands that call the machine language subroutine, the subroutine darkens the display by printing a black square (GRAPHICS SPACE) in every character position. Now the screen looks like this:

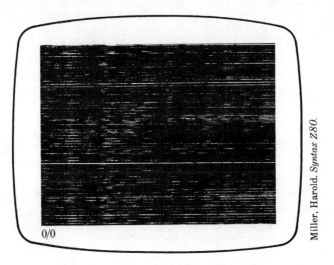

0/0

Miller, Harold. *Syntax Z80.*

In FAST mode, the machine language subroutine runs much faster than the following BASIC program, which produces the same result:

```
10 FOR I=1 TO 704
20 PRINT "▮";
30 NEXT I
```

Published programs with machine language subroutines in REM statements often include an input loop like the one in lines 2-5 above. Regardless of what the machine language subroutine does, the procedure for storing it in a REM statement is usually the same. However, don't try to use a REM statement if the instructions tell you to put the machine language somewhere else in memory. Most machine language routines must be in exactly the right memory addresses in order to work properly.

Some published programs tell you to enter the bytes of the machine language subroutine directly as you type the REM statement. All the characters in the above REM statement appear on the keyboard, so you could type in the REM statement exactly as it appears instead of using an INPUT loop. To try it, execute NEW and enter the following characters, being careful to turn the cursor on and off (with SHIFT-9) at the right places:[9]

| Symbol | How to Make It |
| --- | --- |
| 1 | a number |
| REM | a keyword |
| Y | a letter |
| ■ | GRAPHICS SPACE |
| ▪ | GRAPHICS SHIFT-T |
| ◲ | GRAPHICS SHIFT-4 |
| : | SHIFT-Z |
| ▩ | GRAPHICS K |
| NOT | FUNCTION N |
| $ | SHIFT-U |
| TAB | FUNCTION P |
| ▦ | GRAPHICS SHIFT-H |
| RND | FUNCTION T |
| ◻ | GRAPHICS SHIFT-5 |
| TAB | FUNCTION P |
| ◪ | GRAPHICS SHIFT-Y |
| RND | FUNCTION T |
| TAN | FUNCTION E |

The display should now contain a REM statement exactly like the previous one. Check it very carefully before you call the subroutine. If you make a

[9] Miller, Harold. *Syntax Z80.*

mistake in a machine language subroutine, you may have to unplug the power to the computer in order to get the ▤ cursor again.

Call the subroutine with the same command as before:

```
RAND USR 16514
```

It will produce the same darkened screen. To fill the screen with some other character when the subroutine is called, edit the REM statement to replace the second character (GRAPHICS SPACE) with the new screen-filling character.

Some machine language subroutines are difficult or even impossible to type directly. If the REM statement contains a BASIC command word (such as LET or PRINT), you must enter the command word first on the line, then space backward (SHIFT-5) to enter REM. Also, since there are fewer than 256 keyboard symbols, some byte values do not represent any character (see Appendix C). Such a byte appears as a question mark (?) on the display, but you cannot enter it by typing a question mark or any other character. To enter one of these codes into a REM statement, you must use a POKE command. To avoid such problems, use an INPUT loop instead of typing the machine language directly.

## Machine Language Above RAMTOP

A REM statement disappears when you load another program from cassette or when you execute NEW, but a machine language subroutine above RAM-TOP remains. This is an advantage if several different BASIC programs call the machine language subroutine. The method has disadvantages as well, however: SAVE and LOAD don't preserve or restore the protected space on cassette; the address of the protected space is different for systems with different amounts of read/write memory; and a few extra commands are required to reserve the space in the first place. Published programs using this method will either reserve the space themselves or tell you what commands to give to reserve it. They will usually also include a *loader* routine that POKES the machine language into the reserved space at the beginning.

The following program reserves space above RAMTOP for a machine language subroutine:

```
 10 PRINT "RESERVE HOW MANY BYT
ES?"
 20 INPUT NBYTES
 30 LET RAMTOP=PEEK 16388+256*P
EEK 16389
 40 LET RAMTOP=RAMTOP-NBYTES
 50 POKE 16389,INT (RAMTOP/256)
```

```
   60 POKE 16388,RAMTOP-256*PEEK
16389
   70 NEW
```

Run the program and enter **14** to reserve 14 bytes. The program will disappear from the screen, and the reserved bytes will be ready. To use them, enter the following program:

```
   10 LET RAMTOP=PEEK 16388+256*P
EEK 16389
   15 PRINT "RAMTOP IS ";RAMTOP
   20 FOR X=RAMTOP TO RAMTOP+13
   30 INPUT I
   40 POKE X,I
   50 NEXT X
```

This program is similar to the INPUT loop in the previous section, but it POKES the program into the space above RAMTOP. Run it and enter the following numbers: [10]

```
   62
   149
   6
   4
   14
   176
   215
   13
   32
   252
   5
   32
   247
   201
```

Now enter the command **RAND USR RAMTOP** to call the machine language subroutine, which fills the screen with reverse-video plus signs (+). Delete the entire BASIC program by typing each line number, so that nothing but the ▤ cursor remains. Execute **RAND USR RAMTOP**; the same pattern of reverse-video plus signs appears on the screen. The machine language is safe even if you LOAD another program or execute CLEAR or NEW.

---

[10]Foley, Robert A. *Syntax ZX80* (The Harvard Group, Bolton Road, Harvard, Mass. 01451: September 1982).

You must remember the new value of RAMTOP, however, in order to call the subroutine after executing one of these commands.

## MACHINE LANGUAGE LOADERS

The above programs with INPUT loops are examples of *loader* programs. They *load* machine language into a REM statement or into addresses above RAMTOP using POKE. If you have studied machine language programming, or if you want to enter longer machine language programs written by others, you will need more complete loader programs that make it easy to edit, save, and load machine language. Appendix F describes several more powerful loader programs and explains how to enter and use them. Appendix J gives some longer machine language routines that are both useful and fun.

## FOR MACHINE LANGUAGE PROGRAMMERS ONLY

If you already know the Z80 machine language of the TS1000 and ZX81, the information in this section will help you adapt your knowledge to the special features of these computers.

· Use the RET instruction (decimal value 201) to return to BASIC. The BREAK key does not work for machine language routines.

· The value of the USR function is the value that the machine language subroutine leaves in the BC register pair when it returns to BASIC.

· The master program uses the IY register to store the starting address of the system variables.

· A machine language subroutine may use the stack, but it should restore it to its original state before returning to BASIC.

· If you change the contents of the IY, I, or HL' registers, you must save them first and restore them afterward.

· Machine language subroutines run in either SLOW or FAST mode, whichever was active when the BASIC program called USR.

· In SLOW mode, you must not change the A', F', IX, IY, or R registers, even if you restore them later. The master program uses them for the display while your machine language subroutine is running.

- Appendix L tells how to use several of the subroutines in read-only memory (ROM).

- Appendix N lists sources of further information on TS1000 and ZX81 machine language programming.

Summary of All BASIC
Commands and Functions

# Appendix
# A

This appendix describes all of the commands and functions of BASIC for the TS1000 and ZX81 computers. First it lists the commands and then the functions, each list in alphabetical order. Use this appendix for reference when you need to look up how to use a particular command or function or when you want to scan through the list for one that does what you want to do.

## IMMEDIATE AND PROGRAMMED MODES

All BASIC commands and functions, except the INPUT command, can be used in either immediate mode (also called *command* mode) or in programmed mode. In other words, you can either execute the command without a line number and have the computer carry out the command immediately, or include the command in a program for later execution by *numbering* the line.

## FORMAT CONVENTIONS

The following symbols and abbreviations will be used in the command and function summaries to describe BASIC syntax:

{ }    Braces indicate a choice of items within the statement. The braces are not part of the command; the computer keyboard does not even have braces on it. You must choose one of the items between the braces and include it with the command to make a useful BASIC statement.

[ ]  Brackets enclose optional items. The command is legal with or without the items in brackets; your purpose in using the command determines whether to include these items or not. The brackets themselves are not part of the command.

...  Three dots indicate omitted information or that an optional item may be repeated in the command.

Line numbers  Every program line has a line number. Immediate mode commands do not. The summary does not specify line numbers, but they are implied if you use the item in programmed mode.

Other punctuation  All other punctuation marks—commas, semicolons, quotation marks, and parentheses—must appear exactly as shown.

UPPERCASE  Uppercase words and letters must appear exactly as shown.

*italics*  Items in italics are names of general categories that appear in commands and functions. You must substitute a real variable name, constant, or expression for each italicized item. Use the definitions below and the descriptions of the individual commands and functions to decide exactly what to put in the place of such italicized items.

# DEFINITIONS OF ITALICIZED TERMS

A typical BASIC command may include string or numeric constants or expressions. Some may use array names or FOR-NEXT loop counters, which have special restrictions. This section describes the different categories of acceptable names and specifies an abbreviation (in italics) for each one. After you look up a particular command or function in the alphabetized list, refer to this section for the meaning of the italicized abbreviations that you found there.

*bytexpr*  A numeric expression whose value is between 0 and 255.

*col*  Column number on the display screen or the printer. A numeric constant, variable, or expression should be between 0 and 31 in a PRINT or LPRINT statement and between 0 and 63 in a PLOT or UNPLOT statement.

*expr* Any valid expression or combination of expressions. Includes any combination of constants, variables, or expressions, and may be numeric, string, relational, or logical.

*letter* A single letter (A to Z).

*line* Line number on the display screen or the printer. A numeric constant, variable, or expression in a PRINT or LPRINT statement, with a value between 0 and 21.

*numexpr* Any numeric constant, variable, function, or valid combination of these items.

*row* Row number on the display screen or the printer. A numeric constant, variable, or expression in a PLOT or UNPLOT statement, with a value between 0 and 43.

*statement* Any valid BASIC statement.

*strexpr* Any string constant, variable, function, or any valid combination of these items.

*var* Any numeric or string variable name, including array elements.

## STATEMENTS

This section describes all of the TS1000/ZX81 BASIC statements. Each command is a single symbol on one key; don't try to type in a command letter by letter. The descriptions give the command's purpose, its keyboard location, the general format of the statement in which it is used, and one or more examples of its use.

## BREAK

**Purpose**: halts program execution and returns the computer to immediate mode.

**Location:**   SPACE Key
**Format:**   BREAK

**Example:**   BREAK

Press BREAK while a program is running to terminate the program as soon as the computer finishes the line it is currently executing. This command will interrupt any BASIC line except one with INPUT or USR. It will even interrupt a cassette SAVE or LOAD operation. To terminate INPUT of a numeric variable, enter STOP (SHIFT-A) or any letter that is not the name of a defined variable. To terminate INPUT of a string variable, delete the quotation marks and enter STOP (SHIFT-A).

When a BREAK occurs, the computer finishes the current program line and switches to immediate mode. It displays the report code D, followed by the number of the line that was executing. You can continue program execution with the CONT command (on the C key). Execution will continue with the next line after the one you interrupted.

# CLEAR

**Purpose:** deletes all variables currently defined.

| | |
|---|---|
| **Location:** | x Key |
| **Format:** | CLEAR |
| **Example:** | CLEAR |

The CLEAR command erases the computer's memory of any variables defined by previous LET or INPUT statements. This increases the amount of free memory available. The computer's condition after you press CLEAR is the same as it was immediately after you entered the program but before you ran it.

# CLS

**Purpose:** clears the display screen and frees the memory space the displayed information occupied.

| | |
|---|---|
| **Location:** | v Key |
| **Format:** | CLS |
| **Example:** | CLS |

The display is erased without affecting the stored program or the variables. When a program stops with error report 4 (not enough room in memory), or when EDIT fails for lack of memory to display the edit line, CLS makes more memory available.

# CONT

**Purpose**: resumes program execution after an error, STOP, or BREAK.

| | |
|---|---|
| **Location:** | C Key |
| **Format:** | CONT |
| **Example:** | CONT |

The CONT command attempts to continue after the program terminates with a report code other than 0. Most program errors are not *recoverable*; that is, the same error will occur every time the computer tries to execute the command. Hence, CONT will not work with such errors. It will succeed after BREAK (report code D), STOP (report code 9), and screen full (report code 5). It will also succeed after "undefined variable" (report code 2) if you first define the variable with a LET command in immediate mode. If you accidentally enter a letter instead of a number for a numeric INPUT command, CONT will give you a second chance.

# COPY

**Purpose**: makes a copy of the display screen on the printer.

| | |
|---|---|
| **Location:** | Z Key |
| **Format:** | COPY |
| **Example:** | COPY |

The computer ignores this command if the system does not include a printer.

# DIM

**Purpose**: creates all the members of the array and gives them the value 0 (numeric arrays) or blank (string arrays).

| | |
|---|---|
| **Location:** | D Key |
| **Format:** | DIM *letter*[$](*numexpr*[,*numexpr*...]) |
| **Examples:** | DIM G(12) |
| | DIM Q(4,5,12) |
| | DIM C$(10,2) |

The DIM statement must come before any other statements that use the array. Each array requires a separate DIM statement. The TS1000 and ZX81 allow as many numbers in parentheses as you want to use, provided the system contains enough read-write memory to hold the array. The name of an array must be a single letter (for numeric arrays) or a single letter followed by a dollar sign (for string arrays).

## FAST

**Purpose**: puts the computer into fast mode.

| | |
|---|---|
| **Location:** | SHIFT-F |
| **Format:** | FAST |
| **Example:** | FAST |

In fast mode, the display goes blank while a program is running, except during a PAUSE or an INPUT command. Programs run faster in this mode because the computer devotes all of its time to the program. Fast mode is also better than slow mode for typing and editing program lines because the screen responds more quickly to what you type.

## FOR

**Purpose**: starts a loop that repeats the lines between FOR and NEXT until the loop counter variable reaches a certain value.

| | |
|---|---|
| **Location:** | F Key |
| **Format:** | FOR *letter* = *startexpr* TO *endexpr* [STEP *stepexpr*] |
| **Example:** | FOR I=1 TO 10 |
| | FOR A=TOP TO BOTTOM STEP −1 |
| | FOR D=15 TO 19.95 STEP .05 |

The terms *startexpr*, *endexpr*, and *stepexpr* all represent numeric expressions. *Letter* is the control variable (also called the counter). When the computer first executes the FOR statement, it gives *letter* the value *startexpr*. Then it executes the statements following FOR until it reaches a NEXT statement with the same control variable name *letter*. It adds *stepexpr* to *letter* (or it adds one if STEP is not present). It then compares the result to *endexpr*. If the value of *letter* has not yet reached *endexpr*, the computer branches back to the statement just after FOR. If the value of *letter* has reached or passed *endexpr*, the computer proceeds to the statement after NEXT. If *stepexpr* is positive, *endexpr* should be larger than *startexpr*. If *stepexpr* is negative, *endexpr* should be smaller than *startexpr*. If not, then *letter* is already past *endexpr* before the loop begins, and the computer will skip the loop entirely.

## GOSUB

**Purpose:** calls a subroutine.

| | |
|---|---|
| **Location:** | H Key |
| **Format:** | GOSUB *numexpr* |
| **Example:** | GOSUB 120 |
| | GOSUB 2*SPACE+START |

The computer rounds *numexpr* to the nearest integer and branches to that line number (or to the next higher line number if that one does not exist). Program execution continues from there until it reaches a RETURN statement. The program branches back to the statement immediately following the GOSUB statement. Do not use GOTO instead of RETURN to terminate a subroutine.

## GOTO

**Purpose:** branches to the specified line of the program.

| | |
|---|---|
| **Location:** | G Key |
| **Format:** | GOTO *numexpr* |
| **Example:** | GOTO 50 |
| | GOTO A+LINE |

The computer rounds *numexpr* to the nearest integer and branches to that line number (or to the next highest line number if that one does not exist). Program execution continues normally from that line.

## IF-THEN

**Purpose:** executes the associated statement only if the condition is true.

| | |
|---|---|
| **Location:** | U and SHIFT-3 |
| **Format:** | IF *expr* THEN *statement* |
| **Example:** | IF NUM1>NUM2 THEN PRINT "ILLEGAL DATA" |
| | IF B\$="YES" AND X>100 THEN GOTO 20 |
| | IF 2+VAL THEN RETURN |

If *expr* specifies a true condition, the computer executes the *statement* that follows the keyword THEN on the same program line. If *expr* specifies a false condition, the computer proceeds directly to the next program line without executing the *statement*.

# INPUT

**Purpose:** accepts a string or numeric constant, variable, function, or other expression from the keyboard; evaluates it, and assigns the value to a variable.

| | |
|---|---|
| **Location:** | I Key |
| **Format:** | INPUT *var* |
| **Examples:** | INPUT ANS |
| | INPUT D$ |

The INPUT statement displays the screen contents with a cursor and reads the value of a variable from the keyboard. To read values for several variables, use several INPUT statements or a loop. The computer interprets the entry as a string or a numeric entry, depending on whether *var* is a string variable (with $) or a numeric variable (without $).

# LET

**Purpose:** assigns a value to a specified variable.

| | |
|---|---|
| **Location:** | L Key |
| **Format:** | LET *var=expr* |
| **Examples:** | LET X=24 |
| | LET V$="REPORT" |
| | LET A(5)=15*B+SIN .4 |
| | LET STATUS=D |
| | LET CHOICE=PRICE<LIMIT |

The computer creates a variable named *var* if one did not already exist, evaluates *expr*, and gives the value to *var*. The variable can be a simple numeric or string variable, a numeric or string array element, or a string or string array element with substring slicing notation. A string variable requires a string expression, and a numeric variable requires a numeric, relational, or logical expression.

# LIST

**Purpose:** displays all or part of the program on the television screen.

| | |
|---|---|
| **Location:** | K Key |
| **Format:** | LIST [*numexpr*] |

Example:     LIST
             LIST 400
             LIST 60*BLINE

The LIST command displays the program on the television screen, beginning with line *numexpr* or with the first line if *numexpr* is absent, and makes line *numexpr* the current line for the EDIT cursor.

## LLIST

**Purpose:** displays all or part of the program on the printer.

Location:    SHIFT-G
Format:      LLIST [*numexpr*]
Examples:    LLIST
             LLIST 400
             LLIST 60*BLINE

This command lists the program on the printer, beginning with line *numexpr* or with the first line if *numexpr* is absent.

## LOAD

**Purpose:** transfers a previously recorded BASIC program from cassette to the computer memory.

Location:    J Key
Format:      LOAD *strexpr*
Examples:    LOAD "OLDPROGRAM"
             LOAD W$+"JUNE"
             LOAD ""

## LPRINT

**Purpose:** prints characters on the printer.

Location:    SHIFT-S
Format:      LPRINT [*expr*] [{;}...[*expr*]]...
Examples:    LPRINT "TIMEX-SINCLAIR PRINTER"
             LPRINT SQR 12,A$
             LPRINT "THE ANSWER IS";NUM5
             LPRINT TAB 7;A*B;AT 12,I;CHR$ 40

The LPRINT command prints numbers and strings on the printer. Items allowed in an LPRINT command are constants, variables, functions, more complicated numeric and string expressions, semicolons, commas, TAB, and AT.

# NEW

Purpose: deletes the current program and its variables from memory.

Location:     A Key
Format:       NEW
Examples:     NEW

# NEXT

Purpose: marks the end of the loop started by a previous FOR statement.

Location:     N Key
Format:       NEXT *letter*
Example:      NEXT K

# PAUSE

Purpose: suspends program execution for a specified time, or until you press a key. The television screen remains active during the pause, even in fast mode.

Location:     M Key
Format:       PAUSE *numexpr*
Examples:     PAUSE 120
              PAUSE 60*NSEC

# PLOT

Purpose: darkens the picture element (pixel) at the specified row and column, and moves the print position to just after that location.

Location:     Q Key
Format:       PLOT *col,row*
Examples:     PLOT 20,5
              PLOT 3*I+2,J

A *pixel* is a small square, one-fourth the size of a character on the display. The PLOT command treats the screen as a grid of pixel positions, 64 pixels wide and 44 pixels high. *Col* must be between 0 and 63, and *row* must be between 0 and 43. After PLOT, the print position is the next character after the pixel.

## POKE

**Purpose:** stores a byte of data in a specified memory location.

| | |
|---|---|
| **Location:** | o Key |
| **Format:** | POKE *numexpr,bytexpr* |
| **Examples:** | POKE 16388,221 |

The value of *numexpr* must be between 0 and 65535 and *bytexpr* must be between −255 and 255.

## PRINT

**Purpose:** displays characters on the television display.

| | |
|---|---|
| **Location:** | P Key |
| **Format:** | PRINT [*expr*][{;}...[*expr*]]... |
| **Examples:** | PRINT "TIMEX-SINCLAIR PRINTER" |
| | PRINT SQR 12,A$ |
| | PRINT "THE ANSWER IS";NUM5 |
| | PRINT TAB 7;A*B;AT 12,I;CHR$ 40 |

## REM

**Purpose:** allows you to place explanatory comments (remarks) in a program.

| | |
|---|---|
| **Location:** | E Key |
| **Format:** | REM [*comment*] |
| **Example:** | REM SHOW MENU OF OPTIONS ON SCREEN |

The *comment* is any sequence of characters, although ENTER (character code 118) has a strange effect on the display. The REM statements appear in programs listed using LIST or LLIST, and they are preserved by SAVE and LOAD. Otherwise, BASIC ignores them. They also occupy space in memory and make a program run slightly more slowly. Machine language programmers may POKE bytes of machine code into a REM statement to keep the code from interfering with BASIC and to have it saved and restored with the program on cassette.

## RETURN

**Purpose:** branches to the statement immediately following the most recently executed GOSUB statement.

| | |
|---|---|
| **Location:** | Y Key |
| **Format:** | RETURN |
| **Example:** | RETURN |

A RETURN is placed at the end of a subroutine to branch back and continue execution at the place in the program that is called the subroutine. A RETURN without a previous GOSUB produces error report code 7.

## RAND

**Purpose:** selects the sequence of numbers that the RND function will produce on subsequent calls.

| | |
|---|---|
| **Location:** | T Key |
| **Format:** | RAND [*numexpr*] |
| **Examples:** | RAND |
| | RAND 476 |

## RUN

**Purpose:** erases any existing program variables and starts the program that is in memory.

| | |
|---|---|
| **Location:** | R Key |
| **Format:** | RUN [*numexpr*] |
| **Examples:** | RUN |
| | RUN 150 |

## SAVE

**Purpose:** sends a copy of the program currently in memory, together with its variables, to a cassette.

| | |
|---|---|
| Location: | s Key |
| Format: | SAVE *strexpr* |
| Examples: | SAVE "OLDPROGRAM" |
| | SAVE S$+"JUNE" |

## SCROLL

**Purpose:** moves the display up one line, making room at the bottom of the screen for a new line.

| | |
|---|---|
| Location: | B Key |
| Format: | SCROLL |
| Example: | SCROLL |

## SLOW

**Purpose:** puts the computer into slow mode.

| | |
|---|---|
| Location: | SHIFT-D |
| Format: | SLOW |
| Example: | SLOW |

Slow mode is also called compute-and-display mode. In this mode, the computer maintains the display while the program is running. It is called slow mode because the computer spends much of its time controlling the display, making the program run more slowly.

## STOP

**Purpose:** halts program execution and returns the computer to immediate mode.

| | |
|---|---|
| Location: | SHIFT-A |
| Format: | STOP |
| Example: | STOP |

## UNPLOT

**Purpose:** erases the picture element (pixel) at the specified row and column and moves the print position to just after that location.

| | |
|---|---|
| **Location:** | w Key |
| **Format:** | UNPLOT *col,row* |
| **Examples:** | UNPLOT |
| | UNPLOT 3∗I+2,J |

A *pixel* is a square one-fourth the size of a character on the display. The PLOT and UNPLOT commands treat the screen as a grid of pixel positions, 64 pixels wide and 44 pixels high. *col* must be between 0 and 63, and *row* must be between 0 and 43.

# FUNCTIONS

This section describes the TS1000 and ZX81 BASIC functions. The function symbols are printed below the white key squares. To select a function, first press SHIFT-ENTER, giving you the ▤ cursor. Then press the key for the function you want.

Most of the functions take one argument, but a few take no argument. The argument of a function—the expression on which it operates—goes to the right of the function name. Parentheses around the argument are optional if the argument is a single constant or variable. The value of a function—the information it returns to the program—is a string if the function name ends with a dollar sign; otherwise, its value is a number.

The descriptions below give the keyboard location of each function, its general format, and one or more examples of its use. Refer to the beginning of this chapter for an explanation of the terms and abbreviations in the descriptions.

## ABS

**Purpose:** returns the absolute value (magnitude) of the number that is the argument. The result of this function is always a positive number, regardless of the argument's original sign.

| | |
|---|---|
| **Location:** | G Key |
| **Format:** | ABS *(numexpr)* |
| **Example:** | IF A=ABS A THEN PRINT "POSITIVE" |

## ACS (ARCCOS)

**Purpose:** returns the arccosine of a number.

| | |
|---|---|
| **Location:** | s Key |

| Format: | ACS (*numexpr*) |
|---|---|
| Examples: | LET ANGLE=ACS .5 |

The value of ACS is in radians. *Numexpr* must be between −1 and 1. It is the cosine of the value.

## ASN or ARCSIN

**Purpose:** returns the arcsine of a number.

| Location: | A Key |
|---|---|
| Format: | ASN (*numexpr*) |
| Example: | LET ANGLE=ASN (1/3) |

The value of ASN is in radians. *Numexpr* must be between −1 and 1. It is the sine of the value.

## ATN (ARCTAN)

**Purpose:** returns the arctangent of a number.

| Location: | D Key |
|---|---|
| Format: | ATN (*numexpr*) |
| Example: | PRINT ATN X |

The value of ATN is in radians. *Numexpr* is the tangent of the value.

## CHR$

**Purpose:** returns the string value of the specified character code.

| Location: | U Key |
|---|---|
| Format: | CHR$ (*bytexpr*) |
| Example: | PRINT CHR$ 40 |

*Bytexpr* must be between 0 and 255.

## CODE

**Purpose:** returns the character code number for a specified character.

| Location: | I Key |
|---|---|

| | |
|---|---|
| **Format:** | CODE (*strexpr*) |
| **Example:** | IF CODE A$<28 THEN PRINT "NOT A NUMBER" |

If the string is longer than one character, CODE returns the character code for the first character in the string. If *strexpr* is the empty string, CODE returns 0.

## COS

**Purpose:** returns the cosine of an angle.

| | |
|---|---|
| **Location:** | w Key |
| **Format:** | COS (*numexpr*) |
| **Example:** | PRINT COS Y |

*Numexpr* is an angle, expressed in radians.

## EXP

**Purpose:** returns *e* raised to a power.

| | |
|---|---|
| **Location:** | x Key |
| **Format:** | EXP (*numexpr*) |
| **Example:** | LET A=EXP 2.4 |

This function computes *e* (the base of natural logarithms, 2.7182818) raised to the power *numexpr*.

## INKEY

**Purpose:** reads the key currently pressed on the keyboard.

| | |
|---|---|
| **Location:** | B Key |
| **Format:** | INKEY$ |
| **Example:** | LET R$=INKEY$ |

This function returns the character for the key currently pressed, or the empty string if no key is pressed or if several are pressed. It is useful in controlling program operation while the program is running.

## INT

**Purpose:** returns the integer portion of a number.

**Location:**    R Key
**Format:**    INT (*numexpr*)
**Example:**    IF C< >INT C THEN PRINT "NOT AN INTEGER"

This function returns the largest integer less than or equal to the value of *numexpr*.

## LEN

**Purpose:** returns the length of a string.

**Location:**    K Key
**Format:**    LEN (*strexpr*)
**Example:**    IF LEN S$5 THEN STOP

## LN

**Purpose:** returns the natural logarithm of a number.

**Location:**    Z Key
**Format:**    LN (*numexpr*)
**Example:**    LET A=B*LN C

Computes the natural (base *e*) logarithm of *numexpr*. An error occurs if *numexpr* is zero or negative.

## PEEK

**Purpose:** returns the contents of a memory location.

**Location:**    O Key
**Format:**    PEEK (*numexpr*)
**Example:**    PRINT PEEK 16388

The PEEK function returns the number stored in memory location *numexpr*. An error results if *numexpr* is less than zero or greater than 65535.

## PI

**Purpose:** returns the constant 3.1415927.

**Location:**    M Key
**Format:**      PI
**Example:**    LET CIRCUM=PI*DIAM

## RND

**Purpose:** returns a random number between 0 and 1.

**Location:**    T Key
**Format:**      RND
**Example:**    PRINT 5*RND

The random number is greater than or equal to zero and less than one. The RAND command selects the sequence of numbers for RND.

## SGN

**Purpose:** identifies a number as positive, negative, or zero.

**Location:**    F Key
**Format:**      SGN (*numexpr*)
**Example:**    IF SGN A = −1 THEN PRINT "NEGATIVE"

The SGN function returns 1 if *numexpr* is positive, −1 if it is negative, and 0 if it is zero.

## SIN

**Purpose:** returns the sine of an angle.

**Location:**    Q Key
**Format:**      SIN (*numexpr*)
**Example:**    PRINT SIN X

*Numexpr* is an angle, expressed in radians.

## SQR

**Purpose:** returns the square root of a positive number.

| | |
|---|---|
| **Location:** | H Key |
| **Format:** | SQR (*numexpr*) |
| **Example:** | LET HYPOT=SQR (LEG1**2+LEG2**2) |

This function computes the square root of *numexpr*. Using a negative value for *numexpr* causes an error.

## STR$

**Purpose:** converts a numeric value to a string.

| | |
|---|---|
| **Location:** | Y Key |
| **Format:** | STR$ (*numexpr*) |
| **Example:** | LET A$=STR$ (2/3) |

This function converts the value of *numexpr* to a string. The characters in the string are the same as those that PRINT *numexpr* would display on the screen. An error occurs if *numexpr* exceeds the limits for numeric values.

## TAN

**Purpose:** returns the tangent of an angle.

| | |
|---|---|
| **Location:** | E Key |
| **Format:** | TAN (*numexpr*) |
| **Example:** | PRINT TAN .2 |

*Numexpr* is an angle, expressed in radians.

## USR

**Purpose:** branches to a machine language program.

| | |
|---|---|
| **Location:** | L Key |
| **Format:** | USR (*numexpr*) |
| **Example:** | PRINT USR 16514 |

Report Codes

# Appendix

# B

When the TS1000 or ZX81 finishes executing a program, whether in command or program mode, it displays a pair of numbers or a letter and a number, separated by a slash, in the lower left corner of the screen. If the computer is in programmed mode, the second number will be the number of the last line executed. If the computer is in command mode, the second number will be zero. The first number is the *report code*. It indicates why the computer stopped at that line.

The following descriptions of the different report codes will help you diagnose and fix problems in your programs.

## REPORT CODE 0: SUCCESSFUL COMPLETION

The computer did not detect any errors. Either it executed the last line of the program, or it executed a GOTO or a GOSUB with a line number larger than the last line of the program.

## REPORT CODE 1: UNDEFINED CONTROL VARIABLE

The second number in the report is the line number of a NEXT statement whose control variable (the variable to the right of the NEXT keyword) has not previously appeared in a FOR command. Such an error usually produces report code 2 instead of 1, but code 1 occurs when the program contains a variable with the same name as the control variable, but which is not part of the FOR statement.

The FOR and NEXT statements must always occur in pairs. Every FOR statement marks the beginning of a loop and specifies a control variable (the variable name immediately after the FOR keyword). The corresponding NEXT statement specifies the same control variable and marks the end of the loop. You may have mistyped the name of the control variable in the FOR command or the NEXT command, or you may have branched into the middle of a loop with a GOTO or GOSUB command.

# REPORT CODE 2:
# UNDEFINED VARIABLE

Report code 2 may occur in three situations. First, you must use a LET, INPUT, or FOR statement to give a variable a value before you attempt to use the variable, and the computer must execute this statement before it can use the variable in any other statement. For example, the following program will produce report code 2/30, because the GOTO statement caused the computer to skip giving a value to A:

```
10 GOTO 30
20 LET A=5
30 LET B=2*A
```

Second, report code 2 can mean that you forgot to include a DIM statement before using an array. Every array requires a DIM statement to tell the computer its name and size. The DIM statement also defines the array's initial variables by assigning the value zero to all its elements.

Third, if the line number in the report is the number of a NEXT statement, report code 2 means that the control variable (the variable to the right of the NEXT keyword) was not specified in a FOR command (see report code 1).

# REPORT CODE 3:
# SUBSCRIPT OUT OF RANGE

A reference to an array element produces report code 3 if the subscript is larger than the corresponding DIM statement allows. For example, the following program produces the report 3/20:

```
10 DIM B(10)
20 LET B(11)=3.4
```

A subscript smaller than 1 or larger than 65535 will generate a report code B instead of 3.

# REPORT CODE 4:
# NOT ENOUGH ROOM IN MEMORY

This report means that the computer has used all of the available read/write memory (RAM) and cannot finish executing the program line. Even the report code itself may be incomplete because the computer did not have enough memory to display it. Any one of several BASIC commands can produce this error. It means that your program or its variables use more memory than you have available. Chapter 7 suggests some methods of conserving memory.

## REPORT CODE 5:
## NO MORE ROOM ON THE SCREEN

Your program has tried to write more lines (with PRINT, PLOT, UNPLOT, or LIST), but the screen is full. The TS1000 and ZX81 do not automatically scroll the display upward to make more room at the bottom. To clear the screen and continue printing, execute CONT in command mode.

To avoid this problem entirely, use CLS at places where the screen may be filled, or use SCROLL before each PRINT statement to move the display up one line.

## REPORT CODE 6:
## ARITHMETIC OVERFLOW

The program line tried to create a number that is beyond the range the computer can handle. Many different kinds of calculations can produce this error. The most common one is division by zero, as in the following example, which produces report 6/20:

```
10 LET Z=0
20 LET A=2/Z
```

The rules of mathematics forbid division by zero.

In some cases not involving division by zero, you can redesign the program to use smaller numbers. Arrange the numeric expression so that those operations that make the result smaller occur first. For example, the line

```
10 LET X=100*1E37/1000
```

produces error report code 6 because the computer tries to multiply 100 by 1E37. The intermediate result is 1E39, which is too large. To avoid the error, write the command as follows:

```
10 LET X=100*(1E37/1000)
```

First the computer divides by 1000 to give 1E34. Then it multiplies by 100 to give 1E36. All of these numbers are smaller than 1E38, so no error results.

If you think none of the calculations in the reported line should produce such a large number, insert PRINT statements before the line to display all the variables it uses. The real cause of the problem could be an error earlier in the program that gave one of the variables a very large or very small value.

# REPORT CODE 7:
# NO CORRESPONDING GOSUB
# FOR A RETURN STATEMENT

The computer encountered a RETURN statement without first executing a GOSUB, or it encountered another RETURN statement after returning from all the previous GOSUBS.

# REPORT CODE 8:
# INPUT IN COMMAND MODE

The INPUT statement can be used only in programmed mode. It must have a line number. To give a variable a value in command mode, use LET instead of INPUT.

# REPORT CODE 9:
# STOP STATEMENT EXECUTED

Report code 9 is a normal program termination, not an error. It indicates that the computer executed a STOP statement on the reported line number.

# REPORT CODE A:
# INVALID ARGUMENT TO CERTAIN FUNCTIONS

Report code A means your program violated one of the rules for a mathematical function. For example, the argument of the SQR function cannot be negative; the argument of LN must be greater than zero; and the argument of ACS or ASN must be between −1 and 1.

## REPORT CODE B:
## INTEGER OUT OF RANGE

The computer will generate report code B when an integer is larger or smaller than its allowable range in the computer.

Several commands and functions round their arguments to the nearest integer and require the integer to be within a certain range. Among these, RUN, GOTO, GOSUB, LIST, LLIST, PAUSE, RAND, DIM, PEEK, and USR give error 4 if the integer is larger than 65535 or negative. The POKE command requires its first number to be in this range also, and its second number to be between −255 and 255. The PLOT and UNPLOT commands allow column numbers only from 0 to 63 and line numbers from 0 to 43. Line numbers used with PRINT AT must be between 0 and 21, and column numbers must be between 0 and 31. Specifications for PRINT TAB and arguments of CHR$ must be between 0 and 255.

## REPORT CODE C:
## INVALID ARGUMENT FOR VAL FUNCTION

The string argument of VAL must be a valid numeric expression. That is, it must be an expression that you could use in a LET statement to define a variable.

## REPORT CODE D:
## BREAK

Report code D is a valid termination, not an error. It appears when you interrupt a program with BREAK at the keyboard or when you enter STOP in response to an INPUT statement.

## REPORT CODE F:
## SAVE REQUIRES A NAME FOR THE PROGRAM

The empty string " " cannot follow SAVE. Put at least one character between the quotation marks to identify the saved program on cassette.

## OTHER REPORT CODES

Report codes E, G-Z, graphics symbols, and reverse-video symbols are available to BASIC and machine language programmers, but the master program does not use them for errors it detects. If one of them occurs, look for its meaning in the documentation for the program you were running.

The Character Code

# Appendix
# C

Each keyboard symbol has its own numeric code, which represents the symbol used in BASIC strings, in the BASIC program listing, in variable names, and in the display file. Table C-1 is a complete list of these character codes.

**Table C-1. Character codes**

| Decimal Code | Character | Hexadecimal Code |
|---|---|---|
| 0 | space | 00 |
| 1 | ▘ | 01 |
| 2 | ▝ | 02 |
| 3 | ▀ | 03 |
| 4 | ▖ | 04 |
| 5 | ▌ | 05 |
| 6 | ▞ | 06 |
| 7 | ▛ | 07 |
| 8 | ▒ | 08 |
| 9 | 🮏 | 09 |
| 10 | 🮎 | 0A |
| 11 | " | 0B |
| 12 | | 0C |
| 13 | $ | 0D |
| 14 | : | 0E |
| 15 | ? | 0F |
| 16 | ( | 10 |

Table C-1. (Continued)

| Decimal Code | Character | Hexadecimal Code |
|:---:|:---:|:---:|
| 17 | ) | 11 |
| 18 | > | 12 |
| 19 | < | 13 |
| 20 | = | 14 |
| 21 | + | 15 |
| 22 | − | 16 |
| 23 | * | 17 |
| 24 | / | 18 |
| 25 | ; | 19 |
| 26 | , | 1A |
| 27 | . | 1B |
| 28 | 0 | 1C |
| 29 | 1 | 1D |
| 30 | 2 | 1E |
| 31 | 3 | 1F |
| 32 | 4 | 20 |
| 33 | 5 | 21 |
| 34 | 6 | 22 |
| 35 | 7 | 23 |
| 36 | 8 | 24 |
| 37 | 9 | 25 |
| 38 | A | 26 |
| 39 | B | 27 |
| 40 | C | 28 |
| 41 | D | 29 |
| 42 | E | 2A |
| 43 | F | 2B |
| 44 | G | 2C |
| 45 | H | 2D |
| 46 | I | 2E |
| 47 | J | 2F |
| 48 | K | 30 |
| 49 | L | 31 |
| 50 | M | 32 |
| 51 | N | 33 |
| 52 | O | 34 |
| 53 | P | 35 |
| 54 | Q | 36 |
| 55 | R | 37 |
| 56 | S | 38 |
| 57 | T | 39 |
| 58 | U | 3A |
| 59 | V | 3B |

Table C-1. (Continued)

| Decimal Code | Character | Hexadecimal Code |
|---|---|---|
| 60 | W | 3C |
| 61 | X | 3D |
| 62 | Y | 3E |
| 63 | Z | 3F |
| 64 | RND | 40 |
| 65 | INKEY$ | 41 |
| 66 | PI | 42 |
| 67-111 | Not used | |
| 112 | cursor up | 70 |
| 113 | cursor down | 71 |
| 114 | cursor left | 72 |
| 115 | cursor right | 73 |
| 116 | GRAPHICS | 74 |
| 117 | EDIT | 75 |
| 118 | ENTER | 76 |
| 119 | DELETE | 77 |
| 120 | ▨/▤ mode | 78 |
| 121 | FUNCTION | 79 |
| 122 | not used | 7A |
| 123 | not used | 7B |
| 124 | not used | 7C |
| 125 | not used | 7D |
| 126 | number | 7E |
| 127 | cursor | 7F |
| 128 | ■ | 80 |
| 129 | ▗ | 81 |
| 130 | ▖ | 82 |
| 131 | ▄ | 83 |
| 132 | ▝ | 84 |
| 133 | ▐ | 85 |
| 134 | ▞ | 86 |
| 135 | ▟ | 87 |
| 136 | ▓ | 88 |
| 137 | ▒ | 89 |
| 138 | ▚ | 8A |
| 139 | inverse " | 8B |
| 140 | inverse £ | 8C |
| 141 | inverse $ | 8D |
| 142 | inverse : | 8E |
| 143 | inverse ? | 8F |
| 144 | inverse ( | 90 |
| 145 | inverse ) | 91 |
| 146 | inverse > | 92 |

**Table C-1. (Continued)**

| Decimal Code | Character | Hexadecimal Code |
|:---:|:---:|:---:|
| 147 | inverse < | 93 |
| 148 | inverse = | 94 |
| 149 | inverse + | 95 |
| 150 | inverse − | 96 |
| 151 | inverse * | 97 |
| 152 | inverse / | 98 |
| 153 | inverse ; | 99 |
| 154 | inverse , | 9A |
| 155 | inverse . | 9B |
| 156 | inverse 0 | 9C |
| 157 | inverse 1 | 9D |
| 158 | inverse 2 | 9E |
| 159 | inverse 3 | 9F |
| 160 | inverse 4 | A0 |
| 161 | inverse 5 | A1 |
| 162 | inverse 6 | A2 |
| 163 | inverse 7 | A3 |
| 164 | inverse 8 | A4 |
| 165 | inverse 9 | A5 |
| 166 | inverse A | A6 |
| 167 | inverse B | A7 |
| 168 | inverse C | A8 |
| 169 | inverse D | A9 |
| 170 | inverse E | AA |
| 171 | inverse F | AB |
| 172 | inverse G | AC |
| 173 | inverse H | AD |
| 174 | inverse I | AE |
| 175 | inverse J | AF |
| 176 | inverse K | B0 |
| 177 | inverse L | B1 |
| 178 | inverse M | B2 |
| 179 | inverse N | B3 |
| 180 | inverse O | B4 |
| 181 | inverse P | B5 |
| 182 | inverse Q | B6 |
| 183 | inverse R | B7 |
| 184 | inverse S | B8 |
| 185 | inverse T | B9 |
| 186 | inverse U | BA |
| 187 | inverse V | BB |
| 188 | inverse W | BC |
| 189 | inverse X | BD |

**Table C-1. (Continued)**

| Decimal Code | Character | Hexadecimal Code |
|:---:|:---:|:---:|
| 190 | inverse Y | BE |
| 191 | inverse Z | BF |
| 192 | " " | C0 |
| 193 | AT | C1 |
| 194 | TAB | C2 |
| 195 | not used | C3 |
| 196 | CODE | C4 |
| 197 | VAL | C5 |
| 198 | LEN | C6 |
| 199 | SIN | C7 |
| 200 | COS | C8 |
| 201 | TAN | C9 |
| 202 | ASN | CA |
| 203 | ACS | CB |
| 204 | ATN | CC |
| 205 | LN | CD |
| 206 | EXP | CE |
| 207 | INT | CF |
| 208 | SQR | D0 |
| 209 | SGN | D1 |
| 210 | ABS | D2 |
| 211 | PEEK | D3 |
| 212 | USR | D4 |
| 213 | STR$ | D5 |
| 214 | CHR$ | D6 |
| 215 | NOT | D7 |
| 216 | ** | D8 |
| 217 | OR | D9 |
| 218 | AND | DA |
| 219 | <= | DB |
| 220 | >= | DC |
| 221 | < > | DD |
| 222 | THEN | DE |
| 223 | TO | DF |
| 224 | STEP | E0 |
| 225 | LPRINT | E1 |
| 226 | LLIST | E2 |
| 227 | STOP | E3 |
| 228 | SLOW | E4 |
| 229 | FAST | E5 |
| 230 | NEW | E6 |
| 231 | SCROLL | E7 |
| 232 | CONT | E8 |

**Table C-1. (Continued)**

| Decimal Code | Character | Hexadecimal Code |
|:---:|:---:|:---:|
| 233 | DIM | E9 |
| 234 | REM | EA |
| 235 | FOR | EB |
| 236 | GOTO | EC |
| 237 | GOSUB | ED |
| 238 | INPUT | EE |
| 239 | LOAD | EF |
| 240 | LIST | F0 |
| 241 | LET | F1 |
| 242 | PAUSE | F2 |
| 243 | NEXT | F3 |
| 244 | POKE | F4 |
| 245 | PRINT | F5 |
| 246 | PLOT | F6 |
| 247 | RUN | F7 |
| 248 | SAVE | F8 |
| 249 | RAND | F9 |
| 250 | IF | FA |
| 251 | CLS | FB |
| 252 | UNPLOT | FC |
| 253 | CLEAR | FD |
| 254 | RETURN | FE |
| 255 | COPY | FF |

SOURCE: *Timex User Manual* by Steven Vickers, © 1982, Timex
Corporation, pp. 137-143.

Troubleshooting the Screen Image

# Appendix
# D

Your TS1000 or ZX81 computer probably will work perfectly the first time you plug it in. However, you may encounter a few problems until you find the best combination of settings for the television and the computer. Here are some suggestions to help you correct the most common difficulties.

## No Picture

If the display has nothing on it but "snow," unplug the computer power supply from the wall socket and plug in a lamp or other appliance to verify that the socket has power. Check that the video cable is securely connected to the computer and to the "COMPUTER" terminals on the antenna switch, and confirm that the antenna switch is in the "COMPUTER" position.

## Image Off the Screen

If you still don't see the cursor, your television may be out of adjustment in such a way that the picture is too big to fit on the screen. This can cause the cursor to disappear off the bottom or side of the screen. It also can make the top line or two of a program disappear off the top. To test for this problem, turn the vertical control of the television set until the picture "rolls" up or down the screen. If you still don't see the cursor, try the same thing with the horizontal control. If you can only see the cursor while the screen is unsteady, have your set adjusted by a qualified technician.

## Poor Picture

If a grid of horizontal and vertical lines appears on the screen with the cursor, try switching both the television and the computer to the other channel. Readjust the fine tuning and the other controls if necessary. If the grid is still there, check to make sure that the screws holding the cover on the computer are tight and that none of the plug connections between the different parts of the system are loose. A small black-and-white television set often gives a much clearer picture than a color set. The display will not be as clear if the computer is on a metal table or if there is an electric motor or other source of television interference nearby.

## Intermittent Problems

Occasionally, people have problems with the connection between the computer and the optional accessories at the back edge connector. If you have the printer or the memory expansion pack, and you find that the display sometimes disappears or the computer stops responding to your commands when you jostle or move it, chances are you have a bad connection at the edge connector. To improve the connection, first unplug the power. Then remove the accessory from the edge connector and clean the metal strips on both sides of the connector with a pencil eraser. Be very careful not to cut or damage any of the metal foil connections. All you need to do is to remove any dirt or oxide that may be on the metal surface.

The System Variables

# Appendix
# E

The system variables are locations in read/write memory (RAM) that the master program uses for its internal bookkeeping. Chapter 7 describes those that BASIC programmers might use and explains how to examine and store those that occupy two bytes. BASIC will not work without correct relationships among the system variables. Consult Chapter 7 or the references in Appendix N for further information.

Table E-1 describes all the system variables. The names in the first column are for your use only. They mean nothing to the computer, in BASIC or in any other language. The master program uses only the contents of the addresses.

### Table E-1. System Variables

| Name | Address | Description |
| --- | --- | --- |
| ERR_NR | 16384 | You can POKE a number here to stop a program with a report code at the lower left corner of the screen. The legal codes are |
| | | *POKE Value*     *Error Code Displayed*<br>0 to 8          1 to 9<br>9 to 14        A to F<br>15 to 34       G to Z<br>99 to 109    Graphics symbol<br>110 to 127   Reverse-video character<br>Other POKE values either do nothing or confuse the master program. |
| FLAGS | 16385 | *Flags* (bits set to one or zero to indicate specific conditions) for master program bookkeeping. |

## Table E-1. (Continued)

| Name | Address | Description |
|---|---|---|
| ERR_SP | 16386-16387 | Address of the first item on the machine *stack* (an area for temporary storage of values) |
| RAMTOP | 16388-16389 | Address of the first byte not used by BASIC. Any read/write memory above this point is protected and available for machine language routines. (See Chapter 7.) |
| MODE | 16390 | Specifies ▨, ▤, ▤, or ▤ cursor. |
| PPC | 16391-16392 | Line number of the BASIC statement currently being executed. |
| VERSN | 16393 | Version of master program. Identifies 8K ROM in programs saved on cassette. |
| E_PPC | 16394-16395 | Number of the BASIC line where the program cursor is. |
| D_FILE | 16396-16397 | Address of the first location in the display file (see Figure 7-1). |
| DF_CC | 16398-16399 | Address (in the display file) of the current print position. (See Chapter 7.) |
| VARS | 16400-16401 | Address of the first location in the BASIC variables area. Also the next location after the end of the display file (see Figure 7-1). |
| DEST | 16402-16403 | Address of the variable currently being processed. |
| E_LINE | 16404-16405 | Address of the beginning of the work space. |
| CH_ADD | 16406-16407 | Address of the next character in the string currently being processed. |
| X_PTR | 16408-16409 | Address of the character where syntax error occurred. |
| STKBOT | 16410-16411 | Address of the beginning of the calculator stack in the work space. |
| STKEND | 16412-16413 | Address of the top of the calculator stack, which is the beginning of available memory. |
| BREG | 16414 | Temporary storage while doing calculations. |
| MEM | 16415-16416 | Address of another area used for doing calculations. |
| Not used | 16417 | The master program does not use this byte. Machine language programmers sometimes use it to pass an argument from BASIC to a machine language subroutine. |
| DF_SZ | 16418 | The number of lines in the lower part of the screen. |
| S_TOP | 16419-16420 | The number of the top program line in automatic listings. |
| LAST_K | 16421-16422 | The key value (see Appendix M) of the last key that was pressed. |
| DEBOUNCE | 16423 | Debounce status of the keyboard. |

**Table E-1. (Continued)**

| Name | Address | Description |
|------|---------|-------------|
| MARGIN | 16424 | Number of blank lines above or below the picture. |
| NXTLIN | 16425-16426 | Program line that BASIC will execute next. |
| OLDPPC | 16427-16428 | Previous BASIC line number (for the CONT command). |
| FLAGX | 16429 | Flags for master program bookkeeping. |
| STRLEN | 16430-16431 | Length of the string being processed. |
| T__ADDR | 16432-16433 | Address of the next item in the syntax table. |
| SEED | 16434-16435 | Number that determines the sequence produced by RND, the random number generator function. The command RAND sets the value of SEED. |
| FRAMES | 16436-16437 | Counts the number of frames displayed on the television. Used by PAUSE to measure time intervals. When RAND is executed without a number for SEED, it uses the value of FRAMES. This usually produces a different sequence each time. |
| COORDS | 16438,16439 | The X and Y coordinates, respectively, of the last point for PLOT. |
| PR__CC | 16440 | The less significant byte of the current address in the printer buffer, PRBUFF. |
| S__POSN | 16441,16442 | The column and line numbers, respectively, for the print position. |
| CDFLAG | 16443 | Flags for master program bookkeeping, including the SLOW mode flag (bit 7). |
| PRBUFF | 16444-16476 | Printer buffer. Machine language subroutines may use this area for temporary storage, but printer commands and some other BASIC commands will alter its contents. |
| MEMBOT | 16477-16506 | Temporary storage for calculations. |
| Not used | 16507-16508 | The master program does not use these bytes. Machine language programmers sometimes use them to pass arguments from BASIC to a machine language subroutine. |

SOURCE: *Timex User Manual* by Steven Vickers, © 1982 Timex Corporation, pp. 134-136.

Entering Machine Language Subroutines

# Appendix
# F

This appendix provides convenient programs for loading machine language subroutines such as those in Appendices G and L. It also gives some technical information of interest to machine language programmers.

## MACHINE LANGUAGE LOADER PROGRAMS

The following are two loader programs. One loads a machine language program into a REM statement; the other loads it into space that you reserve above RAMTOP. Each program uses a string variable, which must be the first variable in the BASIC program. This variable contains the hexadecimal representation of the machine language code.

Each routine in Appendices G and L includes a LET statement (at line 20) that defines the machine code for that routine. Read the appropriate loader routine from cassette and type in the hexadecimal lines from Appendix G or L for the machine language routine you want to use. You must type each line exactly as shown, with one space between each pair of hexadecimal digits. Be sure to include a space between the last pair of digits and the closing quotation mark.

### REM Loader

The REM loader program will save you the trouble of typing long REM statements and making sure they contain the correct number of characters. Use it to load the example programs in Appendix L. The loader program has a short machine language routine of its own in the REM statement of line 10.

This routine extends the BASIC program area and lengthens the REM statement in line 200, so that it has exactly the right number of bytes to contain the machine language instructions you specify in the string variable H$. To create the loader program, start with the following INPUT loop:

```
10 REM 123456789
20 FOR I=16516 TO 16522
30 INPUT A
40 POKE I,A
50 NEXT I
```

Run it and enter the decimal numbers **42, 130, 64, 205, 155, 9,** and **201.** Now delete lines 20-50 and enter the rest of the program, as follows:[12]

```
10 REM 12ELRNDLN ▮TAN
40 LET N=LEN H$/3
50 LET D=PEEK 16396+256*PEEK 1
6397-2
60 FOR I=1 TO N
70 POKE 16515,INT ((D+I)/256)
80 POKE 16514,D+I-256*PEEK 165
15
90 RAND USR 16516
100 POKE D+I,16*CODE H$(I*3-2)+
CODE H$(I*3-1)-476
110 NEXT I
120 POKE D-1,INT ((N+2)/256)
130 POKE D-2,N+2-256*PEEK (D-1)
200 REM
```

Enter this program exactly as it appears above and SAVE it on a cassette. When you are ready to enter a machine language program, LOAD the program from tape. Your machine language program will be entered as a string variable, using a LET statement in a new line (use line number 20). Here is an example of how this would be done using the program entered in Chapter 8:

```
20 LET H$="3E 95 06 04 0E 60 D
7 0D 20 FC 05 20 F7 C9 "
```

Note that the data is entered as hexadecimal numbers. Remember that the program requires you to enter a space following the last two digits of the program (as in the previous example).

Appendices G and L give a complete listing of each machine language routine for the benefit of machine language programmers who want to see how they work. If you have not studied machine language programming, you can still enter and use the routines. With the loader program and your line 20

---

[12]Adapted from Frank O'Hara, *Syntax*, August, 1982, p. 8, and William Wentz, *Syntax Quarterly*, Winter, 1982 (The Harvard Group, Bolton Road, Harvard, Mass. 01451), p. 21.

in the computer, execute RUN to translate the hexadecimal code into machine language. The loader program extends the REM statement at line 200, which must be the last line in the program, and POKEs the machine language into it. A peculiar line of symbols appears in the REM statement because the computer treats the bytes of the machine language routine as text.

To run the machine language program, delete all of the loader program except line 200 to make it the first line in the program. This will make the machine language routine in the REM statement begin at address 16514. Do not insert any BASIC lines before it, or you will change its starting address. You can save the REM statement on cassette and load it whenever you want to use the machine language program.

## RAMTOP Loader

If you want to use the same machine language routine with many different BASIC programs, you may prefer to store it in protected space at the top of memory instead of in a REM statement. BASIC does not save this part of memory, but it also does not clear it when you execute NEW or LOAD.

The RAMTOP loader automatically

- determines the length of the machine language routine
- resets RAMTOP without using NEW or destroying the BASIC program
- POKEs the machine language into the reserved space
- displays the new value of RAMTOP, where the routine begins.

The location of the routine in memory will be different on systems that have different amounts of read/write memory, so use this method only for routines that will run correctly regardless of where they are in memory. The routines in Appendix G are all position-independent and can be stored above RAMTOP, but those in Appendix L cannot.

Like the REM loader program in the previous section, this RAMTOP loader begins with a machine language routine of its own in a REM statement. This routine resets RAMTOP and relocates the master program's stack. To enter the loader program, begin with the following input loop:[13]

```
 10 REM 12345678901234567890123
4567890123456789012345678
 20 FOR X=16514 TO 16563
 30 INPUT N
 40 POKE X,N
 50 NEXT X
```

[13]Wentz and Roderick McConnell, *Syntax*, August 1982 (The Harvard Group, Bolton Road, Harvard, Mass., 01451), pp. 20-21.

Run it and enter the following decimal numbers, from left to right, beginning with the top row:[14]

```
175 205   35   15   42    4   64 237
114   68   77    3   57 237   91 123
 64 237   82 235   25 237 184 237
 75 123   64   42    4   64 237   66
 34    4   64   42    2   64 237   66
 34    2   64 237   98   57 237   66
249 201
```

Delete the INPUT loop, leaving only the REM statement, which now looks like line 10 below. Enter the remainder of the following program and SAVE it on cassette:[15]

```
   10 REM ▓LN 77E▪RND GOSUB ???▀T
GOSUB ??RND GOSUB ? FOR ; GOSUB
 ▓ GOSUB ??RNDE▪RND GOSUB PI6▪RN
DE▀RND GOSUB PI6▀RND GOSUB ?T GO
SUB PI RAND TAN
   40 LET L=LEN H$/3
   50 LET M=L
   60 IF L<20 THEN LET M=20
   70 POKE 16507,M
   80 PRINT USR 16514;" BYTES SAV
ED"
   90 LET N=PEEK 16388+256*PEEK 1
6389
  100 PRINT "RECORD USR ADDRESS "
;N
  110 FOR X=3 TO L*3 STEP 3
  120 POKE N,16*CODE H$(X-2)+CODE
H$(X-1)-476
  130 LET N=N+1
  140 NEXT X
  150 PRINT "MACHINE CODE LOADED"
```

To use this loader, LOAD it from cassette and enter your hexadecimal code into a string variable H$, as shown in the REM loader described above. Save the loader program on cassette with the hexadecimal string so you can load the same routine again whenever you need it.

To load your machine language program, run the BASIC program and then execute NEW to delete it. The machine language routine will be stored above RAMTOP. To determine where your machine language program starts, enter and run the following line in immediate mode:

```
 PRINT PEEK 16388 + 256 * PEEK 1
6389
```

Your program will remain there even if you execute NEW or LOAD. Because of this, you can load several adjacent routines above RAMTOP by running the BASIC program several times with different hexadecimal strings each time.

[14]*Ibid.*
[15]*Ibid.*

# FOR MACHINE LANGUAGE PROGRAMMERS

The rest of this appendix is for readers who have studied Z80 machine language routines for the TS1000 or ZX81. If you want to learn more about machine language programming, consult the references in Appendix N.

As a machine language programmer, you must choose a portion of read/write memory to contain your routine. A REM statement is a good choice because the SAVE and LOAD commands preserve it, and because you can easily determine the exact memory address where it begins. Make the REM statement the first line of the BASIC program, and the bytes following the REM keyword will always begin at address 16514 (hexadecimal 4082).

If the byte value 118 occurs in the routine, it breaks the REM statement into two lines and changes the display of several bytes following it. The byte value 126 makes the next five bytes invisible on the display. If either of these is near the end of the REM statement, it also affects the display of the following line. (Character code 118 represents ENTER, and 126 hides the values of floating point constants that the master program stores in the listing.) Programs containing these bytes in REM statements will still work correctly, apart from the effect on the display. However, you cannot use EDIT to change a REM statement that contains 126, because EDIT deletes the byte containing 126 and the next five bytes after it. Therefore, design your REM statement programs to avoid these byte values.

Line Renumbering and Program Merging

# Appendix
# G

The following routines implement two valuable editing functions for BASIC programming. They also demonstrate the machine language capability of the TS1000 and ZX81.

## LINE RENUMBERING

This machine language renumbering program is similar to the BASIC renumbering program used earlier in the book. Because it is in machine language, however, it will remain in memory above RAMTOP while you enter or load different BASIC programs.

To use this program, enter it by means of the RAMTOP loader program from Appendix F. When you enter line 20, it must look exactly like the following lines, including a single space between each pair of digits and a space after the last pair:

```
 20 LET H$="11 7D 40 1A FE 76 C
8 2A 7B 40 7C 12 13 7D 12 1B 3A
21 40 4F 06 00 09 22 7B 40 EB CD
 F2 09 18 E3 "
```

After you run the loader program, it will display the USR address of the machine language routine. Write this down for future use. The routine remains in read/write memory until you disconnect power to the computer.

To renumber a BASIC program, you will need to enter it into the machine by hand or load it from a cassette. Once it is in memory, decide what your new starting line will be and give it the variable name FNUM as follows:

```
LET FNUM=XXXX
```

Replace the X's in the routine above with your starting value (the number you choose must be between 1 and 9999). Then decide what the new line increments will be. (The increment may be any value between 1 and 255.) Give that value to the variable INC in immediate mode, replacing the X's in the following routine with your selected increment value:

```
LET INC=XXX
```

Now store the starting line and increment values in your renumber routine by entering these three lines and running them in immediate mode:

```
POKE 16508,INT (FNUM/256)
POKE 16507,FNUM-256*PEEK 16508
POKE 16417,INC
```

With this data in place, you can now renumber any program by executing the command RAND USR XXXXXX with the starting address you got earlier from the loader routine in place of the X's. When the display returns, the program will have the new line numbers. If it contains any GOTO or GOSUB commands, you will need to edit them to make them agree with the new numbering.

The complete machine language listing follows for those readers who wish to use it. Each line describes one machine language command. The first column gives the hexadecimal contents of the byte or bytes that make up the command. The second column shows the standard name (*mnemonic*) for the command, and the last column is a comment explaining the command's function in the subroutine.

## Line Renumbering Routine

| Machine Code | Instruction | Comment |
| --- | --- | --- |
| 11 7D 40 | LD DE,407D | Get address of first BASIC line |
| 1A | LOOP LD A,(DE) | Store first byte of line number in A |
| FE76 | CP 76 | ENTER code means end of program |
| C8 | RET Z | Return to caller—all done |
| 2A 7B 40 | LD HL,(407B) | Get new value of line number |
| 7C | LD A,H | Store it in the program line |
| 12 | LD (DE),A | High byte first |
| 13 | INC DE | |
| 7D | LD A,L | |
| 12 | LD (DE),A | Low byte of number in next location |
| 1B | DEC DE | Restore starting address of line |
| 3A 21 40 | LD A,(4021) | Get line number increment |
| 4F | LD C,A | Store it in BC |
| 06 00 | LD B,00 | |

| Machine Code | Instruction | Comment |
|---|---|---|
| 09 | ADD HL,BC | Add increment to line number |
| 22 7B 40 | LD (407B),HL | Store line number for next line |
| EB | EX DE,HL | Put address of this line into HL |
| CD F2 09 | CALL NEXT_LINE | Get address of next line into DE |
| 18 E3 | JR LOOP | Process the next line |

## PROGRAM MERGING

The next routines in this section require at least 2K of read/write memory. Therefore, they will not run on a ZX81 without the 16K memory pack.

These machine language routines merge two BASIC programs into a single program. You can keep frequently used subroutines on cassette and merge them with other programs as you need them. Because these merge routines are in machine language, they will remain in memory above RAM-TOP, allowing you to enter or load different BASIC programs.

Once again, use the RAMTOP loader program from Appendix F to load each of the two merge routines. Include the hexadecimal code for each machine language routine in a string variable. As before, the code must appear exactly as shown below, including a single space between each pair of digits and a space after the last pair. There are two routines. To load the first one, enter the following line:

```
  20 LET H$="2A 0C 40 11 7B 40 A
F ED 52 7C A7 20 07 7D FE 14 30
02 2E 14 22 7B 40 AF CD 23 0F 2A
 04 40 ED 72 44 4D 03 39 ED 5B 7
B 40 ED 52 EB 19 ED B8 ED 4B 7B
40 2A 04 40 ED 42 22 04 40 2A 02
 40 ED 42 22 02 40 ED 62 39 ED 4
2 F9 ED 5B 04 40 21 0C 40 ED A0
ED A0 21 7D 40 ED B0 C9 "
```

Run the loader routine and write down the USR address. Now replace line 20 with the code of the second merge routine:

```
  20 LET H$="2A 04 40 5E 23 56 2
3 E5 21 7D 40 EB AF ED 52 E5 44
4D 2A 0C 40 E5 2B CD 9E 09 D1 C1
 E1 ED B0 C9 "
```

Finally, run the loader again and write down the second USR address.

The two routines will remain in read/write memory until you disconnect power. If you have enough read/write memory, you can keep the renumber and the two merge routines in memory at all times in case you need to use them.

To merge two programs, enter or load the BASIC program with larger line numbers and run the first merge routine by entering RAND USR XXXXX, using the first number you wrote down in place of the X's. The routine moves RAMTOP down and copies the program into the reserved space. Now execute NEW and load or enter the BASIC program with smaller line numbers. Run the second merge routine using RAND USR and the second number. The computer will copy the previous BASIC program from the reserved space and merge it with the current BASIC program. It will also execute the previous program before returning to the ▦ cursor. (To prevent this, insert a STOP command at the beginning of the higher-numbered program before running the first merge routine.)

The complete machine language listing for these routines follows.

## First Merge Routine

| Machine Code | Instruction | Comment |
|---|---|---|
| | | **Part 1: Find length of program** |
| 2A 0C 40 | LD HL,(D_FILE) | Get next address after program area |
| 11 7B 40 | LD DE,407B | Get address of start of program − 2 |
| AF | XOR A | Clear carry flag |
| ED 52 | SBC HL,DE | Calculate length of program + 2 |
| 7C | LD A,H | Must not try to reserve < 20 bytes |
| A7 | AND A | |
| 20 07 | JR NZ,LEN_OK | |
| 7D | LD A,L | |
| FE 14 | CP 14 | |
| 30 02 | JR NC,LEN_OK | |
| 2E 14 | LD L,14 | If length < 20, reserve 20 bytes |
| 22 7B 40 | LEN_OK LD (407B),HL | Store length |
| | | **Part 2: Move RAMTOP down** |
| AF | XOR A | Clear carry flag |
| CD 23 0F | CALL FAST_MODE | Go into fast mode |
| 2A 04 40 | LD HL,(RAMTOP) | Get value of RAMTOP |
| ED 72 | SBC HL,SP | Subtract SP to get length of stacks |
| 44 | LD B,H | Transfer length to BC |
| 4D | LD C,L | |
| 03 | INC BC | Add one to length |

| Machine Code | Instruction | Comment |
|---|---|---|
| 39 | ADD HL,SP | Restore value of RAMTOP to HL |
| ED 5B 7B 40 | LD DE,(407B) | Get size of space to reserve |
| ED 52 | SBC HL,DE | Subtract to get new value of RAMTOP |
| EB | EX DE,HL | Store new RAMTOP value in DE |
| 19 | ADD HL,DE | Restore old RAMTOP value to HL |
| ED B8 | LDDR | Move stack down to new RAMTOP |
| ED 4B 7B 40 | LD BC,(407B) | Get size of reserved space |
| 2A 04 40 | LD HL,(RAMTOP) | Get old value of RAMTOP |
| ED 42 | SBC HL,BC | Calculate new value of RAMTOP |
| 22 04 40 | LD (RAMTOP),HL | Store new value |
| 2A 02 40 | LD HL,(ERR_SP) | Get old value of ERR_SP |
| ED 42 | SBC HL,BC | Calculate new value of ERR_SP |
| 22 02 40 | LD (ERR_SP),HL | Store new value |
| ED 62 | SBC HL,HL | Clear HL |
| 39 | ADD HL,SP | Load stack pointer into HL |
| ED 42 | SBC HL,BC | Calculate new value of stack pointer |
| F9 | LD SP,HL | Store new value |

**Part 3: Copy program above RAMTOP**

| Machine Code | Instruction | Comment |
|---|---|---|
| ED 5B 04 40 | LD DE,(RAMTOP) | Get new value of RAMTOP |
| 21 0C 40 | LD HL,D_FILE | Get address of D_FILE system variable |
| ED A0 | LDI | Copy D_FILE into reserved space |
| ED A0 | LDI | |
| 21 7D 40 | LD HL,407D | Get starting address of program |
| ED B0 | LDIR | Copy program into reserved space |
| C9 | RET | Return to BASIC |

## Second Merge Routine

| Machine Code | Instruction | Comment |
|---|---|---|
| 2A 04 40 | LD HL,(RAMTOP) | Get new value of RAMTOP |
| 5E | LD E,(HL) | Copy old D_FILE from reserved space |
| 23 | INC HL | |
| 56 | LD D,(HL) | |
| 23 | INC HL | HL now contains address of old program |
| E5 | PUSH HL | Store address on stack |
| 21 7D 40 | LD HL,407D | Get address of program storage area |
| EB | EX DE,HL | Prepare to subtract |
| AF | XOR A | Clear carry |
| ED 52 | SBC HL,DE | Calculate length of old program |
| E5 | PUSH HL | Store length on stack |
| 44 | LD B,H | Transfer length to BC |
| 4D | LD C,L | |

| Machine Code | Instruction | Comment |
|---|---|---|
| 2A 0C 40 | LD HL,(D_FILE) | Get address of end of current program |
| E5 | PUSH HL | Store end address on stack |
| 2B | DEC HL | Point to actual last byte |
| CD 9E 09 | CALL 099E | Make space for old program at end of new program |
| D1 | POP DE | Get starting address of space |
| C1 | POP BC | Get length of old program |
| E1 | POP HL | Get starting address of old program |
| ED B0 | LDIR | Copy old program into space |
| C9 | RET | Return to BASIC |

Floating Point Format

# Appendix
# H

Most of the time, when you are using the TS1000 or ZX81 computer, the way that numbers are stored in memory is of no importance. This is because you can assign values to variables and use them simply by naming the variable. Or if you need to use a constant, simply enter the value and away you go. If you are dealing with the computer on a more detailed level, however, you may need to understand how numbers are stored within BASIC statements.

The way that numbers are stored in the TS1000 and ZX81 computers is called *floating point format.*

Floating point format is similar to scientific notation except that it uses the binary number system (base 2) instead of the decimal number system (base 10). It takes five bytes to store numbers in ZX81/TS1000 floating point format. These five bytes are located in the BASIC program after the character code bytes for the value.

The first of the five bytes contains the binary exponent, and the next four bytes contain the binary mantissa. The mantissa is the binary representation of the number without regard for the binary point, beginning with the first nonzero digit and padded with zeros on the right. The first binary digit of the mantissa is changed to zero for positive numbers to distinguish them from negative numbers. For most numbers, the exponent is determined by adding 128 to the number of binary digits on the left of the binary point. For numbers between −1 and 1 (excluding zero), the exponent is 128 minus the number of zeros between the binary point and the first nonzero digit to its right. The number zero is a special case, with all five of its bytes being zero.

Table H-1 gives some examples of floating point format.

**Table H-1. Examples of Floating Point Format**

| Decimal Number | Five-Byte Floating Point Representation | | | | |
|---|---|---|---|---|---|
| −5 | 131 | 160 | 0 | 0 | 0 |
| −4 | 131 | 128 | 0 | 0 | 0 |
| −3 | 130 | 192 | 0 | 0 | 0 |
| −2 | 130 | 128 | 0 | 0 | 0 |
| −1 | 129 | 128 | 0 | 0 | 0 |
| −1/2 | 128 | 128 | 0 | 0 | 0 |
| −1/4 | 127 | 128 | 0 | 0 | 0 |
| −1/8 | 126 | 128 | 0 | 0 | 0 |
| 0 | 0 | 0 | 0 | 0 | 0 |
| 1/8 | 126 | 0 | 0 | 0 | 0 |
| 1/4 | 127 | 0 | 0 | 0 | 0 |
| 1/2 | 128 | 0 | 0 | 0 | 0 |
| 1 | 129 | 0 | 0 | 0 | 0 |
| 2 | 130 | 0 | 0 | 0 | 0 |
| 3 | 130 | 64 | 0 | 0 | 0 |
| 4 | 131 | 0 | 0 | 0 | 0 |
| 5 | 131 | 32 | 0 | 0 | 0 |

Storage Formats for BASIC Variables

# Appendix
# I

The master program of the TS1000 and ZX81 stores the BASIC variables in read/write memory. The BASIC commands LET and INPUT create variables in this area. Machine language programmers can use the BASIC variables to communicate with a BASIC program, and the BASIC program itself may even PEEK and POKE into the variable storage area for special purposes.

The system variable VARS gives the address of the beginning of the BASIC variables area, and the system variable E_LINE gives the address of the next byte after the end of this area (see Appendix E).

Within the BASIC variables area, each type of variable has its own format. For example, each single variable or array begins with the character codes for the variable's name. The three highest bits of the first character contain a code that identifies the type of variable. Some types of variables have special information right after the variable name. For example, an array variable has information about its dimensions, while a string variable has two bytes containing its length followed by its value. For strings, the value is the character codes of the characters in the string. As discussed in Appendix H, numeric variables occupy five bytes in a special format.

Figures I-1 through I-6 show the storage format for each kind of BASIC variable. They are adapted from the *Timex User Manual* by Steven Vickers (Timex Corporation, 1982), pp. 129-31.

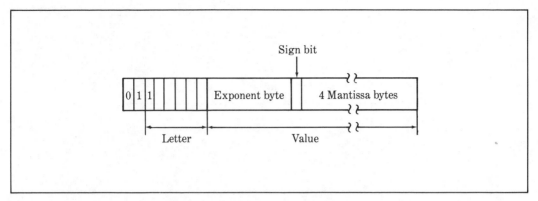

**Figure I-1. Numeric variable with a one-letter name**

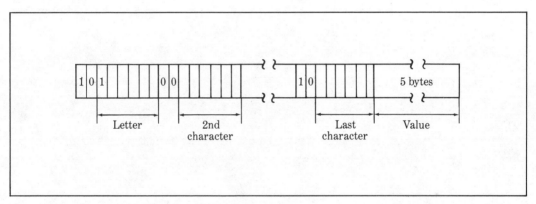

**Figure I-2. Numeric variable with a longer name**

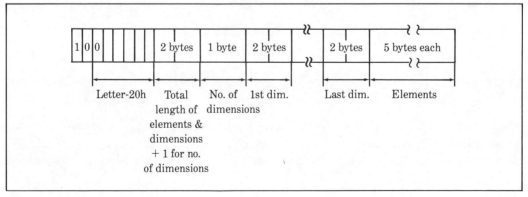

**Figure I-3. Numeric array**

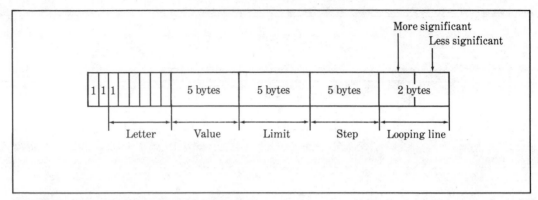

**Figure I-4. FOR-NEXT loop control variable**

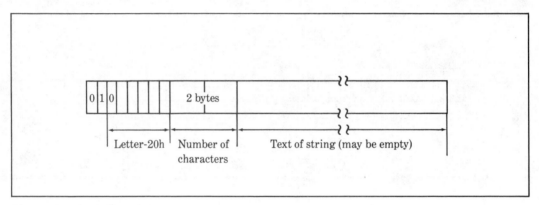

**Figure I-5. String variable**

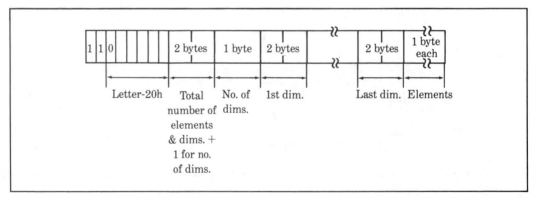

**Figure I-6. String array**

# Hexadecimal Conversion Tables

# Appendix

# J

In the summary of instructions built into the Z80 microprocessor, given in Appendix K, the numeric values of the instructions are given in hexadecimal notation. Descriptions of the contents of computer memory locations often use hexadecimal notation as well. This number system, based on 16, relates more directly to the settings of the individual bits than does decimal notation, and it conveniently represents each byte with only two digits.

The familiar decimal system uses powers of 10. Each digit represents 1's, 10's, 100's, and so on, depending on its position in the number. The hexadecimal system uses powers of 16 instead. Each hexadecimal digit represents 1's, 16's, 256's, and so on (powers of 16). In addition to the digits 0-9, hexadecimal notation uses the single digits A, B, C, D, E, and F to represent the (decimal) numbers 10, 11, 12, 13, 14, and 15.

This appendix contains the following tables:

· Hexadecimal-binary numbers (Table J-1)
· Hexadecimal-decimal integers (Table J-2)
· Powers of 2 (Table J-3)
· Useful mathematical constants in decimal and hexadecimal (Table J-4)
· Powers of 16 (Table J-5)
· Powers of 10 (Table J-6).

Use Table J-1 to make conversions between hexadecimal numbers in the range 00-OFF and binary numbers in the range 0000-1111.

Convert larger binary numbers to hexadecimal numbers by converting four binary digits at a time, working from right to left. If there are fewer than four binary digits in the leftmost group, add leading zeros. Here is an example (the subscripts indicate which number system is being used):

$$100101_2 = \underbrace{\underbrace{0010}_{2}\underbrace{0101}_{5}}_{25_{16}}{}_2$$

Convert hexadecimal numbers larger than 0F to binary one digit at a time. Here is an example:

$$\underbrace{\underbrace{0110}_{3}\quad\underbrace{0111}_{7}}_{01100111_2} \quad 37_{16}$$

### Table J-1. Hexadecimal-Binary Conversion

| Hexadecimal | Binary | Hexadecimal | Binary |
|:-----------:|:------:|:-----------:|:------:|
| 00 | 0000 | 08 | 1000 |
| 01 | 0001 | 09 | 1001 |
| 02 | 0010 | 0A | 1010 |
| 03 | 0011 | 0B | 1011 |
| 04 | 0100 | 0C | 1100 |
| 05 | 0101 | 0D | 1101 |
| 06 | 0110 | 0E | 1110 |
| 07 | 0111 | 0F | 1111 |

## Table J-2. Hexadecimal-Decimal Integer Conversion

The table below provides for direct conversions between hexadecimal integers in the range 0−FFF and decimal integers in the range 0−4095. For conversion of larger integers, the table values may be added to the following figures:

| Hexadecimal | Decimal | Hexadecimal | Decimal |
|---|---|---|---|
| 01 000 | 4 096 | 20 000 | 131 072 |
| 02 000 | 8 192 | 30 000 | 196 608 |
| 03 000 | 12 288 | 40 000 | 262 144 |
| 04 000 | 16 384 | 50 000 | 327 680 |
| 05 000 | 20 480 | 60 000 | 393 216 |
| 06 000 | 24 576 | 70 000 | 458 752 |
| 07 000 | 28 672 | 80 000 | 524 288 |
| 08 000 | 32 768 | 90 000 | 589 824 |
| 09 000 | 36 864 | A0 000 | 655 360 |
| 0A 000 | 40 960 | B0 000 | 720 896 |
| 0B 000 | 45 056 | C0 000 | 786 432 |
| 0C 000 | 49 152 | D0 000 | 851 968 |
| 0D 000 | 53 248 | E0 000 | 917 504 |
| 0E 000 | 57 344 | F0 000 | 983 040 |
| 0F 000 | 61 440 | 100 000 | 1 048 576 |
| 10 000 | 65 536 | 200 000 | 2 097 152 |
| 11 000 | 69 632 | 300 000 | 3 145 728 |
| 12 000 | 73 728 | 400 000 | 4 194 304 |
| 13 000 | 77 824 | 500 000 | 5 242 880 |
| 14 000 | 81 920 | 600 000 | 6 291 456 |
| 15 000 | 86 016 | 700 000 | 7 340 032 |
| 16 000 | 90 112 | 800 000 | 8 388 608 |
| 17 000 | 94 208 | 900 000 | 9 437 184 |
| 18 000 | 98 304 | A00 000 | 10 485 760 |
| 19 000 | 102 400 | B00 000 | 11 534 336 |
| 1A 000 | 106 496 | C00 000 | 12 582 912 |
| 1B 000 | 110 592 | D00 000 | 13 631 488 |
| 1C 000 | 114 688 | E00 000 | 14 680 064 |
| 1D 000 | 118 784 | F00 000 | 15 728 640 |
| 1E 000 | 122 880 | 1 000 000 | 16 777 216 |
| 1F 000 | 126 976 | 2 000 000 | 33 554 432 |

Hexadecimal fractions may be converted to decimal fractions as follows:

1. Express the hexadecimal fraction as an integer times $16^{-n}$, where n is the number of significant hexadecimal places to the right of the hexadecimal point.

$$0.\,CA9BF3_{16} = CA9\,BF3_{16} \times 16^{-6}$$

2. Find the decimal equivalent of the hexadecimal integer

$$CA9\,BF3_{16} = 13\,278\,195_{10}$$

3. Multiply the decimal equivalent by $16^{-n}$

$$\begin{array}{r} 13\,278\,195 \\ \times\ 596\,046\,448 \times 10^{-16} \\ \hline 0.791\,442\,096_{10} \end{array}$$

Decimal fractions may be converted to hexadecimal fractions by successively multiplying the decimal fraction by $16_{10}$. After each multiplication, the integer portion is removed to form a hexadecimal fraction by building to the right of the hexadecimal point. However, since decimal arithmetic is used in this conversion, the integer portion of each product must be converted to hexadecimal numbers.

Example: Convert $0.895_{10}$ to its hexadecimal equivalent

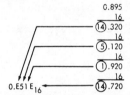

| | 0 | 1 | 2 | 3 | 4 | 5 | 6 | 7 | 8 | 9 | A | B | C | D | E | F |
|---|---|---|---|---|---|---|---|---|---|---|---|---|---|---|---|---|
| 00 | 0000 | 0001 | 0002 | 0003 | 0004 | 0005 | 0006 | 0007 | 0008 | 0009 | 0010 | 0011 | 0012 | 0013 | 0014 | 0015 |
| 01 | 0016 | 0017 | 0018 | 0019 | 0020 | 0021 | 0022 | 0023 | 0024 | 0025 | 0026 | 0027 | 0028 | 0029 | 0030 | 0031 |
| 02 | 0032 | 0033 | 0034 | 0035 | 0036 | 0037 | 0038 | 0039 | 0040 | 0041 | 0042 | 0043 | 0044 | 0045 | 0046 | 0047 |
| 03 | 0048 | 0049 | 0050 | 0051 | 0052 | 0053 | 0054 | 0055 | 0056 | 0057 | 0058 | 0059 | 0060 | 0061 | 0062 | 0063 |
| 04 | 0064 | 0065 | 0066 | 0067 | 0068 | 0069 | 0070 | 0071 | 0072 | 0073 | 0074 | 0075 | 0076 | 0077 | 0078 | 0079 |
| 05 | 0080 | 0081 | 0082 | 0083 | 0084 | 0085 | 0086 | 0087 | 0088 | 0089 | 0090 | 0091 | 0092 | 0093 | 0094 | 0095 |
| 06 | 0096 | 0097 | 0098 | 0099 | 0100 | 0101 | 0102 | 0103 | 0104 | 0105 | 0106 | 0107 | 0108 | 0109 | 0110 | 0111 |
| 07 | 0112 | 0113 | 0114 | 0115 | 0116 | 0117 | 0118 | 0119 | 0120 | 0121 | 0122 | 0123 | 0124 | 0125 | 0126 | 0127 |
| 08 | 0128 | 0129 | 0130 | 0131 | 0132 | 0133 | 0134 | 0135 | 0136 | 0137 | 0138 | 0139 | 0140 | 0141 | 0142 | 0143 |
| 09 | 0144 | 0145 | 0146 | 0147 | 0148 | 0149 | 0150 | 0151 | 0152 | 0153 | 0154 | 0155 | 0156 | 0157 | 0158 | 0159 |
| 0A | 0160 | 0161 | 0162 | 0163 | 0164 | 0165 | 0166 | 0167 | 0168 | 0169 | 0170 | 0171 | 0172 | 0173 | 0174 | 0175 |
| 0B | 0176 | 0177 | 0178 | 0179 | 0180 | 0181 | 0182 | 0183 | 0184 | 0185 | 0186 | 0187 | 0188 | 0189 | 0190 | 0191 |
| 0C | 0192 | 0193 | 0194 | 0195 | 0196 | 0197 | 0198 | 0199 | 0200 | 0201 | 0202 | 0203 | 0204 | 0205 | 0206 | 0207 |
| 0D | 0208 | 0209 | 0210 | 0211 | 0212 | 0213 | 0214 | 0215 | 0216 | 0217 | 0218 | 0219 | 0220 | 0221 | 0222 | 0223 |
| 0E | 0224 | 0225 | 0226 | 0227 | 0228 | 0229 | 0230 | 0231 | 0232 | 0233 | 0234 | 0235 | 0236 | 0237 | 0238 | 0239 |
| 0F | 0240 | 0241 | 0242 | 0243 | 0244 | 0245 | 0246 | 0247 | 0248 | 0249 | 0250 | 0251 | 0252 | 0253 | 0254 | 0255 |

## Table J-2. (Continued)

|    | 0 | 1 | 2 | 3 | 4 | 5 | 6 | 7 | 8 | 9 | A | B | C | D | E | F |
|----|------|------|------|------|------|------|------|------|------|------|------|------|------|------|------|------|
| 10 | 0256 | 0257 | 0258 | 0259 | 0260 | 0261 | 0262 | 0263 | 0264 | 0265 | 0266 | 0267 | 0268 | 0269 | 0270 | 0271 |
| 11 | 0272 | 0273 | 0274 | 0275 | 0276 | 0277 | 0278 | 0279 | 0280 | 0281 | 0282 | 0283 | 0284 | 0285 | 0286 | 0287 |
| 12 | 0288 | 0289 | 0290 | 0291 | 0292 | 0293 | 0294 | 0295 | 0296 | 0297 | 0298 | 0299 | 0300 | 0301 | 0302 | 0303 |
| 13 | 0304 | 0305 | 0306 | 0307 | 0308 | 0309 | 0310 | 0311 | 0312 | 0313 | 0314 | 0315 | 0316 | 0317 | 0318 | 0319 |
| 14 | 0320 | 0321 | 0322 | 0323 | 0324 | 0325 | 0326 | 0327 | 0328 | 0329 | 0330 | 0331 | 0332 | 0333 | 0334 | 0335 |
| 15 | 0336 | 0337 | 0338 | 0339 | 0340 | 0341 | 0342 | 0343 | 0344 | 0345 | 0346 | 0347 | 0348 | 0349 | 0350 | 0351 |
| 16 | 0352 | 0353 | 0354 | 0355 | 0356 | 0357 | 0358 | 0359 | 0360 | 0361 | 0362 | 0363 | 0364 | 0365 | 0366 | 0367 |
| 17 | 0368 | 0369 | 0370 | 0371 | 0372 | 0373 | 0374 | 0375 | 0376 | 0377 | 0378 | 0379 | 0380 | 0381 | 0382 | 0383 |
| 18 | 0384 | 0385 | 0386 | 0387 | 0388 | 0389 | 0390 | 0391 | 0392 | 0393 | 0394 | 0395 | 0396 | 0397 | 0398 | 0399 |
| 19 | 0400 | 0401 | 0402 | 0403 | 0404 | 0405 | 0406 | 0407 | 0408 | 0409 | 0410 | 0411 | 0412 | 0413 | 0414 | 0415 |
| 1A | 0416 | 0417 | 0418 | 0419 | 0420 | 0421 | 0422 | 0423 | 0424 | 0425 | 0426 | 0427 | 0428 | 0429 | 0430 | 0431 |
| 1B | 0432 | 0433 | 0434 | 0435 | 0436 | 0437 | 0438 | 0439 | 0440 | 0441 | 0442 | 0443 | 0444 | 0445 | 0446 | 0447 |
| 1C | 0448 | 0449 | 0450 | 0451 | 0452 | 0453 | 0454 | 0455 | 0456 | 0457 | 0458 | 0459 | 0460 | 0461 | 0462 | 0463 |
| 1D | 0464 | 0465 | 0466 | 0467 | 0468 | 0469 | 0470 | 0471 | 0472 | 0473 | 0474 | 0475 | 0476 | 0477 | 0478 | 0479 |
| 1E | 0480 | 0481 | 0482 | 0483 | 0484 | 0485 | 0486 | 0487 | 0488 | 0489 | 0490 | 0491 | 0492 | 0493 | 0494 | 0495 |
| 1F | 0496 | 0497 | 0498 | 0499 | 0500 | 0501 | 0502 | 0503 | 0504 | 0505 | 0506 | 0507 | 0508 | 0509 | 0510 | 0511 |
| 20 | 0512 | 0513 | 0514 | 0515 | 0516 | 0517 | 0518 | 0519 | 0520 | 0521 | 0522 | 0523 | 0524 | 0525 | 0526 | 0527 |
| 21 | 0528 | 0529 | 0530 | 0531 | 0532 | 0533 | 0534 | 0535 | 0536 | 0537 | 0538 | 0539 | 0540 | 0541 | 0542 | 0543 |
| 22 | 0544 | 0545 | 0546 | 0547 | 0548 | 0549 | 0550 | 0551 | 0552 | 0553 | 0554 | 0555 | 0556 | 0557 | 0558 | 0559 |
| 23 | 0560 | 0561 | 0562 | 0563 | 0564 | 0565 | 0566 | 0567 | 0568 | 0569 | 0570 | 0571 | 0572 | 0573 | 0574 | 0575 |
| 24 | 0576 | 0577 | 0578 | 0579 | 0580 | 0581 | 0582 | 0583 | 0584 | 0585 | 0586 | 0587 | 0588 | 0589 | 0590 | 0591 |
| 25 | 0592 | 0593 | 0594 | 0595 | 0596 | 0597 | 0598 | 0599 | 0600 | 0601 | 0602 | 0603 | 0604 | 0605 | 0606 | 0607 |
| 26 | 0608 | 0609 | 0610 | 0611 | 0612 | 0613 | 0614 | 0615 | 0616 | 0617 | 0618 | 0619 | 0620 | 0621 | 0622 | 0623 |
| 27 | 0624 | 0625 | 0626 | 0627 | 0628 | 0629 | 0630 | 0631 | 0632 | 0633 | 0634 | 0635 | 0636 | 0637 | 0638 | 0639 |
| 28 | 0640 | 0641 | 0642 | 0643 | 0644 | 0645 | 0646 | 0647 | 0648 | 0649 | 0650 | 0651 | 0652 | 0653 | 0654 | 0655 |
| 29 | 0656 | 0657 | 0658 | 0659 | 0660 | 0661 | 0662 | 0663 | 0664 | 0665 | 0666 | 0667 | 0668 | 0669 | 0670 | 0671 |
| 2A | 0672 | 0673 | 0674 | 0675 | 0676 | 0677 | 0678 | 0679 | 0680 | 0681 | 0682 | 0683 | 0684 | 0685 | 0686 | 0687 |
| 2B | 0688 | 0689 | 0690 | 0691 | 0692 | 0693 | 0694 | 0695 | 0696 | 0697 | 0698 | 0699 | 0700 | 0701 | 0702 | 0703 |
| 2C | 0704 | 0705 | 0706 | 0707 | 0708 | 0709 | 0710 | 0711 | 0712 | 0713 | 0714 | 0715 | 0716 | 0717 | 0718 | 0719 |
| 2D | 0720 | 0721 | 0722 | 0723 | 0724 | 0725 | 0726 | 0727 | 0728 | 0729 | 0730 | 0731 | 0732 | 0733 | 0734 | 0735 |
| 2E | 0736 | 0737 | 0738 | 0739 | 0740 | 0741 | 0742 | 0743 | 0744 | 0745 | 0746 | 0747 | 0748 | 0749 | 0750 | 0751 |
| 2F | 0752 | 0753 | 0754 | 0755 | 0756 | 0757 | 0758 | 0759 | 0760 | 0761 | 0762 | 0763 | 0764 | 0765 | 0766 | 0767 |
| 30 | 0768 | 0769 | 0770 | 0771 | 0772 | 0773 | 0774 | 0775 | 0776 | 0777 | 0778 | 0779 | 0780 | 0781 | 0782 | 0783 |
| 31 | 0784 | 0785 | 0786 | 0787 | 0788 | 0789 | 0790 | 0791 | 0792 | 0793 | 0794 | 0795 | 0796 | 0797 | 0798 | 0799 |
| 32 | 0800 | 0801 | 0802 | 0803 | 0804 | 0805 | 0806 | 0807 | 0808 | 0809 | 0810 | 0811 | 0812 | 0813 | 0814 | 0815 |
| 33 | 0816 | 0817 | 0818 | 0819 | 0820 | 0821 | 0822 | 0823 | 0824 | 0825 | 0826 | 0827 | 0828 | 0829 | 0830 | 0831 |
| 34 | 0832 | 0833 | 0834 | 0835 | 0836 | 0837 | 0838 | 0839 | 0840 | 0841 | 0842 | 0843 | 0844 | 0845 | 0846 | 0847 |
| 35 | 0848 | 0849 | 0850 | 0851 | 0852 | 0853 | 0854 | 0855 | 0856 | 0857 | 0858 | 0859 | 0860 | 0861 | 0862 | 0863 |
| 36 | 0864 | 0865 | 0866 | 0867 | 0868 | 0869 | 0870 | 0871 | 0872 | 0873 | 0874 | 0875 | 0876 | 0877 | 0878 | 0879 |
| 37 | 0880 | 0881 | 0882 | 0883 | 0884 | 0885 | 0886 | 0887 | 0888 | 0889 | 0890 | 0891 | 0892 | 0893 | 0894 | 0895 |
| 38 | 0896 | 0897 | 0898 | 0899 | 0900 | 0901 | 0902 | 0903 | 0904 | 0905 | 0906 | 0907 | 0908 | 0909 | 0910 | 0911 |
| 39 | 0912 | 0913 | 0914 | 0915 | 0916 | 0917 | 0918 | 0919 | 0920 | 0921 | 0922 | 0923 | 0924 | 0925 | 0926 | 0927 |
| 3A | 0928 | 0929 | 0930 | 0931 | 0932 | 0933 | 0934 | 0935 | 0936 | 0937 | 0938 | 0939 | 0940 | 0941 | 0942 | 0943 |
| 3B | 0944 | 0945 | 0946 | 0947 | 0948 | 0949 | 0950 | 0951 | 0952 | 0953 | 0954 | 0955 | 0956 | 0957 | 0958 | 0959 |
| 3C | 0960 | 0961 | 0962 | 0963 | 0964 | 0965 | 0966 | 0967 | 0968 | 0969 | 0970 | 0971 | 0972 | 0973 | 0974 | 0975 |
| 3D | 0976 | 0977 | 0978 | 0979 | 0980 | 0981 | 0982 | 0983 | 0984 | 0985 | 0986 | 0987 | 0988 | 0989 | 0990 | 0991 |
| 3E | 0992 | 0993 | 0994 | 0995 | 0996 | 0997 | 0998 | 0999 | 1000 | 1001 | 1002 | 1003 | 1004 | 1005 | 1006 | 1007 |
| 3F | 1008 | 1009 | 1010 | 1011 | 1012 | 1013 | 1014 | 1015 | 1016 | 1017 | 1018 | 1019 | 1020 | 1021 | 1022 | 1023 |

## Table J-2. (Continued)

|     | 0 | 1 | 2 | 3 | 4 | 5 | 6 | 7 | 8 | 9 | A | B | C | D | E | F |
|-----|---|---|---|---|---|---|---|---|---|---|---|---|---|---|---|---|
| 40 | 1024 | 1025 | 1026 | 1027 | 1028 | 1029 | 1030 | 1031 | 1032 | 1033 | 1034 | 1035 | 1036 | 1037 | 1038 | 1039 |
| 41 | 1040 | 1041 | 1042 | 1043 | 1044 | 1045 | 1046 | 1047 | 1048 | 1049 | 1050 | 1051 | 1052 | 1053 | 1054 | 1055 |
| 42 | 1056 | 1057 | 1058 | 1059 | 1060 | 1061 | 1062 | 1063 | 1064 | 1065 | 1066 | 1067 | 1068 | 1069 | 1070 | 1071 |
| 43 | 1072 | 1073 | 1074 | 1075 | 1076 | 1077 | 1078 | 1079 | 1080 | 1081 | 1082 | 1083 | 1084 | 1085 | 1086 | 1087 |
| 44 | 1088 | 1089 | 1090 | 1091 | 1092 | 1093 | 1094 | 1095 | 1096 | 1097 | 1098 | 1099 | 1100 | 1101 | 1102 | 1103 |
| 45 | 1104 | 1105 | 1106 | 1107 | 1108 | 1109 | 1110 | 1111 | 1112 | 1113 | 1114 | 1115 | 1116 | 1117 | 1118 | 1119 |
| 46 | 1120 | 1121 | 1122 | 1123 | 1124 | 1125 | 1126 | 1127 | 1128 | 1129 | 1130 | 1131 | 1132 | 1133 | 1134 | 1135 |
| 47 | 1136 | 1137 | 1138 | 1139 | 1140 | 1141 | 1142 | 1143 | 1144 | 1145 | 1146 | 1147 | 1148 | 1149 | 1150 | 1151 |
| 48 | 1152 | 1153 | 1154 | 1155 | 1156 | 1157 | 1158 | 1159 | 1160 | 1161 | 1162 | 1163 | 1164 | 1165 | 1166 | 1167 |
| 49 | 1168 | 1169 | 1170 | 1171 | 1172 | 1173 | 1174 | 1175 | 1176 | 1177 | 1178 | 1179 | 1180 | 1181 | 1182 | 1183 |
| 4A | 1184 | 1185 | 1186 | 1187 | 1188 | 1189 | 1190 | 1191 | 1192 | 1193 | 1194 | 1195 | 1196 | 1197 | 1198 | 1199 |
| 4B | 1200 | 1201 | 1202 | 1203 | 1204 | 1205 | 1206 | 1207 | 1208 | 1209 | 1210 | 1211 | 1212 | 1213 | 1214 | 1215 |
| 4C | 1216 | 1217 | 1218 | 1219 | 1220 | 1221 | 1222 | 1223 | 1224 | 1225 | 1226 | 1227 | 1228 | 1229 | 1230 | 1231 |
| 4D | 1232 | 1233 | 1234 | 1235 | 1236 | 1237 | 1238 | 1239 | 1240 | 1241 | 1242 | 1243 | 1244 | 1245 | 1246 | 1247 |
| 4E | 1248 | 1249 | 1250 | 1251 | 1252 | 1253 | 1254 | 1255 | 1256 | 1257 | 1258 | 1259 | 1260 | 1261 | 1262 | 1263 |
| 4F | 1264 | 1265 | 1266 | 1267 | 1268 | 1269 | 1270 | 1271 | 1272 | 1273 | 1274 | 1275 | 1276 | 1277 | 1278 | 1279 |
| 50 | 1280 | 1281 | 1282 | 1283 | 1284 | 1285 | 1286 | 1287 | 1288 | 1289 | 1290 | 1291 | 1292 | 1293 | 1294 | 1295 |
| 51 | 1296 | 1297 | 1298 | 1299 | 1300 | 1301 | 1302 | 1303 | 1304 | 1305 | 1306 | 1307 | 1308 | 1309 | 1310 | 1311 |
| 52 | 1312 | 1313 | 1314 | 1315 | 1316 | 1317 | 1318 | 1319 | 1320 | 1321 | 1322 | 1323 | 1324 | 1325 | 1326 | 1327 |
| 53 | 1328 | 1329 | 1330 | 1331 | 1332 | 1333 | 1334 | 1335 | 1336 | 1337 | 1338 | 1339 | 1340 | 1341 | 1342 | 1343 |
| 54 | 1344 | 1345 | 1346 | 1347 | 1348 | 1349 | 1350 | 1351 | 1352 | 1353 | 1354 | 1355 | 1356 | 1357 | 1358 | 1359 |
| 55 | 1360 | 1361 | 1362 | 1363 | 1364 | 1365 | 1366 | 1367 | 1368 | 1369 | 1370 | 1371 | 1372 | 1373 | 1374 | 1375 |
| 56 | 1376 | 1377 | 1378 | 1379 | 1380 | 1381 | 1382 | 1383 | 1384 | 1385 | 1386 | 1387 | 1388 | 1389 | 1390 | 1391 |
| 57 | 1392 | 1393 | 1394 | 1395 | 1396 | 1397 | 1398 | 1399 | 1400 | 1401 | 1402 | 1403 | 1404 | 1405 | 1406 | 1407 |
| 58 | 1408 | 1409 | 1410 | 1411 | 1412 | 1413 | 1414 | 1415 | 1416 | 1417 | 1418 | 1419 | 1420 | 1421 | 1422 | 1423 |
| 59 | 1424 | 1425 | 1426 | 1427 | 1428 | 1429 | 1430 | 1431 | 1432 | 1433 | 1434 | 1435 | 1436 | 1437 | 1438 | 1439 |
| 5A | 1440 | 1441 | 1442 | 1443 | 1444 | 1445 | 1446 | 1447 | 1448 | 1449 | 1450 | 1451 | 1452 | 1453 | 1454 | 1455 |
| 5B | 1456 | 1457 | 1458 | 1459 | 1460 | 1461 | 1462 | 1463 | 1464 | 1465 | 1466 | 1467 | 1468 | 1469 | 1470 | 1471 |
| 5C | 1472 | 1473 | 1474 | 1475 | 1476 | 1477 | 1478 | 1479 | 1480 | 1481 | 1482 | 1483 | 1484 | 1485 | 1486 | 1487 |
| 5D | 1488 | 1489 | 1490 | 1491 | 1492 | 1493 | 1494 | 1495 | 1496 | 1497 | 1498 | 1499 | 1500 | 1501 | 1502 | 1503 |
| 5E | 1504 | 1505 | 1506 | 1507 | 1508 | 1509 | 1510 | 1511 | 1512 | 1513 | 1514 | 1515 | 1516 | 1517 | 1518 | 1519 |
| 5F | 1520 | 1521 | 1522 | 1523 | 1524 | 1525 | 1526 | 1527 | 1528 | 1529 | 1530 | 1531 | 1532 | 1533 | 1534 | 1535 |
| 60 | 1536 | 1537 | 1538 | 1539 | 1540 | 1541 | 1542 | 1543 | 1544 | 1545 | 1546 | 1547 | 1548 | 1549 | 1550 | 1551 |
| 61 | 1552 | 1553 | 1554 | 1555 | 1556 | 1557 | 1558 | 1559 | 1560 | 1561 | 1562 | 1563 | 1564 | 1565 | 1566 | 1567 |
| 62 | 1568 | 1569 | 1570 | 1571 | 1572 | 1573 | 1574 | 1575 | 1576 | 1577 | 1578 | 1579 | 1580 | 1581 | 1582 | 1583 |
| 63 | 1584 | 1585 | 1586 | 1587 | 1588 | 1589 | 1590 | 1591 | 1592 | 1593 | 1594 | 1595 | 1596 | 1597 | 1598 | 1599 |
| 64 | 1600 | 1601 | 1602 | 1603 | 1604 | 1605 | 1606 | 1607 | 1608 | 1609 | 1610 | 1611 | 1612 | 1613 | 1614 | 1615 |
| 65 | 1616 | 1617 | 1618 | 1619 | 1620 | 1621 | 1622 | 1623 | 1624 | 1625 | 1626 | 1627 | 1628 | 1629 | 1630 | 1631 |
| 66 | 1632 | 1633 | 1634 | 1635 | 1636 | 1637 | 1638 | 1639 | 1640 | 1641 | 1642 | 1643 | 1644 | 1645 | 1646 | 1647 |
| 67 | 1648 | 1649 | 1650 | 1651 | 1652 | 1653 | 1654 | 1655 | 1656 | 1657 | 1658 | 1659 | 1660 | 1661 | 1562 | 1663 |
| 68 | 1664 | 1665 | 1666 | 1667 | 1668 | 1669 | 1670 | 1671 | 1672 | 1673 | 1674 | 1675 | 1676 | 1677 | 1678 | 1679 |
| 69 | 1680 | 1681 | 1682 | 1683 | 1684 | 1685 | 1686 | 1687 | 1688 | 1689 | 1690 | 1691 | 1692 | 1693 | 1694 | 1695 |
| 6A | 1696 | 1697 | 1698 | 1699 | 1700 | 1701 | 1702 | 1703 | 1704 | 1705 | 1706 | 1707 | 1708 | 1709 | 1710 | 1711 |
| 6B | 1712 | 1713 | 1714 | 1715 | 1716 | 1717 | 1718 | 1719 | 1720 | 1721 | 1722 | 1723 | 1724 | 1725 | 1726 | 1727 |
| 6C | 1728 | 1729 | 1730 | 1731 | 1732 | 1733 | 1734 | 1735 | 1736 | 1737 | 1738 | 1739 | 1740 | 1741 | 1742 | 1743 |
| 6D | 1744 | 1745 | 1746 | 1747 | 1748 | 1749 | 1750 | 1751 | 1752 | 1753 | 1754 | 1755 | 1756 | 1757 | 1758 | 1759 |
| 6E | 1760 | 1761 | 1762 | 1763 | 1764 | 1765 | 1766 | 1767 | 1768 | 1769 | 1770 | 1771 | 1772 | 1773 | 1774 | 1775 |
| 6F | 1776 | 1777 | 1778 | 1779 | 1780 | 1781 | 1782 | 1783 | 1784 | 1785 | 1786 | 1787 | 1788 | 1789 | 1790 | 1791 |

# Table J-2. (Continued)

| | 0 | 1 | 2 | 3 | 4 | 5 | 6 | 7 | 8 | 9 | A | B | C | D | E | F |
|---|---|---|---|---|---|---|---|---|---|---|---|---|---|---|---|---|
| 70 | 1792 | 1793 | 1794 | 1795 | 1796 | 1797 | 1798 | 1799 | 1800 | 1801 | 1802 | 1803 | 1804 | 1805 | 1806 | 1807 |
| 71 | 1808 | 1809 | 1810 | 1811 | 1812 | 1813 | 1814 | 1815 | 1816 | 1817 | 1818 | 1819 | 1820 | 1821 | 1822 | 1823 |
| 72 | 1824 | 1825 | 1826 | 1827 | 1828 | 1829 | 1830 | 1831 | 1832 | 1833 | 1834 | 1835 | 1836 | 1837 | 1838 | 1839 |
| 73 | 1840 | 1841 | 1842 | 1843 | 1844 | 1845 | 1846 | 1847 | 1848 | 1849 | 1850 | 1851 | 1852 | 1853 | 1854 | 1855 |
| 74 | 1856 | 1857 | 1858 | 1859 | 1860 | 1861 | 1862 | 1863 | 1864 | 1865 | 1866 | 1867 | 1868 | 1869 | 1870 | 1871 |
| 75 | 1872 | 1873 | 1874 | 1875 | 1876 | 1877 | 1878 | 1879 | 1880 | 1881 | 1882 | 1883 | 1884 | 1885 | 1886 | 1887 |
| 76 | 1888 | 1889 | 1890 | 1891 | 1892 | 1893 | 1894 | 1895 | 1896 | 1897 | 1898 | 1899 | 1900 | 1901 | 1902 | 1903 |
| 77 | 1904 | 1905 | 1906 | 1907 | 1908 | 1909 | 1910 | 1911 | 1912 | 1913 | 1914 | 1915 | 1916 | 1917 | 1918 | 1919 |
| 78 | 1920 | 1921 | 1922 | 1923 | 1924 | 1925 | 1926 | 1927 | 1928 | 1929 | 1930 | 1931 | 1932 | 1933 | 1934 | 1935 |
| 79 | 1936 | 1937 | 1938 | 1939 | 1940 | 1941 | 1942 | 1943 | 1944 | 1945 | 1946 | 1947 | 1948 | 1949 | 1950 | 1951 |
| 7A | 1952 | 1953 | 1954 | 1955 | 1956 | 1957 | 1958 | 1959 | 1960 | 1961 | 1962 | 1963 | 1964 | 1965 | 1966 | 1967 |
| 7B | 1968 | 1969 | 1970 | 1971 | 1972 | 1973 | 1974 | 1975 | 1976 | 1977 | 1978 | 1979 | 1980 | 1981 | 1982 | 1983 |
| 7C | 1984 | 1985 | 1986 | 1987 | 1988 | 1989 | 1990 | 1991 | 1992 | 1993 | 1994 | 1995 | 1996 | 1997 | 1998 | 1999 |
| 7D | 2000 | 2001 | 2002 | 2003 | 2004 | 2005 | 2006 | 2007 | 2008 | 2009 | 2010 | 2011 | 2012 | 2013 | 2014 | 2015 |
| 7E | 2016 | 2017 | 2018 | 2019 | 2020 | 2021 | 2022 | 2023 | 2024 | 2025 | 2026 | 2027 | 2028 | 2029 | 2030 | 2031 |
| 7F | 2032 | 2033 | 2034 | 2035 | 2036 | 2037 | 2038 | 2039 | 2040 | 2041 | 2042 | 2043 | 2044 | 2045 | 2046 | 2047 |
| 80 | 2048 | 2049 | 2050 | 2051 | 2052 | 2053 | 2054 | 2055 | 2056 | 2057 | 2058 | 2059 | 2060 | 2061 | 2062 | 2063 |
| 81 | 2064 | 2065 | 2066 | 2067 | 2068 | 2069 | 2070 | 2071 | 2072 | 2073 | 2074 | 2075 | 2076 | 2077 | 2078 | 2079 |
| 82 | 2080 | 2081 | 2082 | 2083 | 2084 | 2085 | 2086 | 2087 | 2088 | 2089 | 2090 | 2091 | 2092 | 2093 | 2094 | 2095 |
| 83 | 2096 | 2097 | 2098 | 2099 | 2100 | 2101 | 2102 | 2103 | 2104 | 2105 | 2106 | 2107 | 2108 | 2109 | 2110 | 2111 |
| 84 | 2112 | 2113 | 2114 | 2115 | 2116 | 2117 | 2118 | 2119 | 2120 | 2121 | 2122 | 2123 | 2124 | 2125 | 2126 | 2127 |
| 85 | 2128 | 2129 | 2130 | 2131 | 2132 | 2133 | 2134 | 2135 | 2136 | 2137 | 2138 | 2139 | 2140 | 2141 | 2142 | 2143 |
| 86 | 2144 | 2145 | 2146 | 2147 | 2148 | 2149 | 2150 | 2151 | 2152 | 2153 | 2154 | 2155 | 2156 | 2157 | 2158 | 2159 |
| 87 | 2160 | 2161 | 2162 | 2163 | 2164 | 2165 | 2166 | 2167 | 2168 | 2169 | 2170 | 2171 | 2172 | 2173 | 2174 | 2175 |
| 88 | 2176 | 2177 | 2178 | 2179 | 2180 | 2181 | 2182 | 2183 | 2184 | 2185 | 2186 | 2187 | 2188 | 2189 | 2190 | 2191 |
| 89 | 2192 | 2193 | 2194 | 2195 | 2196 | 2197 | 2198 | 2199 | 2200 | 2201 | 2202 | 2203 | 2204 | 2205 | 2206 | 2207 |
| 8A | 2208 | 2209 | 2210 | 2211 | 2212 | 2213 | 2214 | 2215 | 2216 | 2217 | 2218 | 2219 | 2220 | 2221 | 2222 | 2223 |
| 8B | 2224 | 2225 | 2226 | 2227 | 2228 | 2229 | 2230 | 2231 | 2232 | 2233 | 2234 | 2235 | 2236 | 2237 | 2238 | 2239 |
| 8C | 2240 | 2241 | 2242 | 2243 | 2244 | 2245 | 2246 | 2247 | 2248 | 2249 | 2250 | 2251 | 2252 | 2253 | 2254 | 2255 |
| 8D | 2256 | 2257 | 2258 | 2259 | 2260 | 2261 | 2262 | 2263 | 2264 | 2265 | 2266 | 2267 | 2268 | 2269 | 2270 | 2271 |
| 8E | 2272 | 2273 | 2274 | 2275 | 2276 | 2277 | 2278 | 2279 | 2280 | 2281 | 2282 | 2283 | 2284 | 2285 | 2286 | 2287 |
| 8F | 2288 | 2289 | 2290 | 2291 | 2292 | 2293 | 2294 | 2295 | 2296 | 2297 | 2298 | 2299 | 2300 | 2301 | 2302 | 2303 |
| 90 | 2304 | 2305 | 2306 | 2307 | 2308 | 2309 | 2310 | 2311 | 2312 | 2313 | 2314 | 2315 | 2316 | 2317 | 2318 | 2319 |
| 91 | 2320 | 2321 | 2322 | 2323 | 2324 | 2325 | 2326 | 2327 | 2328 | 2329 | 2330 | 2331 | 2332 | 2333 | 2334 | 2335 |
| 92 | 2336 | 2337 | 2338 | 2339 | 2340 | 2341 | 2342 | 2343 | 2344 | 2345 | 2346 | 2347 | 2348 | 2349 | 2350 | 2351 |
| 93 | 2352 | 2353 | 2354 | 2355 | 2356 | 2357 | 2358 | 2359 | 2360 | 2361 | 2362 | 2363 | 2364 | 2365 | 2366 | 2367 |
| 94 | 2368 | 2369 | 2370 | 2371 | 2372 | 2373 | 2374 | 2375 | 2376 | 2377 | 2378 | 2379 | 2380 | 2381 | 2382 | 2383 |
| 95 | 2384 | 2385 | 2386 | 2387 | 2388 | 2389 | 2390 | 2391 | 2392 | 2393 | 2394 | 2395 | 2396 | 2397 | 2398 | 2399 |
| 96 | 2400 | 2401 | 2402 | 2403 | 2404 | 2405 | 2406 | 2407 | 2408 | 2409 | 2410 | 2411 | 2412 | 2413 | 2414 | 2415 |
| 97 | 2416 | 2417 | 2418 | 2419 | 2420 | 2421 | 2422 | 2423 | 2424 | 2425 | 2426 | 2427 | 2428 | 2429 | 2430 | 2431 |
| 98 | 2432 | 2433 | 2434 | 2435 | 2436 | 2437 | 2438 | 2439 | 2440 | 2441 | 2442 | 2443 | 2444 | 2445 | 2446 | 2447 |
| 99 | 2448 | 2449 | 2450 | 2451 | 2452 | 2453 | 2454 | 2455 | 2456 | 2457 | 2458 | 2459 | 2460 | 2461 | 2462 | 2463 |
| 9A | 2464 | 2465 | 2466 | 2467 | 2468 | 2469 | 2470 | 2471 | 2472 | 2473 | 2474 | 2475 | 2476 | 2477 | 2478 | 2479 |
| 9B | 2480 | 2481 | 2482 | 2483 | 2484 | 2485 | 2486 | 2487 | 2488 | 2489 | 2490 | 2491 | 2492 | 2493 | 2494 | 2495 |
| 9C | 2496 | 2497 | 2498 | 2499 | 2500 | 2501 | 2502 | 2503 | 2504 | 2505 | 2506 | 2507 | 2508 | 2509 | 2510 | 2511 |
| 9D | 2512 | 2513 | 2514 | 2515 | 2516 | 2517 | 2518 | 2519 | 2520 | 2521 | 2522 | 2523 | 2524 | 2525 | 2526 | 2527 |
| 9E | 2528 | 2529 | 2530 | 2531 | 2532 | 2533 | 2534 | 2535 | 2536 | 2537 | 2538 | 2539 | 2540 | 2541 | 2542 | 2543 |
| 9F | 2544 | 2545 | 2546 | 2547 | 2548 | 2549 | 2550 | 2551 | 2552 | 2553 | 2554 | 2555 | 2556 | 2557 | 2558 | 2559 |

# Table J-2. (Continued)

| | 0 | 1 | 2 | 3 | 4 | 5 | 6 | 7 | 8 | 9 | A | B | C | D | E | F |
|---|---|---|---|---|---|---|---|---|---|---|---|---|---|---|---|---|
| A0 | 2560 | 2561 | 2562 | 2563 | 2564 | 2565 | 2566 | 2567 | 2568 | 2569 | 2570 | 2571 | 2572 | 2573 | 2574 | 2575 |
| A1 | 2576 | 2577 | 2578 | 2579 | 2580 | 2581 | 2582 | 2583 | 2584 | 2585 | 2586 | 2587 | 2588 | 2589 | 2590 | 2591 |
| A2 | 2592 | 2593 | 2594 | 2595 | 2596 | 2597 | 2598 | 2599 | 2600 | 2601 | 2602 | 2603 | 2604 | 2605 | 2606 | 2607 |
| A3 | 2608 | 2609 | 2610 | 2611 | 2612 | 2613 | 2614 | 2615 | 2616 | 2617 | 2618 | 2619 | 2620 | 2621 | 2622 | 2623 |
| A4 | 2624 | 2625 | 2626 | 2627 | 2628 | 2629 | 2630 | 2631 | 2632 | 2633 | 2634 | 2635 | 2636 | 2637 | 2638 | 2639 |
| A5 | 2640 | 2641 | 2642 | 2643 | 2644 | 2645 | 2646 | 2647 | 2648 | 2649 | 2650 | 2651 | 2652 | 2653 | 2654 | 2655 |
| A6 | 2656 | 2657 | 2658 | 2659 | 2660 | 2661 | 2662 | 2663 | 2664 | 2665 | 2666 | 2667 | 2668 | 2669 | 2670 | 2671 |
| A7 | 2672 | 2673 | 2674 | 2675 | 2676 | 2677 | 2678 | 2679 | 2680 | 2681 | 2682 | 2683 | 2684 | 2685 | 2686 | 2687 |
| A8 | 2688 | 2689 | 2690 | 2691 | 2692 | 2693 | 2694 | 2695 | 2696 | 2697 | 2698 | 2699 | 2700 | 2701 | 2702 | 2703 |
| A9 | 2704 | 2705 | 2706 | 2707 | 2708 | 2709 | 2710 | 2711 | 2712 | 2713 | 2714 | 2715 | 2716 | 2717 | 2718 | 2719 |
| AA | 2720 | 2721 | 2722 | 2723 | 2724 | 2725 | 2726 | 2727 | 2728 | 2729 | 2730 | 2731 | 2732 | 2733 | 2734 | 2735 |
| AB | 2736 | 2737 | 2738 | 2739 | 2740 | 2741 | 2742 | 2743 | 2744 | 2745 | 2746 | 2747 | 2748 | 2749 | 2750 | 2751 |
| AC | 2752 | 2753 | 2754 | 2755 | 2756 | 2757 | 2758 | 2759 | 2760 | 2761 | 2762 | 2763 | 2764 | 2765 | 2766 | 2767 |
| AD | 2768 | 2769 | 2770 | 2771 | 2772 | 2773 | 2774 | 2775 | 2776 | 2777 | 2778 | 2779 | 2780 | 2781 | 2782 | 2783 |
| AE | 2784 | 2785 | 2786 | 2787 | 2788 | 2789 | 2790 | 2791 | 2792 | 2793 | 2794 | 2795 | 2796 | 2797 | 2798 | 2799 |
| AF | 2800 | 2801 | 2802 | 2803 | 2804 | 2805 | 2806 | 2807 | 2808 | 2809 | 2810 | 2811 | 2812 | 2813 | 2814 | 2815 |
| B0 | 2816 | 2817 | 2818 | 2819 | 2820 | 2821 | 2822 | 2823 | 2824 | 2825 | 2826 | 2827 | 2828 | 2829 | 2830 | 2831 |
| B1 | 2832 | 2833 | 2834 | 2835 | 2836 | 2837 | 2838 | 2839 | 2840 | 2841 | 2842 | 2843 | 2844 | 2845 | 2846 | 2847 |
| B2 | 2848 | 2849 | 2850 | 2851 | 2852 | 2853 | 2854 | 2855 | 2856 | 2857 | 2858 | 2859 | 2860 | 2861 | 2862 | 2863 |
| B3 | 2864 | 2865 | 2866 | 2867 | 2868 | 2869 | 2870 | 2871 | 2872 | 2873 | 2874 | 2875 | 2876 | 2877 | 2878 | 2879 |
| B4 | 2880 | 2881 | 2882 | 2883 | 2884 | 2885 | 2886 | 2887 | 2888 | 2889 | 2890 | 2891 | 2892 | 2893 | 2894 | 2895 |
| B5 | 2896 | 2897 | 2898 | 2899 | 2900 | 2901 | 2902 | 2903 | 2904 | 2905 | 2906 | 2907 | 2908 | 2909 | 2910 | 2911 |
| B6 | 2912 | 2913 | 2914 | 2915 | 2916 | 2917 | 2918 | 2919 | 2920 | 2921 | 2922 | 2923 | 2924 | 2925 | 2926 | 2927 |
| B7 | 2928 | 2929 | 2930 | 2931 | 2932 | 2933 | 2934 | 2935 | 2936 | 2937 | 2938 | 2939 | 2940 | 2941 | 2942 | 2943 |
| B8 | 2944 | 2945 | 2946 | 2947 | 2948 | 2949 | 2950 | 2951 | 2952 | 2953 | 2954 | 2955 | 2956 | 2957 | 2958 | 2959 |
| B9 | 2960 | 2961 | 2962 | 2963 | 2964 | 2965 | 2966 | 2967 | 2968 | 2969 | 2970 | 2971 | 2972 | 2973 | 2974 | 2975 |
| BA | 2976 | 2977 | 2978 | 2979 | 2980 | 2981 | 2982 | 2983 | 2984 | 2985 | 2986 | 2987 | 2988 | 2989 | 2990 | 2991 |
| BB | 2992 | 2993 | 2994 | 2995 | 2996 | 2997 | 2998 | 2999 | 3000 | 3001 | 3002 | 3003 | 3004 | 3005 | 3006 | 3007 |
| BC | 3008 | 3009 | 3010 | 3011 | 3012 | 3013 | 3014 | 3015 | 3016 | 3017 | 3018 | 3019 | 3020 | 3021 | 3022 | 3023 |
| BD | 3024 | 3025 | 3026 | 3027 | 3028 | 3029 | 3030 | 3031 | 3032 | 3033 | 3034 | 3035 | 3036 | 3037 | 3038 | 3039 |
| BE | 3040 | 3041 | 3042 | 3043 | 3044 | 3045 | 3046 | 3047 | 3048 | 3049 | 3050 | 3051 | 3052 | 3053 | 3054 | 3055 |
| BF | 3056 | 3057 | 3058 | 3059 | 3060 | 3061 | 3062 | 3063 | 3064 | 3065 | 3066 | 3067 | 3068 | 3069 | 3070 | 3071 |
| C0 | 3072 | 3073 | 3074 | 3075 | 3076 | 3077 | 3078 | 3079 | 3080 | 3081 | 3082 | 3083 | 3084 | 3085 | 3086 | 3087 |
| C1 | 3088 | 3089 | 3090 | 3091 | 3092 | 3093 | 3094 | 3095 | 3096 | 3097 | 3098 | 3099 | 3100 | 3101 | 3102 | 3103 |
| C2 | 3104 | 3105 | 3106 | 3107 | 3108 | 3109 | 3110 | 3111 | 3112 | 3113 | 3114 | 3115 | 3116 | 3117 | 3118 | 3119 |
| C3 | 3120 | 3121 | 3122 | 3123 | 3124 | 3125 | 3126 | 3127 | 3128 | 3129 | 3130 | 3131 | 3132 | 3133 | 3134 | 3135 |
| C4 | 3136 | 3137 | 3138 | 3139 | 3140 | 3141 | 3142 | 3143 | 3144 | 3145 | 3146 | 3147 | 3148 | 3149 | 3150 | 3151 |
| C5 | 3152 | 3153 | 3154 | 3155 | 3156 | 3157 | 3158 | 3159 | 3160 | 3161 | 3162 | 3163 | 3164 | 3165 | 3166 | 3167 |
| C6 | 3168 | 3169 | 3170 | 3171 | 3172 | 3173 | 3174 | 3175 | 3176 | 3177 | 3178 | 3179 | 3180 | 3181 | 3182 | 3183 |
| C7 | 3184 | 3185 | 3186 | 3187 | 3188 | 3189 | 3190 | 3191 | 3192 | 3193 | 3194 | 3195 | 3196 | 3197 | 3198 | 3199 |
| C8 | 3200 | 3201 | 3202 | 3203 | 3204 | 3205 | 3206 | 3207 | 3208 | 3209 | 3210 | 3211 | 3212 | 3213 | 3214 | 3215 |
| C9 | 3216 | 3217 | 3218 | 3219 | 3220 | 3221 | 3222 | 3223 | 3224 | 3225 | 3226 | 3227 | 3228 | 3229 | 3230 | 2231 |
| CA | 3232 | 3233 | 3234 | 3235 | 3236 | 3237 | 3238 | 3239 | 3240 | 3241 | 3242 | 3243 | 3244 | 3245 | 3246 | 3247 |
| CB | 3248 | 3249 | 3250 | 3251 | 3252 | 3253 | 3254 | 3255 | 3256 | 3257 | 3258 | 3259 | 3260 | 3261 | 3262 | 3263 |
| CC | 3264 | 3265 | 3266 | 3267 | 3268 | 3269 | 3270 | 3271 | 3272 | 3273 | 3274 | 3275 | 3276 | 3277 | 3278 | 3279 |
| CD | 3280 | 3281 | 3282 | 3283 | 3284 | 3285 | 3286 | 3287 | 3288 | 3289 | 3290 | 3291 | 3292 | 3293 | 3294 | 3295 |
| CE | 3296 | 3297 | 3298 | 3299 | 3300 | 3301 | 3302 | 3303 | 3304 | 3305 | 3306 | 3307 | 3308 | 3309 | 3310 | 3311 |
| CF | 3312 | 3313 | 3314 | 3315 | 3316 | 3317 | 3318 | 3319 | 3320 | 3321 | 3322 | 3323 | 3324 | 3325 | 3326 | 3327 |

# Table J-2. (Continued)

| | 0 | 1 | 2 | 3 | 4 | 5 | 6 | 7 | 8 | 9 | A | B | C | D | E | F |
|---|---|---|---|---|---|---|---|---|---|---|---|---|---|---|---|---|
| D0 | 3328 | 3329 | 3330 | 3331 | 3332 | 3333 | 3334 | 3335 | 3336 | 3337 | 3338 | 3339 | 3340 | 3341 | 3342 | 3343 |
| D1 | 3344 | 3345 | 3346 | 3347 | 3348 | 3349 | 3350 | 3351 | 3352 | 3353 | 3354 | 3355 | 3356 | 3357 | 3358 | 3359 |
| D2 | 3360 | 3361 | 3362 | 3363 | 3364 | 3365 | 3366 | 3367 | 3368 | 3369 | 3370 | 3371 | 3372 | 3373 | 3374 | 3375 |
| D3 | 3376 | 3377 | 3378 | 3379 | 3380 | 3381 | 3382 | 3383 | 3384 | 3385 | 3386 | 3387 | 3388 | 3389 | 3390 | 3391 |
| D4 | 3392 | 3393 | 3394 | 3395 | 3396 | 3397 | 3398 | 3399 | 3400 | 3401 | 3402 | 3403 | 3404 | 3405 | 3406 | 3407 |
| D5 | 3408 | 3409 | 3410 | 3411 | 3412 | 3413 | 3414 | 3415 | 3416 | 3417 | 3418 | 3419 | 3420 | 3421 | 3422 | 3423 |
| D6 | 3424 | 3425 | 3426 | 3427 | 3428 | 3429 | 3430 | 3431 | 3432 | 3433 | 3434 | 3435 | 3436 | 3437 | 3438 | 3439 |
| D7 | 3440 | 3441 | 3442 | 3443 | 3444 | 3445 | 3446 | 3447 | 3448 | 3449 | 3450 | 3451 | 3452 | 3453 | 3454 | 3455 |
| D8 | 3456 | 3457 | 3458 | 3459 | 3460 | 3461 | 3462 | 3463 | 3464 | 3465 | 3466 | 3467 | 3468 | 3469 | 3470 | 3471 |
| D9 | 3472 | 3473 | 3474 | 3475 | 3476 | 3477 | 3478 | 3479 | 3480 | 3481 | 3482 | 3483 | 3484 | 3485 | 3486 | 3487 |
| DA | 3488 | 3489 | 3490 | 3491 | 3492 | 3493 | 3494 | 3495 | 3496 | 3497 | 3498 | 3499 | 3500 | 3501 | 3502 | 3503 |
| DB | 3504 | 3505 | 3506 | 3507 | 3508 | 3509 | 3510 | 3511 | 3512 | 3513 | 3514 | 3515 | 3516 | 3517 | 3518 | 3519 |
| DC | 3520 | 3521 | 3522 | 3523 | 3524 | 3525 | 3526 | 3527 | 3528 | 3529 | 3530 | 3531 | 3532 | 3533 | 3534 | 3535 |
| DD | 3536 | 3537 | 3538 | 3539 | 3540 | 3541 | 3542 | 3543 | 3544 | 3545 | 3546 | 3547 | 3548 | 3549 | 3550 | 3551 |
| DE | 3552 | 3553 | 3554 | 3555 | 3556 | 3557 | 3558 | 3559 | 3560 | 3561 | 3562 | 3563 | 3564 | 3565 | 3566 | 3567 |
| DF | 3568 | 3569 | 3570 | 3571 | 3572 | 3573 | 3574 | 3575 | 3576 | 3577 | 3578 | 3579 | 3580 | 3581 | 3582 | 3583 |
| E0 | 3584 | 3585 | 3586 | 3587 | 3588 | 3589 | 3590 | 3591 | 3592 | 3593 | 3594 | 3595 | 3596 | 3597 | 3598 | 3599 |
| E1 | 3600 | 3601 | 3602 | 3603 | 3604 | 3605 | 3606 | 3607 | 3608 | 3609 | 3610 | 3611 | 3612 | 3613 | 3614 | 3615 |
| E2 | 3616 | 3617 | 3618 | 3619 | 3620 | 3621 | 3622 | 3623 | 3624 | 3625 | 3626 | 3627 | 3628 | 3629 | 3630 | 3631 |
| E3 | 3632 | 3633 | 3634 | 3635 | 3636 | 3637 | 3638 | 3639 | 3640 | 3641 | 3642 | 3643 | 3644 | 3645 | 3646 | 3647 |
| E4 | 3648 | 3649 | 3650 | 3651 | 3652 | 3653 | 3654 | 3655 | 3656 | 3657 | 3658 | 3659 | 3660 | 3661 | 3662 | 3663 |
| E5 | 3664 | 3665 | 3666 | 3667 | 3668 | 3669 | 3670 | 3671 | 3672 | 3673 | 3674 | 3675 | 3676 | 3677 | 3678 | 3679 |
| E6 | 3680 | 3681 | 3682 | 3683 | 3684 | 3685 | 3686 | 3687 | 3688 | 3689 | 3690 | 3691 | 3692 | 3693 | 3694 | 3695 |
| E7 | 3696 | 3697 | 3698 | 3699 | 3700 | 3701 | 3702 | 3703 | 3704 | 3705 | 3706 | 3707 | 3708 | 3709 | 3710 | 3711 |
| E8 | 3712 | 3713 | 3714 | 3715 | 3716 | 3717 | 3718 | 3719 | 3720 | 3721 | 3722 | 3723 | 3724 | 3725 | 3726 | 3727 |
| E9 | 3728 | 3729 | 3730 | 3731 | 3732 | 3733 | 3734 | 3735 | 3736 | 3737 | 3738 | 3739 | 3740 | 3741 | 3742 | 3743 |
| EA | 3744 | 3745 | 3746 | 3747 | 3748 | 3749 | 3750 | 3751 | 3752 | 3753 | 3754 | 3755 | 3756 | 3757 | 3758 | 3759 |
| EB | 3760 | 3761 | 3762 | 3763 | 3764 | 3765 | 3766 | 3767 | 3768 | 3769 | 3770 | 3771 | 3772 | 3773 | 3774 | 3775 |
| EC | 3776 | 3777 | 3778 | 3779 | 3780 | 3781 | 3782 | 3783 | 3784 | 3785 | 3786 | 3787 | 3788 | 3789 | 3790 | 3791 |
| ED | 3792 | 3793 | 3794 | 3795 | 3796 | 3797 | 3798 | 3799 | 3800 | 3801 | 3802 | 3803 | 3804 | 3805 | 3806 | 3807 |
| EE | 3808 | 3809 | 3810 | 3811 | 3812 | 3813 | 3814 | 3815 | 3816 | 3817 | 3818 | 3819 | 3820 | 3821 | 3822 | 3823 |
| EF | 3824 | 3825 | 3826 | 3827 | 3828 | 3829 | 3830 | 3831 | 3832 | 3833 | 3834 | 3835 | 3836 | 3837 | 3838 | 3839 |
| F0 | 3840 | 3841 | 3842 | 3843 | 3844 | 3845 | 3846 | 3847 | 3848 | 3849 | 3850 | 3851 | 3852 | 3853 | 3854 | 3855 |
| F1 | 3856 | 3857 | 3858 | 3859 | 3860 | 3861 | 3862 | 3863 | 3864 | 3865 | 3866 | 3867 | 3868 | 3869 | 3870 | 3871 |
| F2 | 3872 | 3873 | 3874 | 3875 | 3876 | 3877 | 3878 | 3879 | 3880 | 3881 | 3882 | 3883 | 3884 | 3885 | 3886 | 3887 |
| F3 | 3888 | 3889 | 3890 | 3891 | 3892 | 3893 | 3894 | 3895 | 3896 | 3897 | 3898 | 3899 | 3900 | 3901 | 3902 | 3903 |
| F4 | 3904 | 3905 | 3906 | 3907 | 3908 | 3909 | 3910 | 3911 | 3912 | 3913 | 3914 | 3915 | 3916 | 3917 | 3918 | 3919 |
| F5 | 3920 | 3921 | 3922 | 3923 | 3924 | 3925 | 3926 | 3927 | 3928 | 3929 | 3930 | 3931 | 3932 | 3933 | 3934 | 3935 |
| F6 | 3936 | 3937 | 3938 | 3939 | 3940 | 3941 | 3942 | 3943 | 3944 | 3945 | 3946 | 3947 | 3948 | 3949 | 3950 | 3951 |
| F7 | 3952 | 3953 | 3954 | 3955 | 3956 | 3957 | 3958 | 3959 | 3960 | 3961 | 3962 | 3963 | 3964 | 3965 | 3966 | 3967 |
| F8 | 3968 | 3969 | 3970 | 3971 | 3972 | 3973 | 3974 | 3975 | 3976 | 3977 | 3978 | 3979 | 3980 | 3981 | 3982 | 3983 |
| F9 | 3984 | 3985 | 3986 | 3987 | 3988 | 3989 | 3990 | 3991 | 3992 | 3993 | 3994 | 3995 | 3996 | 3997 | 3998 | 3999 |
| FA | 4000 | 4001 | 4002 | 4003 | 4004 | 4005 | 4006 | 4007 | 4008 | 4009 | 4010 | 4011 | 4012 | 4013 | 4014 | 4015 |
| FB | 4016 | 4017 | 4018 | 4019 | 4020 | 4021 | 4022 | 4023 | 4024 | 4025 | 4026 | 4027 | 4028 | 4029 | 4030 | 4031 |
| FC | 4032 | 4033 | 4034 | 4035 | 4036 | 4037 | 4038 | 4039 | 4040 | 4041 | 4042 | 4043 | 4044 | 4045 | 4046 | 4047 |
| FD | 4048 | 4049 | 4050 | 4051 | 4052 | 4053 | 4054 | 4055 | 4056 | 4057 | 4058 | 4059 | 4060 | 4061 | 4062 | 4063 |
| FE | 4064 | 4065 | 4066 | 4067 | 4068 | 4069 | 4070 | 4071 | 4072 | 4073 | 4074 | 4075 | 4076 | 4077 | 4078 | 4079 |
| FF | 4080 | 4081 | 4082 | 4083 | 4084 | 4085 | 4086 | 4087 | 4088 | 4089 | 4090 | 4091 | 4092 | 4093 | 4094 | 4095 |

# Table J-3. Powers of Two

| $2^n$ | n | $2^{-n}$ |
|---|---|---|
| 1 | 0 | 1.0 |
| 2 | 1 | 0.5 |
| 4 | 2 | 0.25 |
| 8 | 3 | 0.125 |
| 16 | 4 | 0.062 5 |
| 32 | 5 | 0.031 25 |
| 64 | 6 | 0.015 625 |
| 128 | 7 | 0.007 812 5 |
| 256 | 8 | 0.003 906 25 |
| 512 | 9 | 0.001 953 125 |
| 1 024 | 10 | 0.000 976 562 5 |
| 2 048 | 11 | 0.000 488 281 25 |
| 4 096 | 12 | 0.000 244 140 625 |
| 8 192 | 13 | 0.000 122 070 312 5 |
| 16 384 | 14 | 0.000 061 035 156 25 |
| 32 768 | 15 | 0.000 030 517 578 125 |
| 65 536 | 16 | 0.000 015 258 789 062 5 |
| 131 072 | 17 | 0.000 007 629 394 531 25 |
| 262 144 | 18 | 0.000 003 814 697 265 625 |
| 524 288 | 19 | 0.000 001 907 348 632 812 5 |
| 1 048 576 | 20 | 0.000 000 953 674 316 406 25 |
| 2 097 152 | 21 | 0.000 000 476 837 158 203 125 |
| 4 194 304 | 22 | 0.000 000 238 418 579 101 562 5 |
| 8 388 608 | 23 | 0.000 000 119 209 289 550 781 25 |
| 16 777 216 | 24 | 0.000 000 059 604 644 775 390 625 |
| 33 554 432 | 25 | 0.000 000 029 802 322 387 695 312 5 |
| 67 108 864 | 26 | 0.000 000 014 901 161 193 847 656 25 |
| 134 217 728 | 27 | 0.000 000 007 450 580 596 923 828 125 |
| 268 435 456 | 28 | 0.000 000 003 725 290 298 461 914 062 5 |
| 536 870 912 | 29 | 0.000 000 001 862 645 149 230 957 031 25 |
| 1 073 741 824 | 30 | 0.000 000 000 931 322 574 615 478 515 625 |
| 2 147 483 648 | 31 | 0.000 000 000 465 661 287 307 739 257 8i. 5 |
| 4 294 967 296 | 32 | 0.000 000 000 232 830 643 653 869 628 906 25 |
| 8 589 934 592 | 33 | 0.000 000 000 116 415 321 826 934 814 453 125 |
| 17 179 869 184 | 34 | 0.000 000 000 058 207 66'' 913 467 407 226 562 5 |
| 34 359 738 368 | 35 | 0.000 000 000 029 103 83. 456 733 703 613 281 25 |
| 68 719 476 736 | 36 | 0.000 000 000 014 551 915 228 366 851 806 640 625 |
| 137 438 953 472 | 37 | 0.000 000 000 007 275 957 614 183 425 903 320 312 5 |
| 274 877 906 944 | 38 | 0.000 000 000 003 637 978 807 091 712 951 660 156 25 |
| 549 755 813 888 | 39 | 0.000 000 000 001 818 989 403 545 856 475 830 078 125 |
| 1 099 511 627 776 | 40 | 0.000 000 000 000 909 494 701 772 928 237 915 039 062 5 |
| 2 199 023 235 552 | 41 | 0.000 000 000 000 454 747 350 886 464 118 957 519 531 25 |
| 4 398 046 511 104 | 42 | 0.000 000 000 000 227 373 675 443 232 059 478 759 765 625 |
| 8 796 093 022 208 | 43 | 0.000 000 000 000 113 686 837 721 616 029 739 379 882 812 5 |
| 17 592 186 044 416 | 44 | 0.000 000 000 000 056 843 418 860 808 014 869 689 941 406 25 |
| 35 184 372 088 832 | 45 | 0.000 000 000 000 028 421 709 430 404 007 434 844 970 703 125 |
| 70 368 744 177 664 | 46 | 0.000 000 000 000 014 210 854 715 202 003 717 422 485 351 562 5 |
| 140 737 488 355 328 | 47 | 0.000 000 000 000 007 105 427 357 601 001 858 711 242 675 781 25 |
| 281 474 976 710 656 | 48 | 0.000 000 000 000 003 552 713 678 800 500 929 355 621 337 890 625 |
| 562 949 953 421 312 | 49 | 0.000 000 000 000 001 776 356 839 400 250 464 677 810 668 945 312 5 |
| 1 125 899 906 842 624 | 50 | 0.000 000 000 000 000 888 178 419 700 125 232 338 905 334 472 656 25 |
| 2 251 799 813 685 248 | 51 | 0.000 000 000 000 000 444 089 209 850 062 616 169 452 667 236 328 125 |
| 4 503 599 627 370 496 | 52 | 0.000 000 000 000 000 222 044 604 925 031 308 084 726 333 618 164 062 5 |
| 9 007 199 254 740 992 | 53 | 0.000 000 000 000 000 111 022 302 462 515 654 042 363 166 809 082 031 25 |
| 18 014 398 509 481 984 | 54 | 0.000 000 000 000 000 055 511 151 231 257 827 021 181 583 404 541 015 625 |
| 36 028 797 018 963 968 | 55 | 0.000 000 000 000 000 027 755 575 615 628 913 510 590 791 702 270 507 812 5 |
| 72 057 594 037 927 936 | 56 | 0.000 000 000 000 000 013 877 787 807 814 456 755 295 395 851 135 253 906 25 |
| 144 115 188 075 855 872 | 57 | 0.000 000 000 000 000 006 938 893 903 907 228 377 647 697 925 567 626 953 125 |
| 288 230 376 151 711 744 | 58 | 0.000 000 000 000 000 003 469 446 951 953 614 188 823 848 962 783 813 476 562 5 |
| 576 460 752 303 423 488 | 59 | 0.000 000 000 000 000 001 734 723 475 976 807 094 411 924 481 391 906 738 281 25 |
| 1 152 921 504 606 846 976 | 60 | 0.000 000 000 000 000 000 867 361 737 988 403 547 205 962 240 695 953 369 140 625 |
| 2 305 843 009 213 693 952 | 61 | 0.000 000 000 000 000 000 433 680 868 994 201 773 602 981 120 347 976 684 570 312 5 |
| 4 611 686 018 427 387 904 | 62 | 0.000 000 000 000 000 000 216 840 434 497 100 886 801 490 560 173 988 342 285 156 25 |
| 9 223 372 036 854 775 808 | 63 | 0.000 000 000 000 000 000 108 420 217 248 550 443 400 745 280 086 994 171 142 578 125 |

## Table J-4. Mathematical Constants

| Constant | Decimal Value | Hexadecimal Value |
|---|---|---|
| $\pi$ | 3.14159 26535 89793 | 3.243F 6A89 |
| $\pi^{-1}$ | 0.31830 98861 83790 | 0.517C C1B7 |
| $\sqrt{\pi}$ | 1.77245 38509 05516 | 1.C5BF 891C |
| $\ln \pi$ | 1.14472 98858 49400 | 1.250D 048F |
| $e$ | 2.71828 18284 59045 | 2.B7E1 5163 |
| $e^{-1}$ | 0.36787 94411 71442 | 0.5E2D 58D9 |
| $\sqrt{e}$ | 1.64872 12707 00128 | 1.A612 98E2 |
| $\log_{10} e$ | 0.43429 44819 03252 | 0.6F2D EC55 |
| $\log_2 e$ | 1.44269 50408 88963 | 1.7154 7653 |
| $\gamma$ | 0.57721 56649 01533 | 0.93C4 67E4 |
| $\ln \gamma$ | -0.54953 93129 81645 | -0.8CAE 9BC1 |
| $\sqrt{2}$ | 1.41421 35623 73095 | 1.6A09 E668 |
| $\ln 2$ | 0.69314 71805 59945 | 0.B172 17F8 |
| $\log_{10} 2$ | 0.30102 99956 63981 | 0.4D10 4D42 |
| $\sqrt{10}$ | 3.16227 76601 68379 | 3.29BB 075C |
| $\ln 10$ | 2.30258 40929 94046 | 2.4D75 3777 |

## Table J-5. Powers of Sixteen

| $16^n$ | $n$ | $16^{-n}$ |
|---|---|---|
| 1 | 0 | 0.10000 00000 00000 00000 × $10$ |
| 16 | 1 | 0.62500 00000 00000 00000 × $10^{-1}$ |
| 256 | 2 | 0.39062 50000 00000 00000 × $10^{-2}$ |
| 4 096 | 3 | 0.24414 06250 00000 00000 × $10^{-3}$ |
| 65 536 | 4 | 0.15258 78906 25000 00000 × $10^{-4}$ |
| 1 048 576 | 5 | 0.95367 43164 06250 00000 × $10^{-6}$ |
| 16 777 216 | 6 | 0.59604 64477 53906 25000 × $10^{-7}$ |
| 268 435 456 | 7 | 0.37252 90298 46191 40625 × $10^{-8}$ |
| 4 294 967 296 | 8 | 0.23283 06436 53869 62891 × $10^{-9}$ |
| 68 719 476 736 | 9 | 0.14551 91522 83668 51807 × $10^{-10}$ |
| 1 099 511 627 776 | 10 | 0.90949 47017 72928 23792 × $10^{-12}$ |
| 17 592 186 044 416 | 11 | 0.56843 41886 08080 14870 × $10^{-13}$ |
| 281 474 976 710 656 | 12 | 0.35527 13678 80050 09294 × $10^{-14}$ |
| 4 503 599 627 370 496 | 13 | 0.22204 46049 25031 30808 × $10^{-15}$ |
| 72 057 594 037 927 936 | 14 | 0.13877 78780 78144 56755 × $10^{-16}$ |
| 1 152 921 504 606 846 976 | 15 | 0.86736 17379 88403 54721 × $10^{-18}$ |

## Table J-6. Powers of Ten Converted to Hexadecimal Values

| $10^n$ | $n$ | $10^{-n}$ | | | | |
|---|---|---|---|---|---|---|
| 1 | 0 | 1.0000 | 0000 | 0000 | 0000 | |
| A | 1 | 0.1999 | 9999 | 9999 | 999A | |
| 64 | 2 | 0.28F5 | C28F | 5C28 | F5C3 | $\times\ 16^{-1}$ |
| 3E8 | 3 | 0.4189 | 374B | C6A7 | EF9E | $\times\ 16^{-2}$ |
| 2710 | 4 | 0.68DB | 8BAC | 710C | B296 | $\times\ 16^{-3}$ |
| 1 86A0 | 5 | 0.A7C5 | AC47 | 1B47 | 8423 | $\times\ 16^{-4}$ |
| F 4240 | 6 | 0.10C6 | F7A0 | B5ED | 8D37 | $\times\ 16^{-4}$ |
| 98 9680 | 7 | 0.1AD7 | F29A | BCAF | 4858 | $\times\ 16^{-5}$ |
| 5F5 E100 | 8 | 0.2AF3 | 1DC4 | 6118 | 73BF | $\times\ 16^{-6}$ |
| 3B9A CA00 | 9 | 0.44B8 | 2FA0 | 9B5A | 52CC | $\times\ 16^{-7}$ |
| 2 540B E400 | 10 | 0.6DF3 | 7F67 | 5EF6 | EADF | $\times\ 16^{-8}$ |
| 17 4876 E800 | 11 | 0.AFEB | FF0B | CB24 | AAFF | $\times\ 16^{-9}$ |
| E8 D4A5 1000 | 12 | 0.1197 | 9981 | 2DEA | 1119 | $\times\ 16^{-9}$ |
| 916 4E72 A000 | 13 | 0.1C25 | C268 | 4976 | 81C2 | $\times\ 16^{-10}$ |
| 5AF3 107A 4000 | 14 | 0.2D09 | 370D | 4257 | 3604 | $\times\ 16^{-11}$ |
| 3 8D7E A4C6 8000 | 15 | 0.480E | BE7B | 9D58 | 566D | $\times\ 16^{-12}$ |
| 23 8652 6FC1 0000 | 16 | 0.734A | CA5F | 6226 | F0AE | $\times\ 16^{-13}$ |
| 163 4578 5D8A 0000 | 17 | 0.B877 | AA32 | 36A4 | B449 | $\times\ 16^{-14}$ |
| DE0 B6B3 A764 0000 | 18 | 0.1272 | 5DD1 | D243 | ABA1 | $\times\ 16^{-14}$ |
| 8AC7 2304 89E8 0000 | 19 | 0.1D83 | C94F | B6D2 | AC35 | $\times\ 16^{-15}$ |

The Machine Language Instruction Set

# Appendix K

Table K-4 lists the instructions built into the Z80 microprocessor, which is the central processing unit of the TS1000 and the ZX81. The table gives the instructions in hexadecimal notation (see Appendix J).

Some of the instructions in Table K-4 require one or two bytes of data. Tables K-1 through K-3 explain notation used for these instructions. Table K-1 defines the symbols that represent data bytes in Table K-4. In some cases, a single line in Table K-4 represents several instructions. Special symbols shown in Table K-2 represent the portion (called a *field*) that differs from one instruction to the next. Table K-3 shows the values that should replace these depending on the register involved.

**Table K-1. Symbols for Data Bytes**

| Symbol | Meaning |
|--------|---------|
| yy | One byte of data |
| yyyy | Two bytes of data |
| ppqq | Two bytes of data giving an address. The least significant byte is always first. |
| disp | One byte of data, containing the displacement for a relative branch |

**Table K-2. Symbols for Instruction Fields**

| Symbol | Meaning |
|--------|---------|
| bbb | Bit number |
| ddd | Destination register |
| rrr | Register |
| sss | Source register |
| xx | Register pair |

## Table K-3. Contents of Instruction Fields

| Symbol | Value | Meaning |
|---|---|---|
| ddd, rrr, sss | 111 | Register A |
| | 000 | Register B |
| | 001 | Register C |
| | 010 | Register D |
| | 011 | Register E |
| | 100 | Register H |
| | 101 | Register L |
| xx | 00 | Register pair BC |
| | 01 | Register pair DE |
| | 10 | Register pair HL |
| | 11 | Register SP or AF |
| bbb | 000 to 111 | Bit number |

# Table K-4. A Summary of the Z80 Instruction Set

** Address Bus: A0-A7: [C]
A8-A15: [B]

| Type | Mnemonic | Operand | Object Code | Bytes | Clock Cycles | C | Z | S | P/O | Ac | N | Operation Performed |
|---|---|---|---|---|---|---|---|---|---|---|---|---|
| O/I | IN | A,(port) | DB yy | 2 | 10 | | | | | | 0 | [A] ← [ port ]<br>Input to Accumulator from directly addressed I/O port.<br>Address Bus: A0-A7: port<br>A8-A15: [ A ] |
| | IN | reg,(C) | ED 01ddd000 | 2 | 11 | | X | X | P | X | 0 | [ reg ] ← [[ C ]]<br>Input to register from I/O port addressed by the contents of C.**<br>If second byte is $70_{16}$ only the flags will be affected. |
| | INIR | | ED B2 | 2 | 21/16** | | 1 | ? | ? | ? | 1 | Repeat until [ B ] = 0:<br>[[ HL ]] ← [[ C ]]<br>[ B ] ← [ B ] - 1<br>[ HL ] ← [ HL ] + 1<br>Transfer a block of data from I/O port addressed by contents of C to memory location addressed by contents of HL, going from low addresses to high. Contents of B serve as a count of bytes remaining to be transferred.** |
| | INDR | | ED BA | 2 | 21/16** | | 1 | ? | ? | ? | 1 | Repeat until [ B ] = 0:<br>[[ HL ]] ← [[ C ]]<br>[ B ] ← [ B ] - 1<br>[ HL ] ← [ HL ] - 1<br>Transfer a block of data from I/O port addressed by contents of C to memory location addressed by contents of HL, going from high addresses to low. Contents of B serve as a count of bytes remaining to be transferred.** |
| | INI | | ED A2 | 2 | 16 | | X | ? | ? | ? | 1 | [[ HL ]] ← [[ C ]]<br>[ B ] ← [ B ] - 1<br>[ HL ] ← [ HL ] + 1<br>Transfer a byte of data from I/O port addressed by contents of C to memory location addressed by contents of HL. Decrement byte count and increment destination address.** |

Table K-4. (Continued)

**Address Bus: A0-A7: [C]
A8-A15: [B]

| Type | Mnemonic | Operand | Object Code | Bytes | Clock Cycles | C | Z | S | P/O | Ac | N | Operation Performed |
|------|----------|---------|-------------|-------|--------------|---|---|---|-----|----|----|---------------------|
| | IND | | ED AA | 2 | 16 | | X | ? | ? | ? | 1 | $[[HL]] \leftarrow [[C]]$<br>$[B] \leftarrow [B] - 1$<br>$[HL] \leftarrow [HL] - 1$<br>Transfer a byte of data from I/O port addressed by contents of C to memory location addressed by contents of HL. Decrement both byte count and destination address. ** |
| | OUT | (port),A | D3 yy | 2 | 11 | | | | | | | $[port] \leftarrow [A]$<br>Output from Accumulator to directly addressed I/O port.<br>Address Bus: A0-A7: port<br>A8-A15: [A] |
| | OUT | (C),reg | ED 01sss001 | 2 | 12 | | | | | | | $[[C]] \leftarrow [reg]$<br>Output from register to I/O port addressed by the contents of C. ** |
| | OTIR | | ED B3 | 2 | 2 1/16** | | 1 | ? | ? | ? | 1 | Repeat until [ B ] = 0:<br>$[[C]] \leftarrow [[HL]]$<br>$[B] \leftarrow [B] - 1$<br>$[HL] \leftarrow [HL] + 1$<br>Transfer a block of data from memory location addressed by contents of HL to I/O port addressed by contents of C, going from low memory to high. Contents of B serve as a count of bytes remaining to be transferred. ** |
| I/O (Continued) | OTDR | | ED BB | 2 | 2 1/16** | | 1 | ? | ? | ? | 1 | Repeat until [ B ] = 0:<br>$[[C]] \leftarrow [[HL]]$<br>$[B] \leftarrow [B] - 1$<br>$[HL] \leftarrow [HL] - 1$<br>Transfer a block of data from memory location addressed by contents of HL to I/O port addressed by contents of C, going from high memory to low. Contents of B serve as a count of bytes remaining to be transferred. ** |

## Table K-4. (Continued)

| Type | Mnemonic | Operand | Object Code | Bytes | Clock Cycles | C | Z | S | P/O | A_C | N | Operation Performed |
|---|---|---|---|---|---|---|---|---|---|---|---|---|
| I/O (Continued) | OUTI | | ED A3 | 2 | 16 | | X | ? | ? | ? | 1 | [[C]] ← [[HL]]<br>[B] ← [B] - 1<br>[HL] ← [HL] + 1<br>Transfer a byte of data from memory location addressed by contents of HL to I/O port addressed by contents of C. Decrement byte count and increment source address.** |
| | OUTD | | ED AB | 2 | 16 | | X | ? | ? | ? | 1 | [[C]] ← [[HL]]<br>[B] ← [B] - 1<br>[HL] ← [HL] - 1<br>Transfer a byte of data from memory location addressed by contents of HL to I/O port addressed by contents of C. Decrement both byte count and source address.** |
| Primary Memory Reference | LD | A,(addr) | 3A ppqq | 3 | 13 | | | | | | | [A] ← [.addr]<br>Load Accumulator from directly addressed memory location. |
| | LD | HL,(addr) | 2A ppqq | 3 | 16 | | | | | | | [H] ← [ addr + 1], [L] ← [ addr]<br>Load HL from directly addressed memory. |
| | LD | rp,(addr)<br>xy,(addr) | ED 01xx1011 ppqq<br>11x11101 2A ppqq | 4<br>4 | 20<br>20 | | | | | | | [rp(HI)] ← [ addr + 1], [rp(LO)] ← [ addr] or<br>[xy(HI)] ← [ addr + 1], [xy(LO)] ← [ addr]<br>Load register pair or Index register from directly addressed memory. |
| | LD | (addr),A | 32 ppqq | 3 | 13 | | | | | | | [addr] ← [A]<br>Store Accumulator contents in directly addressed memory location. |
| | LD | (addr),HL | 22 ppqq | 3 | 16 | | | | | | | [addr + 1] ← [H], [addr] ← [L]<br>Store contents of HL to directly addressed memory location. |
| | LD | (addr),rp<br>(addr),xy | ED 01xx0011 ppqq<br>11x11101 22 ppqq | 4<br>4 | 20<br>20 | | | | | | | [addr + 1] ← [rp(HI)], [addr] ← [rp(LO)] or<br>[addr + 1] ← [xy(HI)], [addr] ← [xy(LO)]<br>Store contents of register pair or Index register to directly addressed memory. |
| | LD | A,(BC)<br>A,(DE) | 0A<br>1A | 1<br>1 | 7<br>7 | | | | | | | [A] ← [[BC]] or [A] ← [[DE]]<br>Load Accumulator from memory location addressed by the contents of the specified register pair. |

| Type | Mnemonic | Operand | Object Code | Bytes | Clock Cycles | Status C | Z | N | S | P/O | A_C | N | Operation Performed |
|---|---|---|---|---|---|---|---|---|---|---|---|---|---|
| Primary Memory Reference (Continued) | LD | reg,(HL) | 01ddd110 | 1 | 7 | | | | | | | | [reg] ← [[HL]] Load register from memory location addressed by contents of HL. |
| | LD | (BC),A (DE),A | 02 12 | 1 | 7 | | | | | | | | [[BC]] ← [A] or [[DE]] ← [A] Store Accumulator to memory location addressed by the contents of the specified register pair. |
| | LD | (HL),reg | 01110sss | 1 | 7 | | | | | | | | [[HL]] ← [reg] Store register contents to memory location addressed by the contents of HL |
| | LD | reg,(xy+displ) | 11x11101 01ddd110 disp | 3 | 19 | | | | | | | | [reg] ← [[xy] + displ] Load register from memory location using base relative addressing. |
| | LD | (xy+displ),reg | 11x11101 01110sss disp | 3 | 19 | | | | | | | | [[xy] + displ] ← [reg] Store register to memory location addressed relative to contents of Index register. |
| Block Transfer and Search | LDIR | | ED B0 | 2 | 21/16** | | | | | 0 | 0 | 0 | Repeat until [BC] = 0: [[DE]] ← [[HL]] [DE] ← [DE] + 1 [HL] ← [HL] + 1 [BC] ← [BC] - 1 Transfer a block of data from the memory location addressed by the contents of HL to the memory location addressed by the contents of DE, going from low addresses to high. Contents of BC serve as a count of bytes to be transferred. |
| | LDDR | | ED B8 | 2 | 21/16** | | | | | 0 | 0 | 0 | Repeat until [BC] = 0: [[DE]] ← [[HL]] [DE] ← [DE] - 1 [HL] ← [HL] - 1 [BC] ← [BC] - 1 Transfer a block of data from the memory location addressed by the contents of HL to the memory location addressed by the contents of DE, going from high addresses to low. Contents of BC serve as a count of bytes to be transferred. |

| Type | Mnemonic | Operand | Object Code | Bytes | Clock Cycles | Status |  |  |  |  |  | Operation Performed |
|---|---|---|---|---|---|---|---|---|---|---|---|---|
|  |  |  |  |  |  | C | Z | S | P/O | Ac | N |  |
| Block Transfer and Search (Continued) | LDI |  | ED A0 | 2 | 16 |  |  |  | X | 0 | 0 | [[DE]] ← [[HL]]<br>[DE] ← [DE] + 1<br>[HL] ← [HL] + 1<br>[BC] ← [BC] - 1<br>Transfer one byte of data from the memory location addressed by the contents of HL to the memory location addressed by the contents of DE. Increment source and destination addresses and decrement byte count. |
|  | LDD |  | ED A8 | 2 | 16 |  |  |  | X | 0 | 0 | [[DE]] ← [[HL]]<br>[DE] ← [DE] - 1<br>[HL] ← [HL] - 1<br>[BC] ← [BC] - 1<br>Transfer one byte of data from the memory location addressed by the contents of HL to the memory location addressed by the contents of DE. Decrement source and destination addresses and byte count. |
|  | CPIR |  | ED B1 | 2 | 20/16** |  | X | X | X | X | 1 | Repeat until [ A] = [[ HL]] or [ BC] = 0:<br>[ A] - [[ HL]] (only flags are affected)<br>[ HL] ← [ HL] + 1<br>[ BC] ← [ BC] - 1<br>Compare contents of Accumulator with those of memory block addressed by contents of HL, going from low addresses to high. Stop when a match is found or when the byte count becomes zero. |
|  | CPDR |  | ED B9 | 2 | 20/16** |  | X | X | X | X | 1 | Repeat until [ A] = [[ HL]] or [ BC] = 0:<br>[ A] - [[ HL]] (only flags are affected)<br>[ HL] ← [ HL] - 1<br>[ BC] ← [ BC] - 1<br>Compare contents of Accumulator with those of memory block addressed by contents of HL, going from high addresses to low. Stop when a match is found or when the byte count becomes zero. |

# Table K-4. (Continued)

| Type | Mnemonic | Operand | Object Code | Bytes | Clock Cycles | C | Z | S | P/O | AC | N | Operation Performed |
|---|---|---|---|---|---|---|---|---|---|---|---|---|
| Block Transfer and Search (Continued) | CPI | | ED A1 | 2 | 16 | × | × | × | × | × | 1 | [A] - [[HL]] (only flags are affected); [HL] ← [HL] + 1; [BC] ← [BC] - 1; Compare contents of Accumulator with those of memory location addressed by contents of HL. Increment address and decrement byte count. |
| | CPD | | ED A9 | 2 | 16 | × | × | × | × | × | 1 | [A] - [[HL]] (only flags are affected); [HL] ← [HL] - 1; [BC] ← [BC] - 1; Compare contents of Accumulator with those of memory location addressed by contents of HL. Decrement address and byte count. |
| Secondary Memory Reference | ADD | A,(HL)<br>A,(xy + disp) | 86<br>11x11101 86 disp | 1<br>3 | 7<br>19 | × | × | × | × | × | 0 | [A] ← [A] + [[HL]] or [A] ← [A] + [[xy] + disp] Add to Accumulator using implied addressing or base relative addressing. |
| | ADC | A,(HL)<br>A,(xy + disp) | 8E<br>11x11101 8E disp | 1<br>3 | 7<br>19 | × | × | × | × | × | 0 | [A] ← [A] + [[HL]] + C or [A] ← [A] + [[xy] + disp] + C Add with Carry using implied addressing or base relative addressing. |
| | SUB | (HL)<br>A,(xy + disp) | 96<br>11x11101 96 disp | 1<br>3 | 7<br>19 | × | × | × | O | × | 1 | [A] ← [A] - [[HL]] or [A] ← [A] - [[xy] + disp] Subtract from Accumulator using implied addressing or base relative addressing. |
| | SBC | A,(HL)<br>A,(xy + disp) | 9E<br>11x11101 9E disp | 1<br>3 | 7<br>19 | × | × | × | O | × | 1 | [A] ← [A] - [[HL]] - C or [A] ← [A] - [[xy] + disp] - C Subtract with Carry using implied addressing or base relative addressing. |
| | AND | (HL)<br>(xy + disp) | A6<br>11x11101 A6 disp | 1<br>3 | 7<br>19 | O | × | × | P | 1 | 0 | [A] ← [A] ∧ [[HL]] or [A] ← [A] ∧ [[xy] + disp] AND with Accumulator using implied addressing or base relative addressing. |
| | OR | (HL)<br>(xy + disp) | B6<br>11x11101 B6 disp | 1<br>3 | 7<br>19 | O | × | × | P | 1 | 0 | [A] ← [A] ∨ [[HL]] or [A] ← [A] ∨ [[xy] + disp] OR with Accumulator using implied addressing or base relative addressing. |

# Table K-4. (Continued)

| Type | Mnemonic | Operand | Object Code | Bytes | Clock Cycles | C | Z | S | P/O | Ac | N | Operation Performed |
|---|---|---|---|---|---|---|---|---|---|---|---|---|
| Secondary Memory Reference (Continued) | XOR | (HL) | AE | 1 | 7 | 0 | X | X | P | 1 | 0 | [A] ← [A] ⊻ [[HL]] or [A] ← [A] ⊻ [[xy] + disp] Exclusive-OR with Accumulator using implied addressing or base relative addressing. |
| | | (xy + disp) | 11x11101 AE disp | 3 | 19 | | | | | | | |
| | CP | (HL) | BE | 1 | 7 | X | X | X | O | X | 1 | [A] - [[HL]] or [A] - [[xy] + disp] Compare with Accumulator using implied addressing or base relative addressing. Only the flags are affected. |
| | | (xy + disp) | 11x11101 BE disp | 3 | 19 | | | | | | | |
| | INC | (HL) | 34 | 1 | 11 | | X | X | O | X | 0 | [[HL]] ← [[HL]] + 1 or [[xy] + disp] ← [[xy] + disp] + 1 Increment using implied addressing or base relative addressing. |
| | | (xy + disp) | 11x11101 34 disp | 3 | 23 | | | | | | | |
| | DEC | (HL) | 35 | 1 | 11 | | X | X | O | X | 1 | [[HL]] ← [[HL]] - 1 or [[xy] + disp] ← [[xy] + disp] - 1 Decrement using implied addressing or base relative addressing. |
| | | (xy + disp) | 11x11101 35 disp | 3 | 23 | | | | | | | |
| Memory Shift and Rotate | RLC | (HL) | CB 06 | 2 | 15 | X | X | X | P | 0 | 0 | [[HL]] or [[xy] + disp] Rotate contents of memory location (implied or base relative addressing) left with branch Carry. |
| | | (xy + disp) | 11x11101 CB disp 06 | 4 | 23 | | | | | | | |
| | RL | (HL) | CB 16 | 2 | 15 | X | X | X | P | 0 | 0 | [[HL]] or [[xy] + disp] Rotate contents of memory location left through Carry. |
| | | (xy + disp) | 11x11101 CB disp 16 | 4 | 23 | | | | | | | |
| | RRC | (HL) | CB 0E | 2 | 15 | X | X | X | P | 0 | 0 | [[HL]] or [[xy] + disp] Rotate contents of memory location right with branch Carry. |
| | | (xy + disp) | 11x11101 CB disp 0E | 4 | 23 | | | | | | | |

| Type | Mnemonic | Operand | Object Code | Bytes | Clock Cycles | C | Z | S | P/O | AC | N | Operation Performed |
|---|---|---|---|---|---|---|---|---|---|---|---|---|
| Memory Shift and Rotate (Continued) | RR | (HL)<br>(xy + disp) | CB 1E<br>11x11101 CB disp<br>1E | 2<br>4 | 15<br>23 | X | X | X | P | 0 | 0 | Rotate contents of memory location right through Carry.<br>[[HL]] or [[xy] + disp] |
| | SLA | (HL)<br>(xy + disp) | CB 26<br>11x11101 CB disp<br>26 | 2<br>4 | 15<br>23 | X | X | X | P | 0 | 0 | Shift contents of memory location left and clear LSB (Arithmetic Shift).<br>[[HL]] or [[xy] + disp] |
| | SRA | (HL)<br>(xy + disp) | CB 2E<br>11x11101 CB disp<br>2E | 2<br>4 | 15<br>23 | X | X | X | P | 0 | 0 | Shift contents of memory location right and preserve MSB (Arithmetic Shift).<br>[[HL]] or [[xy] + disp] |
| | SRL | (HL)<br>(xy + disp) | CB 3E<br>11x11101 CB disp<br>3E | 2<br>4 | 15<br>23 | X | X | X | P | 0 | 0 | Shift contents of memory location right and clear MSB (Logical Shift).<br>[[HL]] or [[xy] + disp] |

| Type | Mnemonic | Operand | Object Code | Bytes | Clock Cycles | Status | | | | | | Operation Performed |
|---|---|---|---|---|---|---|---|---|---|---|---|---|
| | | | | | | C | Z | S | P/O | A$_C$ | N | |
| Immediate | LD | reg,data | 00ddd110 yy | 2 | 7 | | | | | | | [reg] ← data<br>Load immediate into register. |
| | LD | rp,data16<br>xy,data16 | 00xx0001 yyyy<br>11x11101 21 yyyy | 3<br>4 | 10<br>14 | | | | | | | [rp] ← data16 or [xy] ← data16<br>Load 16 bits of immediate data into register pair or index register. |
| | LD | (HL),data<br>(xy + disp),<br>data | 36 yy<br>11x11101 36 disp yy | 2<br>4 | 10<br>19 | | | | | | | [[HL]] ← data or [[xy] + disp] ← data<br>Load immediate into memory location using implied or base relative addressing. |
| Jump | JP | label | C3 ppqq | 3 | 10 | | | | | | | [PC] ← label<br>Jump to instruction at address represented by label. |
| | JR | disp | 18 (disp-2) | 2 | 12 | | | | | | | [PC] ← [PC] + 2 + (disp-2)<br>Jump relative to present contents of Program Counter. |
| | JP | (HL)<br>(xy) | E9<br>11x11101 E9 | 1<br>2 | 4<br>8 | | | | | | | [PC] ← [HL] or [PC] ← [xy]<br>Jump to address contained in HL or Index register. |
| Subroutine Call and Return | CALL | label | CD ppqq | 3 | 17 | | | | | | | [[SP] - 1] ← [PC(HI)]<br>[[SP] - 2] ← [PC(LO)]<br>[SP] ← [SP] - 2<br>[PC] ← label<br>Jump to subroutine starting at address represented by label. |
| | CALL | cond,label | 11ccc100 ppqq | 3 | 10/17 | | | | | | | Jump to subroutine if condition is satisfied; otherwise, continue in sequence. |
| | RET | | C9 | 1 | 10 | | | | | | | [PC(LO)] ← [[SP]]<br>[PC(HI)] ← [[SP] + 1]<br>[SP] ← [SP] + 2<br>Return from subroutine. |
| | RET | cond | 11ccc000 | 1 | 5/11 | | | | | | | Return from subroutine if condition is satisfied; otherwise, continue in sequence. |

# Table K-4. (Continued)

| Type | Mnemonic | Operand | Object Code | Bytes | Clock Cycles | C | Z | S | P/O | Ac | N | Operation Performed |
|---|---|---|---|---|---|---|---|---|---|---|---|---|
| Immediate Operate | ADD | A,data | C6 yy | 2 | 7 | X | X | X | O | X | 0 | $[A] \leftarrow [A] + \text{data}$ <br> Add immediate to Accumulator. |
| | ADC | A,data | CE yy | 2 | 7 | X | X | X | O | X | 0 | $[A] \leftarrow [A] + \text{data} + C$ <br> Add immediate with Carry. |
| | SUB | data | D6 yy | 2 | 7 | X | X | X | O | X | 1 | $[A] \leftarrow [A] - \text{data}$ <br> Subtract immediate from Accumulator. |
| | SBC | A,data | DE yy | 2 | 7 | X | X | X | O | X | 1 | $[A] \leftarrow [A] - \text{data} - C$ <br> Subtract immediate with Carry. |
| | AND | data | E6 yy | 2 | 7 | 0 | X | X | P | 1 | 0 | $[A] \leftarrow [A] \wedge \text{data}$ <br> AND immediate with Accumulator. |
| | OR | data | F6 yy | 2 | 7 | 0 | X | X | P | 1 | 0 | $[A] \leftarrow [A] \vee \text{data}$ <br> OR immediate with Accumulator. |
| | XOR | data | EE yy | 2 | 7 | 0 | X | X | P | 1 | 0 | $[A] \leftarrow [A] \veebar \text{data}$ <br> Exclusive-OR immediate with Accumulator. |
| | CP | data | FE yy | 2 | 7 | X | X | X | O | X | 1 | $[A] - \text{data}$ <br> Compare immediate data with Accumulator contents; only the flags are affected. |
| Jump on Condition | JP | cond,label | 11ccc010 ppqq | 3 | 10 | | | | | | | If cond, then $[PC] \leftarrow \text{label}$ <br> Jump to instruction at address represented by label if the condition is true. |
| | JR | C,disp | 38 (disp-2) | 2 | 7/12 | | | | | | | If $C = 1$, then $[PC] \leftarrow [PC] + 2 + (\text{disp} - 2)$ <br> Jump relative to contents of Program Counter if Carry flag is set. |
| | JR | NC,disp | 30 (disp-2) | 2 | 7/12 | | | | | | | If $C = 0$, then $[PC] \leftarrow [PC] + 2 + (\text{disp} - 2)$ <br> Jump relative to contents of Program Counter if Carry flag is reset. |
| | JR | Z,disp | 28 (disp-2) | 2 | 7/12 | | | | | | | If $Z = 1$, then $[PC] \leftarrow [PC] + 2 + (\text{disp} - 2)$ <br> Jump relative to contents of Program Counter if Zero flag is set. |
| | JR | NZ,disp | 20 (disp-2) | 2 | 7/12 | | | | | | | If $Z = 0$, then $[PC] \leftarrow [PC] + 2 + (\text{disp} - 2)$ <br> Jump relative to contents of Program Counter if Zero flag is reset. |
| | DJNZ | disp | 10 (disp-2) | 2 | 8/13 | | | | | | | $[B] \leftarrow [B] - 1$ <br> If $[B] \neq 0$, then $[PC] \leftarrow [PC] + 2 + (\text{disp} - 2)$ <br> Decrement contents of B and Jump relative to contents of Program Counter if result is not 0. |

## Table K-4. (Continued)

| Type | Mnemonic | Operand | Object Code | Bytes | Clock Cycles | C | Z | S | P/O | A_C | N | Operation Performed |
|---|---|---|---|---|---|---|---|---|---|---|---|---|
| Register-Register Move | LD | dst,src | 01dddsss | 1 | 4 | | | | | | | [dst] ← [src] Move contents of source register to destination register. Register designations src and dst may each be A, B, C, D, E, H or L. |
| | LD | A,I | ED 57 | 2 | 9 | | × | × | I | 0 | 0 | [A] ← [I] Move contents of Interrupt Vector register to Accumulator. |
| | LD | A,R | ED 5F | 2 | 9 | | × | × | I | 0 | 0 | [A] ← [R] Move contents of Refresh register to Accumulator. |
| | LD | I,A | ED 47 | 2 | 9 | | | | | | | [I] ← [A] Load Interrupt Vector register from Accumulator. |
| | LD | R,A | ED 4F | 2 | 9 | | | | | | | [R] ← [A] Load Refresh register from Accumulator. |
| | LD | SP,HL | F9 | 1 | 6 | | | | | | | [SP] ← [HL] Move contents of HL to Stack Pointer. |
| | LD | SP,xy | 11x11101 F9 | 2 | 10 | | | | | | | [SP] ← [xy] Move contents of Index register to Stack Pointer. |
| | EX | DE,HL | EB | 1 | 4 | | | | | | | [DE] ⟶ [HL] Exchange contents of DE and HL. |
| | EX | AF,AF' | 08 | 1 | 4 | | | | | | | [AF] ⟶ [AF'] Exchange program status and alternate program status. |
| | EXX | | D9 | 1 | 4 | | | | | | | ([BC] ⟶ [BC'], [DE] ⟶ [DE'], [HL] ⟶ [HL']) Exchange register pairs and alternate register pairs. |

| Type | Mnemonic | Operand | Object Code | Bytes | Clock Cycles | C | Z | S | P/O | Ac | N | Operation Performed |
|---|---|---|---|---|---|---|---|---|---|---|---|---|
| Register-Register Operate | ADD | A,reg | 10000rrr | 1 | 4 | x | x | x | 0 | x | 0 | [A] ← [A] + [reg] Add contents of register to Accumulator. |
| | ADC | A,reg | 10001rrr | 1 | 4 | x | x | x | 0 | x | 0 | [A] ← [A] + [reg] + C Add contents of register and Carry to Accumulator. |
| | SUB | reg | 10010rrr | 1 | 4 | x | x | x | 0 | x | 1 | [A] ← [A] - [reg] Subtract contents of register from Accumulator. |
| | SBC | A,reg | 10011rrr | 1 | 4 | x | x | x | 0 | x | 1 | [A] ← [A] - [reg] - C Subtract contents of register and Carry from Accumulator. |
| | AND | reg | 10100rrr | 1 | 4 | 0 | x | x | P | 1 | 0 | [A] ← [A] ∧ [reg] AND contents of register with contents of Accumulator. |
| | OR | reg | 10110rrr | 1 | 4 | 0 | x | x | P | 1 | 0 | [A] ← [A] ∨ [reg] OR contents of register with contents of Accumulator. |
| | XOR | reg | 10101rrr | 1 | 4 | 0 | x | x | P | 1 | 0 | [A] ← [A] ⊻ [reg] Exclusive-OR contents of register with contents of Accumulator. |
| | CP | reg | 10111rrr | 1 | 4 | x | x | x | 0 | x | 1 | [A] - [reg] Compare contents of register with contents of Accumulator. Only the flags are affected. |
| | ADD | HL,rp | 00xx1001 | 1 | 11 | x | | | | ? | 0 | [HL] ← [HL] + [rp] 16-bit add register pair contents to contents of HL. |
| | ADC | HL,rp | ED 01xx1010 | 2 | 15 | x | x | x | 0 | ? | 0 | [HL] ← [HL] + [rp] + C 16-bit add with Carry register pair contents to contents of HL. |
| | SBC | HL,rp | ED 01xx0010 | 2 | 15 | x | x | x | 0 | ? | 1 | [HL] ← [HL] - [rp] - C 16-bit subtract with Carry register pair contents from contents of HL. |
| | ADD | IX,pp | DD 00xx1001 | 2 | 15 | x | | | | ? | 0 | [IX] ← [IX] + [pp] 16-bit add register pair contents to contents of Index register IX (pp = BC, DE, IX, SP). |
| | ADD | IY,rr | FD 00xx1001 | 2 | 15 | x | | | | ? | 0 | [IY] ← [IY] + [rr] 16-bit add register pair contents to contents of Index register IY (rr = BC, DE, IY, SP). |

Table K-4.  (Continued)

| Type | Mnemonic | Operand | Object Code | Bytes | Clock Cycles | C | Z | S | P/O | Ac | N | Operation Performed |
|---|---|---|---|---|---|---|---|---|---|---|---|---|
| Register Operate | DAA | | 27 | 1 | 4 | X | X | X | P | X | 1 | Decimal adjust Accumulator, assuming that Accumulator contents are the sum or difference of BCD operands. |
| | CPL | | 2F | 1 | 4 | | | | | 1 | 1 | [A] ← [Ā] Complement Accumulator (ones complement). |
| | NEG | | ED 44 | 2 | 8 | X | X | X | O | X | 1 | [A] ← [Ā] + 1 Negate Accumulator (twos complement). |
| | INC | reg | 00rrr100 | 1 | 4 | | X | X | O | X | 0 | [reg] ← [reg] + 1 Increment register contents. |
| | INC | rp | 00xx0011 | 1 | 6 | | | | | | | [rp] ← [rp] + 1 or [xy] ← [xy] + 1 Increment contents of register or Index register. |
| | INC | xy | 11x11101 23 | 2 | 10 | | | | | | | |
| | DEC | reg | 00rrr101 | 1 | 4 | | X | X | O | X | 1 | [reg] ← [reg] - 1 Decrement register contents. |
| | DEC | rp | 00xx1011 | 1 | 6 | | | | | | | [rp] ← [rp] - 1 or [xy] ← [xy] - 1 Decrement contents of register pair or Index register. |
| | DEC | xy | 11x11101 2B | 2 | 10 | | | | | | | |
| Register Shift and Rotate | RLCA | | 07 | 1 | 4 | X | | | | 0 | 0 | Rotate Accumulator left with branch Carry. |
| | RLA | | 17 | 1 | 4 | X | | | | 0 | 0 | Rotate Accumulator left through Carry. |
| | RRCA | | 0F | 1 | 4 | X | | | | 0 | 0 | Rotate Accumulator right with branch Carry. |

Table K-4. (Continued)

| Type | Mnemonic | Operand | Object Code | Bytes | Clock Cycles | C | Z | S | P/O | Ac | N | Operation Performed |
|---|---|---|---|---|---|---|---|---|---|---|---|---|
| Register Shift and Rotate (Continued) | RRA | | 1F | 1 | 4 | X | X | X | | 0 | 0 | Rotate Accumulator right through Carry. |
| | RLC | reg | CB 00000rrr | 2 | 8 | X | X | X | P | 0 | 0 | Rotate contents of register left with branch Carry. |
| | RL | reg | CB 00010rrr | 2 | 8 | X | X | X | P | 0 | 0 | Rotate contents of register left through Carry. |
| | RRC | reg | CB 00001rrr | 2 | 8 | X | X | X | P | 0 | 0 | Rotate contents of register right with branch Carry. |
| | RR | reg | CB 00011rrr | 2 | 8 | X | X | X | P | 0 | 0 | Rotate contents of register right through Carry. |
| | SLA | reg | CB 00100rrr | 2 | 8 | X | X | X | P | 0 | 0 | Shift contents of register left and clear LSB (Arithmetic Shift). |

| Type | Mnemonic | Operand | Object Code | Bytes | Clock Cycles | C | Z | S | P/O | AC | N | Operation Performed |
|---|---|---|---|---|---|---|---|---|---|---|---|---|
| Register Shift and Rotate (Continued) | SRA | reg | CB 00101rrr | 2 | 8 | X | X | X | P | 0 | 0 | Shift contents of register right and preserve MSB (Arithmetic Shift). |
| | SRL | reg | CB 00111rrr | 2 | 8 | X | X | X | P | 0 | 0 | Shift contents of register right and clear MSB (Logical Shift). |
| | RLD | | ED 6F | 2 | 18 | X | X | X | P | 0 | 0 | Rotate one BCD digit left between the Accumulator and memory location (implied addressing).Contents of the upper half of the Accumulator are not affected. |
| | RRD | | ED 67 | 2 | 18 | X | X | X | P | 0 | 0 | Rotate one BCD digit right between the Accumulator and memory location (implied addressing).Contents of the upper half of the Accumulator are not affected. |

## Table K-4. (Continued)

| Type | Mnemonic | Operand | Object Code | Bytes | Clock Cycles | C | Z | S | P/O | Ac | N | Operation Performed |
|---|---|---|---|---|---|---|---|---|---|---|---|---|
| Bit Manipulation | BIT | b,reg | CB 01bbbrrr | 2 | 8 | | X | ? | ? | 1 | 0 | Z ← reg(b). Zero flag contains complement of the selected register bit. |
| | BIT | b,(HL)<br>b,(xy + disp) | CB 01bbb110<br>11x11101 CB disp<br>01bbb110 | 2<br>4 | 12<br>20 | | X | ? | ? | 1 | 0 | Z ← [[HL]](b) or Z ← [[xy] + displ(b). Zero flag contains complement of selected bit of the memory location (implied addressing or base relative addressing). |
| | SET | b,reg | CB 11bbbrrr | 2 | 8 | | | | | | | reg(b) ← 1. Set indicated register bit. |
| | SET | b,(HL)<br>b,(xy + disp) | CB 11bbb110<br>11x11101 CB disp<br>11bbb110 | 2<br>4 | 15<br>23 | | | | | | | [[HL]](b) ← 1 or [[xy] + displ(b) ← 1. Set indicated bit of memory location (implied addressing or base relative addressing). |
| | RES | b,reg | CB 10bbbrrr | 2 | 8 | | | | | | | reg(b) ← 0. Reset indicated register bit. |
| | RES | b,(HL)<br>b,(xy + disp) | CB 10bbb110<br>11x11101 CB disp<br>10bbb110 | 2<br>4 | 15<br>23 | | | | | | | [[HL]](b) ← 0 or [[xy] + displ(b) ← 0. Reset indicated bit in memory location (implied addressing or base relative addressing). |
| Stack | PUSH | pr<br>xy | 11xx0101<br>11x11101 E5 | 1<br>2 | 11<br>15 | | | | | | | [[SP]-1] ← [pr(HI)]<br>[[SP]-2] ← [pr(LO)]<br>[SP] ← [SP]-2<br>Put contents of register pair or Index register on top of Stack and decrement Stack Pointer. |
| | POP | pr<br>xy | 11xx0001<br>11x11101 E1 | 1<br>2 | 10<br>14 | | | | | | | [pr(LO)] ← [[SP]]<br>[pr(HI)] ← [[SP] + 1]<br>[SP] ← [SP] + 2<br>Put contents of top of Stack in register pair or Index register and increment Stack Pointer. |
| | EX | (SP),HL<br>(SP),xy | E3<br>11x11101 E3 | 1<br>2 | 19<br>23 | | | | | | | [H] ↔ [[SP] + 1]<br>[L] ↔ [[SP]]<br>Exchange contents of HL or Index register and top of Stack. |

| Type | Mnemonic | Operand | Object Code | Bytes | Clock Cycles | C | Z | S | P/O | AC | N | Operation Performed |
|------|----------|---------|-------------|-------|--------------|---|---|---|-----|----|----|---------------------|
| Interrupt | DI | | F3 | 1 | 4 | | | | | | | Disable interrupts. |
| | EI | | FB | 1 | 4 | | | | | | | Enable interrupts. |
| | RST | n | 11xxx111 | 1 | 11 | | | | | | | $[[SP]-1] \leftarrow [PC(HI)]$; $[[SP]-2] \leftarrow [PC(LO)]$; $[SP] \leftarrow [SP]-2$; $[PC] \leftarrow (8 \cdot n)_{16}$; Restart at designated location. |
| | RETI | | ED 4D | 2 | 14 | | | | | | | Return from interrupt. |
| | RETN | | ED 45 | 2 | 14 | | | | | | | Return from nonmaskable interrupt. |
| | IM | 0 | ED 46 | 2 | 8 | | | | | | | Set interrupt mode 0, 1, or 2. |
| | IM | 1 | ED 56 | 2 | 8 | | | | | | | |
| | IM | 2 | ED 5E | 2 | 8 | | | | | | | |
| Status | SCF | | 37 | 1 | 4 | 1 | | | | 0 | 0 | $C \leftarrow 1$; Set Carry flag. |
| | CCF | | 3F | 1 | 4 | X | | | | ? | 0 | $C \leftarrow \overline{C}$; Complement Carry flag. |
| | NOP | | 00 | 1 | 4 | | | | | | | No operation — volatile memories are refreshed. |
| | HALT | | 76 | 1 | 4 | | | | | | | CPU halts, executes NOPs to refresh volatile memories. |

**Execution time shown is for one iteration.

# Using Routines in Read-Only Memory

# Appendix L

The TS1000/ZX81 master program contains subroutines that read the keyboard, print on the television display, evaluate functions, manipulate strings, perform arithmetic with floating-point numbers, and perform many other tasks. The master program calls these subroutines to carry out its usual operations, but machine language programmers can also call them from machine language subroutines. This capability makes machine language extremely powerful and versatile on the TS1000 or ZX81.

This appendix explains how to use some of the subroutines in the master program. It assumes that you already know how to write machine language routines for the Z80 processor, and that you understand some of the technical terms that machine language programmers use.

In many cases, the subroutines described in this appendix change the contents of the processor's registers. Some of them also use the alternate register set. Before calling them, save the contents of any registers you are currently using (with PUSH instructions) and restore them after the call (with POP instructions). (These instructions are part of the instruction set of the Z80 processor.)

To find out exactly what each of these subroutines does, or to learn the detailed inner workings of other parts of the master program, consult the annotated ROM disassembly by Ian Logan and Frank O'Hara (see bibliography in Appendix N).

Unfortunately, there are two versions of the master program. Some early models of the ZX81 have one version while the TS1000 and later models of the ZX81 have the second version. Both versions contain all of the subroutines described in this appendix, but some of the subroutines begin at different addresses. To determine which version of the master program your computer has, calculate the square of 0.25 and PEEK the contents of location 54. If the results are 0.0625 and 136, you have the second version. If either result is different, you have the first version.[18]

Table L-1 gives the calling addresses for some of the more useful subroutines in the master program. Use the first column of addresses if your computer has the older version of the master program. Use the second column if it has the newer version.

---

[18]Ian Logan, *Understanding Your ZX81 ROM* (Leighton Buzzard: Melbourne House, 1981), p.1.

# HOW TO USE THE SUBROUTINES

To use one of the subroutines in Table L-1, replace the symbolic name of the routine (such as SCAN_KBD) with the corresponding hexadecimal address

Table L-1. Selected Program Routines

| Symbolic Name | Old ROM Address | New ROM Address | Effect |
|---|---|---|---|
| **Keyboard Routines** | | | |
| SCAN_KBD | 02BB | 02BB | Determine key value of pressed key |
| DECODE_KEY | 07BD | 07BD | Convert key value to character code |
| **Display Routines** | | | |
| PRINT_CHAR | 0010 | 0010 | Print a character on the display |
| PRINT_ENTER | 0847 | 0847 | Move to beginning of next display line |
| PRINT_POS | 08F5 | 08F5 | Change the print position |
| CLEAR_SCR | 0A2A | 0A2A | Clear the display |
| POP_PRINT | 0B55 | 0B55 | (See calculator stack routines below) |
| PRINT_STR | 0B6B | 0B6B | Print a string |
| SCROLL_DISP | 0C0E | 0C0E | Move display up one line |
| FAST_MODE | 0F20 | 0F23 | Enter FAST mode |
| SLOW_MODE | 0F28 | 0F2B | Enter SLOW mode |
| PAUSE_DISP | 0F32 | 0F35 | Wait a specified time with display on |
| **Report Code Routines** | | | |
| REPORT_CODE | 0008 | 0008 | Display a report code |
| TEST_BREAK | 0F43 | 0F46 | Check for BREAK pressed |
| **Search Routines** | | | |
| LOOK_VARS | 111B | 111C | Find a BASIC variable |
| FIND_LINE | 09DB | 09DB | Find beginning of a BASIC line |
| **Calculator Stack Routines** | | | |
| START_CALC | 0028 | 0028 | Begin a series of calculator operations |
| POP_PRINT | 0B55 | 0B55 | Print the top item on the stack |
| POP_BYTE | 0C02 | 0C02 | Round and store top stack number in a byte |
| POP_WORD | 0EA7 | 0EA7 | Round and store top stack number in a word |
| PUSH_STR | 12BE | 12C2 | Move a string descriptor onto stack |
| FLOAT_STR | 14D5 | 14D9 | Convert a string to floating point |
| PUSH_BYTE | 1519 | 151D | Convert a byte to floating point |
| PUSH_WORD | 151C | 1520 | Convert two bytes to floating point |
| TEST_STACK | 19EA | 19EB | Check for room to add an item to stack |

from the table.

In the examples in this appendix, the calling addresses used are taken from the list of addresses for the newer version of the master program. If your computer has the older version, substitute the calling addresses used in the first column of Table L-1. Each example appears first as it should be entered using the REM loader from Appendix F. Following this is a complete assembly language listing of the routine, including comments. Unless you have an assembler program, you cannot enter the assembly listing directly, but it will help you understand how the routine works. To enter one of the example routines, insert the LET H$ statement in either of the REM loader programs, delete any other LET H$ statements or filled REM statements from previous runs, and make certain the following line is present with nothing following it:

```
200 REM
```

Then execute RUN. Since none of the example programs contains the byte value 7E, you can edit line 200 to make it line 1 instead of deleting all the other lines of the program. Execute each machine language example by entering RAND USR 16514, unless that particular example specifies a different command.

## KEYBOARD ROUTINES

The master program routine SCAN_KBD checks every row on the keyboard and returns a number in the HL register pair to tell which key, if any, was pressed. The numbers it returns (given in Appendix M) are called key values. They contain information about the physical location of the key (its row and column on the keyboard). Addresses 007E-0110 contain a similar table, which the master program routine DECODE_KEY uses to convert the key value into a character code (given in Appendix C).

The first program illustrates the SCAN_KBD and DECODE_KEY routines. It can be called with the following BASIC command:

```
PRINT CHR$ USR 16514
```

(Use SLOW mode.) The routine waits until you press a key, decodes the key value, and returns the corresponding character code to the USR function. To print the character code that this program returns, you must release the ENTER key quickly after entering the BASIC command, or the routine will detect the ENTER key itself.

Here is the program line to include in the REM loader:

```
20 LET H$="CD BB 02 44 4D 2C 2
8 F8 CD BD 07 4E 06 00 C9 "
```

The complete machine language listing of the program follows:

| Address | Contents | Instruction | Comment |
|---------|----------|-------------|---------|
| 4082 | CD BB 02 | L1 CALL SCAN__KBD | Read the keyboard |
| 4085 | 44 | LD B,H | Transfer the key value |
| 4086 | 4D | LD C,L | from BC to HL |
| 4087 | 2C | INC L | FF in L means no key pressed |
| 4088 | 28 F8 | JR Z,L1 | Loop until key pressed |
| 408A | CD BD 07 | CALL DECODE__KEY | Decode the key value |
| 408D | 4E | LD C,(HL) | Put character code in C register |
| 408E | 06 00 | LD B,00 | Clear the B register |
| 4090 | C9 | RET | Return character code in BC |

This program uses the fact that the key value FFFF (which SCAN__KBD returns when no key is pressed) is the only key value with FF in the low byte. The INC L instruction produces zero in that case, and the following JR Z instruction causes the program to loop until some other key value appears.

# DISPLAY ROUTINES

The master program's routine to display a single character is at hexadecimal location 10. This routine is called PRINT__CHAR. It

1. verifies that the current print position is valid
2. determines whether to start a new line
3. expands the display file if necessary to make room for the new character
4. displays the character
5. increases the print position by one.

You can call this routine directly by loading the character code of the character into register A and executing the instruction RST 10 in machine code, or you can call it using one of the higher-level routines described in this appendix. The screen fill program from Chapter 8 is an example of a direct call to the PRINT__CHAR routine.[19]

Here is the line that will load this routine:

```
20 LET H$="3E 95 06 04 0E 80 D
7 0D 20 FC 05 20 F7 C9 "
```

[19]Harold Miller, *Syntax ZX80* (The Harvard Group, Bolton Road, Harvard, MA 01451), August 1982, pp 6-7.

Robert A. Foley, *Syntax ZX80*, September 1982, p. 17.

The complete assembly-language listing of the program follows:

| Address | Contents | Instruction | Comment |
| --- | --- | --- | --- |
| 4082 | 3E 95 | LD A,95 | Load char. code for ▓ into A |
| 4084 | 06 04 | LD B,04 | Load first loop counter into B |
| 4086 | 0E B0 | L1 LD C,B0 | Second loop counter into C |
| 4088 | D7 | L2 RST 10 | Print the character in A |
| 4089 | 0D | DEC C | Subtract 1 from counter in C |
| 408A | 20 FC | JR NZ,L2 | Loop until it reaches 0 |
| 408C | 05 | DEC B | Subtract 1 from counter in B |
| 408D | 20 F7 | JR NZ,L1 | Loop until it reaches 0 |
| 408F | C9 | RET | Return to BASIC |

To begin a new line on the display, do not call PRINT_CHAR with the character code for ENTER (hexadecimal 76). Call the special routine PRINT_ENTER instead.

Like most of the routines in this appendix, PRINT_CHAR and the routines that call it will return to BASIC and display a report code if one of the standard errors (such as screen full or out of memory) occurs. If your system is a ZX81 without the 16K memory expansion, it will report error code 4 (out of memory) before the screen fills completely unless you delete the loader program after you run it, leaving only the REM statement.

## Print a String

You can print a string by writing a loop that calls the PRINT_CHAR routine. However, the master program already contains such a loop. To use it, load the length of the string into BC and the string's starting address into DE, and call PRINT_STR. The example of PRINT_POS in the next section includes an example of PRINT_STR.

## Change the Print Position

To make the equivalent of a PRINT AT command in machine language, load the line number into the B register, load the column number into the C register, and call PRINT_POS. PRINT_POS does not print anything itself, but it moves the print position so that the next call to PRINT_CHAR or PRINT_STR begins printing at the new line and column. The following subroutine illustrates PRINT_POS followed by PRINT_STR. It prints the word **HERE** at line 10, column 20. To load it with the REM loader, include the following line in the loader program:

```
20 LET H$="06 0A 0E 14 CD F5 0
8 01 04 00 11 93 40 CD 6B 0B C9
2D 2A 37 2A "
```

The complete assembly-language listing of the program follows:

| Address | Contents | Instruction | Comment |
|---|---|---|---|
| 4082 | 06 0A | LD B,0A | Load line number into A register |
| 4084 | 0E 14 | LD C,14 | Load column number into C register |
| 4086 | CD F5 08 | CALL PRINT_POS | Change the print position |
| 4089 | 01 04 00 | LD BC,0004 | Load string length into BC |
| 408C | 11 93 40 | LD DE,4093 | Load string address into DE |
| 408F | CD 6B 0B | CALL PRINT_STR | Print the string |
| 4092 | C9 | RET | Return to BASIC |
| 4093 | 2D 2A 37 2A | DEFS HERE | Store the bytes of the string |

## Control Routines for the Display

The following routines perform the same function as the corresponding BASIC command given (in parentheses):

· CLEAR_SCR—Clear the display (CLS)
· SCROLL_DISP—Move the display up one line (SCROLL)
· FAST_MODE—Select fast mode (FAST)
· SLOW_MODE—Select slow mode (SLOW)
· PAUSE_DISP—Activate display and wait a specified time or until a key is pressed (PAUSE). Load the parameter (the number that would come after PAUSE in the BASIC command) into the BC register before calling the routine.

## REPORT CODE ROUTINES

REPORT_CODE generates a report code at the lower left corner of the screen, then returns to BASIC in command mode. Use the machine language instruction RST 8 to call REPORT_CODE, and store one less than the desired error number in the next byte. For example, to generate error report 3, store 2 in the next byte. Appendix B describes the standard BASIC report codes, and Appendix E gives the nonstandard ones that you can also use. If you attempt to use any other byte values for error codes, you may confuse the master program and have to pull the plug.

## TEST BREAK

TEST BREAK checks the keyboard to determine whether the BREAK key has been pressed. The BREAK key does not automatically interrupt a machine language routine the way it interrupts a BASIC program. Because of this, if you accidentally write an endless loop, you will be unable to return to BASIC. To prevent this, include calls to TEST_BREAK in your routine loops, and use REPORT_CODE to exit and generate report D if BREAK has been pressed. The following lines show how to do this:

```
CD 46 0F    CALL TEST_BREAK
30 02       JR NC,NEXT
CF          RST 8
0C          DEFB 0C
      NEXT:    continue with program
```

## SEARCH ROUTINES

The master program contains a routine to find the memory location of a BASIC variable and another to find a BASIC Program line. With these routines, you can use BASIC variables to pass parameters between BASIC and your machine language routines. This can make it easier to write programs that modify the text of BASIC programs (to renumber or merge them, for example).

### LOOK_VARS

The master program routine LOOK_VARS searches the BASIC variables area for a variable with a specified name. Before calling it, create a sequence of bytes containing the character codes for the variable name, followed by a terminator byte, such as FF. Store the starting address of the name in the HL register pair and in the system variable CH_ADD. If the variable is not found, the carry flag will be clear after the call to LOOK_VARS. If the carry flag is set, then HL will contain the address of the last character of the variable name. Use the information in Appendix I to find the actual bytes of the variable. The examples at the end of the following section illustrate the use of LOOK_VARS.

### FIND LINE

FIND LINE finds the starting address in read/write memory of a BASIC line. Load the line number of the line into HL before calling it. The routine returns the address of the line in HL if the line exists, or the address of the next line if the specified one does not exist. It also sets the zero flag if the line number matched exactly. If the line number is larger than any of the program lines present, FIND_LINE returns in HL the address of a byte containing hexadecimal 76.

# CALCULATOR STACK ROUTINES

A machine language routine can do arithmetic with floating point numbers, concatenate strings, compare numbers or strings, execute numeric and string functions, and perform other powerful operations just by calling the appropriate master program routine. Thus, machine language routines can do essentially anything that BASIC can do. However, a machine language routine that performs many such operations runs almost as slowly as a BASIC program, because it executes the same machine language instructions. Floating point arithmetic and function evaluation are especially slow, and machine language programmers who need faster programs should use *integer* (non-floating point) arithmetic instead of floating point wherever they can.

The master program uses a calculator stack, or temporary storage area, to evaluate most operations, functions, and other specialized tasks. This stack is separate from the machine stack that the stack pointer register (SP) accesses. The system variables STKBOT and STKEND (Appendix E) contain the addresses of the beginning and end of the calculator stack. This stack is at the end of the first "work space" region in read/write memory (Figure 7-1). Like any other stack, it permits two operations: pushing (adding) a new element onto the stack, and popping (removing) the item most recently added to the stack. Each item on the stack is either a five-byte floating point number or a five-byte *string descriptor*, which gives the address and length of a string stored somewhere else in read/write memory.

Each of the calculator's functions gets its arguments by popping them from the calculator stack, and it pushes its output value onto the stack. You can evaluate a complicated expression very efficiently by arranging the calculation so that the input parameters for each operation are already on the stack as the output parameters from previous operations.

The computer uses a special memory area for temporary storage of numbers from the stack. The system variable MEMBOT (Appendix E) contains the location of this storage area. The master program contains routines to transfer items between this area and the stack.

Using the calculator entails three operations: pushing the arguments onto the stack; calling the calculator functions; and accessing the output value on the stack. The following sections describe each of these tasks.

## Pushing Arguments onto
## The Stack (Adding an Item)

The master program has different subroutines for pushing different kinds of items onto the stack. Some of these also convert bytes, integers, or character strings into floating point format, so that you should never need to know the internal details of the format. Refer to Table L-1 for the numeric addresses of the routines below.

### PUSH_BYTE

To push an integer between 0 and 255, load the number into the A register and call PUSH_BYTE, which converts the byte value to a floating point number and stores it on the calculator stack.

### PUSH_WORD

To push a 16-bit integer, load it into the BC register and call PUSH_WORD, which converts the 16-bit value to a floating point number and stores it on the calculator stack.

### FLOAT_STR

To convert a character string to a floating point number and push its value onto the stack, (1) store the address of the first byte of the string in HL and in the system variable CH_ADD (see Appendix E), (2) store the contents of the first byte in the A register, and (3) call FLOAT_STR. The character string must be a series of adjacent bytes containing character codes and ending with a non-numeric code (such as FF). The string must represent either an ordinary number or a number in scientific notation, just as the PRINT command in BASIC would display it on the television screen. For example, the following line creates machine language instructions to convert and push the number 1.45. Enter it into the REM loader program with:

```
20 LET H$="21 8E 40 22 16 40 4
6 78 CD D9 14 C9 1D 1B 20 21 FF
"
```

The following assembly listing explains more clearly how the subroutine works:

| Address | Contents | Instruction | Comment |
| --- | --- | --- | --- |
| 4082 | 21 8E 40 | LD HL,408E | Load address of string into HL |
| 4085 | 22 16 40 | LD (CH_ADD),HL | Store same address in CH_ADD |
| 4088 | 46 | LD B, (HL) | Load first byte of string into A |
| 4089 | 78 | LD A,B | register |
| 408A | CD D9 14 | CALL FLOAT_STR | Push string's value on the stack |
| 408D | C9 | RET | Return to BASIC |
| 408E | 1D 1B 20 21 | DEFS 1.45 | Store the string itself |
| 4092 | FF | DEFB FF | Store the terminator byte |

With this method, you can create and push any floating point number within the computer's range. (The single instruction LD A,(HL) would be shorter than the two instructions at addresses 4088 and 4089, but its byte value (7E) causes problems when you edit the REM line.)

This routine does not produce any visible result when you run it unless you combine it with other instructions that perform calculations on the stack or are used to display items taken from the stack.

## PUSH_STR

To push a string descriptor, load the address of the first byte of the string into DE and the string's length (in bytes) into BC. Then call PUSH_STR. The string can be any sequence of bytes. By pushing a string descriptor onto the stack, you make the string available as an argument to the string operators and functions.

To push a number that is already in five-byte floating point format, store the address of the first byte in HL and execute the following instructions:

| Address | Contents | Instruction | Comment |
|---------|----------|-------------|---------|
| 4082 | CD EB 19 | CALL TEST_STACK | Make sure there is room in memory and store 0005 in BC |
| 4085 | ED 5B 1C 40 | LD DE, (STKEND) | Get address of top of stack |
| 4088 | ED B0 | LDIR | Transfer 5 bytes |
| 408A | ED 53 1C 40 | LD (STKEND), DE | Store new top of stack |

## Accessing Items on the Stack

The master program has different subroutines for popping (removing) different kinds of items from the stack. Some of these also convert floating point format into bytes or integers, and some print the popped item on the television display. With these routines, you will never need to learn the internal details of floating point format. Refer to Table L-1 for the numeric addresses of the routines below.

### POP_BYTE

Call POP_BYTE to pop a number whose value is between 0 and 255, round it to an 8-bit integer, and store it in the A register. Report code B results if the result is not between 0 and 255. Register C contains the value 1 if the floating point number was positive, or FF if it was negative.

### POP_WORD

Call POP_WORD to pop a number whose value is between 0 and 65535, round it to a 16-bit integer, and store it in the BC register pair. Error report B results if the floating point number was not in the range 0-65535.

## POP_PRINT

Call POP_PRINT to pop a number or a string from the calculator stack and print the number or string at the current print position on the television display. This routine examines the system variable FLAGS at address 4001 to determine whether the stack item is a floating point number or a string descriptor.

To pop a number and store it elsewhere in five-byte floating point format, load the destination address of the first byte into HL and execute the following instructions:

| Address | Contents | Instruction | Comment |
|---------|----------|-------------|---------|
| 4082 | 01 05 00 | LD BC,0005 | Prepare to move five bytes |
| 4085 | 09 | ADD HL,BC | HL now contains address of last byte |
| 4086 | EB | EX DE,HL | DE now contains address of last byte |
| 4087 | 2A 1C 40 | LD HL,(STKEND) | Put next address after stack in HL |
| 408A | 2B | DEC HL | HL now holds last address on stack |
| 408B | ED B8 | LDDR | Transfer five bytes |
| 408D | 23 | INC HL | Get next address after new stack |
| 408E | 22 1C 40 | LD (STKEND),HL | Store it |

## Calling Calculator Routines

The instruction RST 28 calls calculator routines. Immediately after, the RST 28 instruction stores one or more bytes to tell the calculator which operations you want. These bytes are called *calculator codes*. The calculator will perform the operations in order, leaving the output of each operation on the stack and expecting to find the input or inputs for the next operation on the stack. Table L-2 lists the calculator routines and gives the calculator code to put after RST 28 for each one.

After the byte for the last operation, enter a byte containing hexadecimal 34 to mark the end of the calculator calls, and continue with the rest of your subroutine.

You can pass the operation code from Table L-2 to the calculator by placing it between the RST 28 instruction and the byte value 34, or you can load the operation code into the B register and use 37 after the RST 28 instruction. The byte value 37 tells the calculator to use the value in the B register as the operation code. The comparison operations (greater than, less than, and so on) will not work correctly unless you load them in this fashion. The other operations will work with either kind of call. To use byte 37, you will need to exit calculator mode (by entering hex 34). Then set the B register and enter RST 28, hex 36, and hex 34.

## Table L-2. Calculator Codes

| Code | Operation | Value Left on Stack | Comments |
|------|-----------|---------------------|----------|
| | | | **Constants** |
| A0 | | 0 | |
| A1 | | 1 | |
| A2 | | 0.5 | |
| A3 | | 3.1415927 / 2 | |
| A4 | | 10 | |
| | | | **Arithmetic Operations** |
| 03 | Subtract | UNDER − TOP | |
| 04 | Multiply | UNDER * TOP | |
| 05 | Divide | UNDER / TOP | |
| 06 | Take number to a power | UNDER ** TOP | |
| 0F | Add two numbers | UNDER + TOP | |
| 18 | Negate (unary minus) | − TOP | |
| 2E | Modulus | UNDER MOD TOP | Remainder is second on stack |
| | | | **Numeric Functions** |
| 1C | Sine | SIN TOP | |
| 1D | Cosine | COS TOP | |
| 1E | Tangent | TAN TOP | |
| 1F | Arcsine | ASN TOP | |
| 20 | Arccosine | ACS TOP | |
| 21 | Arctangent | ATN TOP | |
| 22 | Natural logarithm | LN TOP | |
| 23 | Exponential (base $e$) | EXP TOP | |
| 24 | Integer part | INT TOP | Rounds down |
| 25 | Square root | SQR TOP | |
| 26 | Signum | SGN TOP | |
| 27 | Absolute value | ABS TOP | |
| 28 | Contents of address | PEEK TOP | |
| 29 | Subroutine parameter | USR TOP | Calls a subroutine |
| 36 | Truncate | Truncation of TOP | Rounds toward zero |
| | | | **Relational Operations on Numbers** (Value is 1 if true, 0 if false) |
| 37 | Less than or equal | UNDER <= TOP | Call with 09 in B register |
| 37 | Greater than or equal | UNDER >= TOP | Call with 0A in B register |
| 37 | Not equal | UNDER <> TOP | Call with 0B in B register |
| 37 | Greater than | UNDER > TOP | Call with 0C in B register |
| 37 | Less than | UNDER < TOP | Call with 0D in B register |
| 37 | Equal | UNDER = TOP | Call with 0E in B register |

**Table L-2. (Continued)**

|  | **Relational Operations on Numbers**<br>**(Value is 1 if true, 0 if false)** |  |
|---|---|---|
| 32 | Less than zero | TOP $<$ 0 |
| 33 | Greater than TOP $>$ 0 | TOP $>$ 0 |

|  | **Logical Operations on Numbers**<br>**(Value follows rules for BASIC,**<br>**Chapter Six)** |  |
|---|---|---|
| 07 | Or | UNDER OR TOP |
| 08 | And | UNDER AND TOP |
| 2C | Not | NOT TOP |

|  | **Operations on Strings** |  |  |
|---|---|---|---|
| 17 | Concatenate | UNDER + TOP | Both UNDER and TOP are strings |
| 10 | And | UNDER AND TOP | UNDER is a string, TOP is a number |
| 11 | Less than or equal | UNDER $<=$ TOP | Both UNDER and TOP are strings |
| 12 | Greater than or equal | UNDER $>=$ TOP | Both UNDER and TOP are strings |
| 13 | Not equal | UNDER $<>$ TOP | Both UNDER and TOP are strings |
| 14 | Greater than | UNDER $>$ TOP | Both UNDER and TOP are strings |
| 15 | Less than | UNDER $<$ TOP | Both UNDER and TOP are strings |
| 16 | Equal | UNDER $=$ TOP | Both UNDER and TOP are strings |

|  | **String Functions** |  |  |
|---|---|---|---|
| 19 | Character code | CODE TOP | String argument, numeric value |
| 1A | Value of string | VAL TOP | String argument, numeric value |
| 1B | Length of string | LEN TOP | String argument, numeric value |
| 2A | String representation | STR$ TOP | Numeric argument, string value |
| 2B | Character string | CHR$ TOP | Numeric argument, string value |

|  | **Stack Manipulation** |  |
|---|---|---|
| 01 | Exchange (switch) top and second items on stack | |
| 02 | Delete top item on stack | |
| 2D | Duplicate top item on stack | |
| C0 | Copy top item from stack to memory cell zero | Stack does not change |
| C1 | Copy top item from stack to memory cell one | Stack does not change |
| C2 | Copy top item from stack to memory cell two | Stack does not change |
| C3 | Copy top item from stack to memory cell three | Stack does not change |
| C4 | Copy top item from stack to memory cell four | Stack does not change |
| C5 | Copy top item from stack to memory cell five | Stack does not change |
| E0 | Push contents of memory cell zero onto stack | |
| E1 | Push contents of memory cell one onto stack | |
| E2 | Push contents of memory cell two onto stack | |
| E3 | Push contents of memory cell three onto stack | |

**Table L-2. (Continued)**

| Stack Manipulation | |
|---|---|
| E4 | Push contents of memory cell four onto stack |
| E5 | Push contents of memory cell five onto stack |

| Control Operations | |
|---|---|
| 2F | Branch forward or backward in the list of character codes currently being executed. The byte following the 2F code contains the positive or negative offset for the branch |
| 00 | Jump (as described above) if the top item on the stack is true (not zero) |

**Note:** The symbols TOP and UNDER denote the top item on the stack and the second item from the top, respectively.

## Using the Auxiliary Memory

Since each calculator routine gets its parameters from the calculator stack and returns its value to this stack, you must arrange the operations on the stack so that the right parameters are there in the right order for the next operation.

The stack operations DUPLICATE, EXCHANGE, and DELETE can rearrange items on the stack.

The computer has six (five-byte) auxiliary storage cells that can store floating point numbers from the stack. You can use these cells as you would use the memories of a pocket calculator.

Each of the code bytes C0-C5 pops a number from the calculator stack and stores it in the corresponding cell (0-5). Conversely, the code bytes E0-E5 each retrieves a number from one of the cells and pushes it onto the stack.

## Calculator Examples

The following subroutines illustrate the calculator routines. Use either REM loader program from Appendix F to enter them, and run them using the command RAND USR 16514 unless the example specifies differently.

1. The first subroutine converts a decimal number to floating point, takes its square root, and prints the result. The REM loader program line is:

```
20 LET H$="21 94 40 22 16 40 4
6 78 CD ▓▓ 14 EF 25 34 CD 55 0B
C9 23 1B 22 2A 21 FF "
```

The complete assembly listing is

| Address | Contents | Instruction | Comment |
|---------|----------|-------------|---------|
| 4082 | 21 94 40 | LD HL,4094 | Load address of string into HL |
| 4085 | 22 16 40 | LD (CH_ADD),HL | Store same address in CH_ADD |
| 4088 | 46 | LD B, (HL) | Load first byte of string into A |
| 4089 | 78 | LD A,B | register |
| 408A | CD D9 14 | CALL FLOAT_STR | Push string's value on the stack |
| 408D | EF | RST 28 | Call the calculator routine |
| 408E | 25 | DEFB 25 | Take the square root |
| 408F | 34 | DEFB 34 | End of call to calculator |
| 4090 | CD 55 0B | CALL POP_PRINT | Display the result |
| 4093 | C9 | RET | Return to BASIC |
| 4094 | 23 1B 22 2A 21 | DEFS 7.6E5 | Store the string |
| 4099 | FF | DEFB FF | Store the end-of-string marker |

This example illustrates a single calculator call, with one command byte (25) and the stop byte (34) after the RST 28 instruction. It also shows how to convert a string into a floating point number with FLOAT_STR and how to print the last item on the stack with POP_PRINT.

You can change the numeric string and try the routine again using the EDIT key. As long as you leave the terminator byte FF at the end of the string (it appears as the COPY keyword on the display), you are free to lengthen or shorten the string. Try several different strings, both in ordinary decimal notation and in scientific notation. To see what happens, try some illegal strings too, such as 2E99 (out of range) and A%3K (not a number).

2. The second routine pushes two string descriptors onto the stack, concatenates them with the + operator, and prints the result. The program line for the REM loader is

```
 20 LET H$="11 9B 40 01 06 00 C
D ▓ 12 11 A2 40 01 05 00 CD ▓
 12 EF 17 34 CD 55 0B C9 28 34 33
  28 26 39 FF 2A 33 26 39 2A FF "
```

The complete assembly listing follows:

| Address | Contents | Instruction | Comment |
|---------|----------|-------------|---------|
| 4082 | 11 9B 40 | LD DE,409B | Address of first string |
| 4085 | 01 06 00 | LD BC,0006 | Length of first string |
| 4088 | CD C2 12 | CALL PUSH_STR | Push first string descriptor |
| 408B | 11 A2 40 | LD DE,40A2 | Address of second string |
| 408E | 01 05 00 | LD BC,0005 | Length of second string |
| 4091 | CD C2 12 | CALL PUSH_STR | Push second string descriptor |
| 4094 | EF | RST 28 | Call the calculator |
| 4095 | 17 | DEFB 17 | Concatenate the strings |

| 4096 | 34 | DEFB 34 | End of calculator call |
|------|------|------|------|
| 4097 | CD 55 0B | CALL POP_PRINT | Print the concatenated string |
| 409A | C9 | RET | Return to BASIC |
| 409B | 28 34 33 28 26 39 | DEFS CONCAT | Store the first string |
| 40A1 | FF | DEFB FF | Store the string terminator |
| 40A2 | 2A 33 26 39 2A | DEFS ENATE | Store the second string |
| 40A7 | FF | DEFB FF | Store the string terminator |

Unlike the earlier example of decimal string conversion, this routine requires you to specify the length of the string in the BC register so you can push its descriptor onto the stack. You can edit the REM statement containing this routine to change bytes in the strings, but you cannot use EDIT to change the length of the strings. Instead, you must edit the hexadecimal listing in line 20 and run the loader program again.

3. The third subroutine converts two integers to floating point, takes the first to the power specified by the second, and prints the result. The REM loader line is

```
20 LET H$="ED 4B 7B 40 CD ▇▇ 1
5 3A 21 40 CD ▇▇ 15 EF 06 34 CD
A7 0E C9 "
```

The complete assembly listing is

| Address | Contents | Instruction | Comment |
|------|------|------|------|
| 4082 | ED 4B 7B 40 | LD BC,(407B) | Load base number into BC |
| 4086 | CD 20 15 | CALL PUSH_WORD | Convert and push on stack |
| 4089 | 3A 21 40 | LD A,(4021) | Load exponent into A |
| 408C | CD 1D 15 | CALL PUSH_BYTE | Convert and push onto stack |
| 408F | EF | RST 28 | Call the calculator |
| 4090 | 06 | DEFB 06 | Calculator exponential |
| 4091 | 34 | DEFB 34 | End of calculator call |
| 4092 | CD A7 0E | CALL POP_WORD | Pop and convert to integer in BC |
| 4095 | C9 | RET | Return to BASIC |

After you have stored this program in a REM statement with the REM loader program, POKE the exponent into location 16417. The exponent must be between 0 and 255. Then POKE the low byte of the other number into 16507 and the high byte into 16508 (as described in Chapter 7).

Since this routine uses POP_WORD instead of POP_PRINT, you must execute it with PRINT USR 16514 in order to see the value that it returns in the BC register pair. Try POKEing different values for the two numbers. Does the routine interpret a negative exponent correctly? What happens if the resulting value is out of range?

4. The next subroutine converts two integers to floating point, takes the cosine of each, compares the two cosines, and prints them in numerical order (the smaller one first). Load it with:

```
  20 LET H$="3A 7B 40 CD ▓▓ 15 E
F 1D 2D 34 3A 7C 40 CD ▓▓ 15 EF
1D C0 01 E0 34 06 0C EF 37 00 02
 01 34 CD 55 0B 3E 76 D7 CD 55 0
B C9 "
```

| Address | Contents | Instruction | Comment |
|---|---|---|---|
| 4082 | 3A 7B 40 | LD A,(407B) | Load first number into A |
| 4085 | CD 1D 15 | CALL PUSH_BYTE | Convert and push it |
| 4088 | EF | RST 28 | Call the calculator |
| 4089 | 1D | DEFB 1D | Take cosine of first number |
| 408A | 2D | DEFB 2D | Duplicate cosine on stack |
| 408B | 34 | DEFB 34 | End of calculator call |
| 408C | 3A 7C 40 | LD A,(407C) | Load second number into A |
| 408F | CD 1D 15 | CALL PUSH_BYTE | Convert and push it |
| 4092 | EF | RST 28 | Call the calculator |
| 4093 | 1D | DEFB 1D | Take cosine of second number |
| 4094 | C0 | DEFB C0 | Store it in memory 0 |
| 4095 | 01 | DEFB 01 | Exchange top 2 numbers on stack |
| 4096 | E0 | DEFB E0 | Push number from memory 0 |
| 4097 | 34 | DEFB 34 | End of calculator call |
| 4098 | 06 0C | LD B,0C | Load compare > byte into B |
| 409A | EF | RST 28 | Call the calculator |
| 409B | 37 | DEFB 37 | Compare top 2 numbers on stack |
| 409C | 00 | DEFB 00 | Jump if greater |
| 409D | 02 | DEFB 02 | Jump length is 2 bytes |
| 409E | 01 | DEFB 01 | Exchange top 2 numbers on stack |
| 409F | 34 | DEFB 34 | End of calculator call |
| 40A0 | CD 55 0B | CALL POP_PRINT | Pop and print top number |
| 40A3 | 3E 76 | LD A,76 | Load ENTER code into A |
| 40A5 | D7 | RST 10 | Print it to go to next line |
| 40A6 | CD 55 0B | CALL POP_PRINT | Pop and print from stack |
| 40A9 | C9 | RET | Return to BASIC |

This routine gets two integers, which must be between 0 and 255, from the byte values you POKE into locations 16507 and 16508 before you execute RAND USR 16514. Begin by POKEing the numbers 2 into 16507 and 3 into 16508. Then run the routine and observe the result. Next, **POKE** 3 into 16507 and 2 into 16508, and run the routine again. Each time the computer prints the numbers like this:

$-0.9899925$
$-0.41614684$

It compares the cosines of the two inputs, printing the smaller one first, regardless of their original order.

This example illustrates several kinds of stack manipulations. First, it stores the cosine of the first number on the stack twice, using calculator code 2D to duplicate it. Then it pushes the cosine of the second number onto the stack so it will look like this:

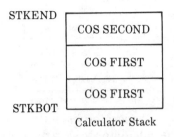

Calculator Stack

After that, the computer stores the top cosine in memory location zero (a copy of it remains on the stack) and exchanges the top two items on the stack (calculator code 01), like this:

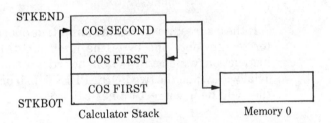

Calculator Stack                    Memory 0

Next the computer pushes the cosine of the second number from memory location zero onto the stack, which now contains alternating copies of the two cosines:

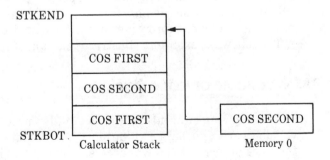

Calculator Stack                    Memory 0

With the cosines stored in this way, the routine uses calculator code 0C to pop and compare the top two values on the stack. Notice that the routine calls the comparison operator with byte value 37 and with the comparison code 0C in the B register. Comparisons do not work with the other calling method. The test removes the top two items, leaving 1 (true) on the stack if the second value on the stack is greater than the top value. Otherwise, it leaves 0.

| 1 or 0 |
| :---: |
| COS SECOND |
| COS FIRST |

Calculator Stack

The jump-true operator (calculator code 00) will remove the test result, causing the calculator to skip the exchange instruction (calculator code 01) if the test result is true.

> **Note:** The jump length in the byte following the jump-true operator is 2 because it must skip both the jump length and the exchange operator following it.

If the test result is false, the jump-true operator will cause the calculator to skip only one byte (the jump length), executing the exchange instruction, which will switch the order of the top two items on the stack. That way, when the two POP_PRINT instructions print their numbers, they will be in correct numerical order.

## CALCULATIONS WITH BASIC VARIABLES

The master program routine LOOK_VARS searches the BASIC variables area for a variable that you specify. By using this routine and the calculator stack, you can pass floating point parameters between BASIC and machine language subroutines in the form of BASIC variables.

The following examples illustrate this capability.

### Push a BASIC Variable onto the Stack

The following subroutine finds a simple numeric variable in the BASIC variables area, pushes its value onto the calculator stack, and prints it from the stack to verify that it was accessed correctly. The BASIC program line to load this routine with the REM loader is

```
 20 LET H$="21 A0 40 22 16 40 C
D 1C 11 DA 4B 0D 23 CD ▓▓ 19 ED
5B 1C 40 ED B0 ED 53 1C 40 CD 55
  0B C9 33 FF "
```

The complete assembly listing is

| Address | Contents | Instruction | Comment |
|---------|----------|-------------|---------|
| 4082 | 21 A0 40 | LD HL,40A0 | Load string address into HL |
| 4085 | 22 16 40 | LD (CH_ADD),HL | Also store it in CH_ADD |
| 4088 | CD 1C 11 | CALL LOOK_VARS | Find variable with that name |
| 408B | DA 4B 0D | JP C,ERR_2 | Report error if undefined |
| 408E | 23 | INC HL | Get address of first byte |
| 408F | CD EB 19 | CALL TEST_STACK | Enough memory to push on stack? |
| 4092 | ED 5B 1C 40 | LD DE,(STKEND) | Get address of top of stack |
| 4096 | ED B0 | LDIR | Transfer five bytes |
| 4098 | ED 53 1C 40 | LD (STKEND),DE | Store new top of stack |
| 409C | CD 55 0B | CALL POP_PRINT | Print value of variable |
| 409F | C9 | RET | Return to BASIC |
| 40A0 | 33 | DEFS N | Create variable name |
| 40A1 | FF | DEFB FF | Terminate name string |

To test this routine, first define a BASIC variable N with a LET statement. Then execute RAND USR 16514, followed by PRINT N. The computer should print the value you assigned to N in the LET statement. To use a different variable name (of any length), edit the REM statement to incorporate the new variable name.

## Transfer a Number from the Stack to a BASIC Variable

The following subroutine pushes the value 2 onto the calculator stack, takes its square root, finds a numeric variable N in the BASIC variables area, and stores the square root in that variable. The BASIC program line to load this routine with the REM loader is

```
 20 LET H$="3E 02 CD ▓▓ 15 EF 2
5 34 21 A6 40 22 16 40 CD ▓▓ 11
DA 4B 0D 01 05 00 09 EB 2A 1C 40
  2B ED B8 23 22 1C 40 C9 33 FF "
```

The complete assembly listing is

| Address | Contents | Instruction | Comment |
|---------|----------|-------------|---------|
| 4082 | 3E 02 | LD A,02 | Store 2 in register A |
| 4084 | CD 1D 15 | CALL PUSH_BYTE | Store 2 on stack in floating point |
| 4087 | EF | RST 28 | Start the calculator routine |
| 4088 | 25 | DEFB 25 | Take square root of stack value |
| 4089 | 34 | DEFB 34 | Exit the calculator routine |
| 408A | 21 A6 40 | LD HL,40A6 | Store string address in HL |
| 408D | 22 16 40 | LD (CH_ADD),HL | And in CH_ADD |
| 4090 | CD 1C 11 | CALL LOOK_VARS | Find the specified variable |
| 4093 | DA 4B 0D | JP C,ERR_2 | Report error if variable undefined |
| 4096 | 01 05 00 | LD BC,0005 | Prepare to move five bytes |
| 4099 | 09 | ADD HL,BC | HL holds address of last byte |
| 409A | EB | EX DE,HL | DE holds address of last byte |
| 409B | 2A 1C 40 | LD HL,(STKEND) | Put address after stack in HL |
| 409E | 2B | DEC HL | HL now holds last stack address |
| 409F | ED B8 | LDDR | Transfer five bytes |
| 40A1 | 23 | INC HL | Get next address after new stack |
| 40A2 | 22 1C 40 | LD (STKEND),HL | Store it |
| 40A5 | C9 | RET | Return to BASIC |
| 40A6 | 33 | DEFS N | Create variable name |
| 40A7 | FF | DEFB FF | Terminate name string |

Before running this routine, you must define a variable N using a LET statement. The value you give it does not matter. Run the routine with RAND USR 16514 and PRINT N. The computer will print 1.4142136, which is the square root of 2.

Key Values

# Appendix
# M

If you access the master program routine, SCAN_KBD, it will return a value that indicates which keys, if any, have just been pressed. Figure M-1 shows the hexadecimal values that will be returned each time a single key is pressed.

If the SHIFT key and one of the keys are pressed together, one of the hexadecimal values shown in Figure M-2 will be returned.

When no keys are pressed, SCAN_KBD will return the hexadecimal value FFFF.

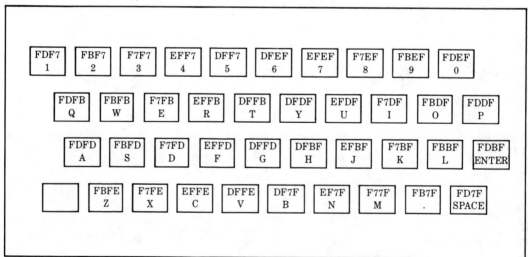

Figure M-1. Hexadecimal key values for unshifted keys

Adapted from *Understanding Your ZX81 ROM* by Ian Logan (Cheddington, Leighton Buzzard, Bedfordshire, UK: Melbourne House Ltd., 1982).

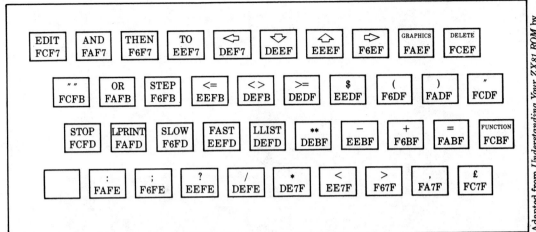

Figure M-2. Hexadecimal key values for shifted keys

Adapted from *Understanding Your ZX81 ROM* by Ian Logan (Cheddington, Leighton Buzzard, Bedfordshire, UK: Melbourne House Ltd., 1982).

References and Further Reading

# Appendix
# N

## BASIC

Albrecht, Finkel, and LeBaron. *What to Do After You Hit Return*. Rochelle Park, N.J.: Hayden Book Co., 1980.

Coan, James S. *Advanced BASIC*. Rochelle Park, N.J.: Hayden Book Co., 1976.

————. *Basic BASIC*. 2nd ed. Rochelle Park, N.J.: Hayden Book Co., 1978.

Dwyer, Thomas A., and Margot A. Critchfield. *BASIC and the Personal Computer*. Reading, Mass.: Addison-Wesley, 1978.

Hurley, Randle. *The Sinclair ZX81. Programming for Real Applications*. Beaverton, Oregon: Dilithium Press, 1982.

Nevison, John M. *The Little Book of BASIC Style*. Reading, Mass.: Addison-Wesley, 1978.

## Assembly Language Programming

Leventhal, Lance A. *Z80 Assembly Language Programming*. Berkeley: Osborne/McGraw-Hill, 1979.

Baker, Toni. *Mastering Machine Code on Your ZX81*. Reston, Virginia: Reston Publishing Co., 1982.

Larsen, Sally G. *Computers for Kids—Sinclair ZX81 Edition*. Morris Plains, N.J.: Creative Computing Press, 1982.

Logan, Ian. *Understanding Your ZX81 ROM*. Leighton Buzzard, Bedfordshire, U.K.: Melbourne House, 1981.

———. *Sinclair ZX81 ROM Disassembly. Part A: 0000H-0F54H*. Leighton Buzzard, Bedfordshire, U.K.: Melbourne House, 1981.

Logan, Ian, and Frank O'Hara. *Sinclair ZX81 ROM Disassembly. Part B: 0F55H-1DFFH*. Leighton Buzzard, Bedfordshire, U.K.: Melbourne House, 1982.

Nichols, Joseph C. et al. *Z80 Microprocessor Programming Interfacing*, Vols. 1 and 2. Indianapolis: Howard W. Sams, 1979.

Osborne, Adam. *An Introduction to Microcomputers: Volume I—Basic Concepts*. 2nd ed. Berkeley: Osborne/McGraw-Hill, 1980.

## Periodicals

*BYTE*. 70 Main Street, Peterborough, NH 03458.

*Creative Computing*. 39 East Hanover Avenue, Morris Plains, NJ 07950.

*Personal Computing*. 50 Essex Street, Rochelle Park, NJ 07662.

*Popular Computing*. 70 Main Street, Peterborough, NH 03458.

*Sinclair Computing*. Box 95-SC, Glenmont, NY 12077.

*Syntax*. The Harvard Group, Bolton Road, Harvard, MA 01451.

*Syntax Quarterly*. The Harvard Group, Bolton Road, Harvard, MA 01451.

# INDEX